verticaleditions.com

THE INSIDE STORY OF SHEFFIELD
WEDNESDAY'S 1990/91 SEASON

ALEX MILLER

First published in the United Kingdom in 2021 by Vertical
Editions, Unit 41 Regency Court, Sheffield, S35 9ZQ

www.verticaleditions.com

Follow us on Twitter:
@VerticalEds
@AlexMiller91

2

ISBN 978-1-908847-22-5

A CIP catalogue record for this book
is available from the British Library

Printed and bound by Jellyfish
Print Solutions, Swanmore, Hants

*To Peter Bryett, who taught a
shy boy how to talk to people.*

*He didn't care much for football,
but would have read this book
from cover to cover.*

CONTENTS

FOREWORD

by Ron Atkinson

I joined Sheffield Wednesday almost accidentally. But boy, am I glad I did. When my time in Spain with Atletico Madrid was cut short, my intention was to sit tight and wait for another chance at a club over there. A couple of Spanish clubs had mentioned their interest and, to be fair, it's not a bad life out there! But on the weekend I was back in England, I went to watch a game at Villa Park and by chance they were playing Wednesday. Villa weren't much cop, but they beat Wednesday fairly comfortably. I was there as a punter, not in any football capacity; just showing my face and seeing a few people I knew. At the end of the game I was coming out of the directors' box and saw Bert McGee, the great Sheffield Wednesday chairman.

I knew Bert – years earlier I'd been offered the Wednesday job when I was at Cambridge United, but I felt it was too early and I went to West Brom – and we had a good chat. But there wasn't really too much talk of an approach. I wasn't exactly touting my name around. The next day I got a phone call from Bert's secretary asking if I'd speak to them. I went up to meet them on the Monday and explained I had a contractual thing going on with Madrid – they owed me a fortune – and the club agreed to cover me against that loss.

So I went to Wednesday until the end of the season. It was February 1989 and in my head I was only going to stay a few months, because I knew there would be the opportunity to head back out to Spain with Valencia or Sevilla sounding me out. I'd felt a little bit short-changed from my time out there and wanted to give it another go.

When I got to Wednesday, we scrambled our way to safety and I liked it. They were great lads; some of the best lads I'd worked with. And we developed a rapport with the supporters. I was lucky enough to manage many teams with great fan bases, but they, in my mind, are the very best. And I'm not just saying that! I lived in the Midlands and it wasn't easy doing all that travelling back and forth, but I loved it at Wednesday that much that I did it, staying at the old Hallam Towers Hotel during the week. I'd brought my old mate Carlton Palmer with me and we'd done some good business, bringing in the likes of John Sheridan and Roland Nilsson, who I regard as of one of the very best buys of my career.

Relegation in 1990 was a great shock to all of us. People go on now about the West Ham side that went down a few years later and one or two others, but in my mind there is no doubt we were the best team ever to get relegated from the First Division. To go down with the highest points total was a slap in the face. We said very early that we wanted to stick together and put things right.

We played our first game the next season at Ipswich, which got us rolling, and a while later we went down to play Leicester and won 4-2. I had a drink with David Pleat afterwards – one of my eventual successors at Hillsborough – and the first thing he said to me was that it was the best display of passing he'd ever seen in that league. Back then you had to kick your way out of trouble, play it long, kick and scratch your way back up. They were the type of teams, playing in that way, that were successful. But we had quality players and we weren't going to start doing that. We wanted to do it in style.

Well, what a season. Promotion was always the primary aim, but to win the cup down at Wembley, against my old club Manchester United, was special. I've always said that the fact it was United made no difference to me, but for the supporters, who that day were nothing short of incredible and went some way to winning us the thing, it added that bit of glamour. If you're going to win a cup at Wembley, there aren't many teams you'd rather do it against!

There were, of course, difficult circumstances at Sheffield Wednesday. The terrible Hillsborough disaster took a toll on the club and I think it is testament to the players and people that we had there that, from a football standpoint at least, we were able to bring a little joy back to the scene of such an unimaginable tragedy. But some wounds don't heal. The experience of being manager of that club at that time will live with me forever.

The circumstances of my move away from Sheffield is one covered later on these pages, I understand, but it's fair to say I regret the way it was done and can understand why the Wednesday supporters were so disappointed. I was of course lucky enough to meet those supporters again when I returned for a second spell in 1997 and we were able to keep the club up in difficult circumstances.

How that might have gone differently. We avoided relegation handsomely and I wanted to stay. I had a good relationship with Dave Richards, who took over from Bert as chairman and who initially offered me a three-year contract. I said that I'd take one to the end of the season, at which point hopefully we'd stayed up and then everything else could be sorted out. I floated the idea of Nigel Pearson, our great leader in the story you're about to read, re-joining the club as my number two.

But, with all this going on, I was sent a contract offer that was for far less money than I'd arrived on. I rang Dave who said to me: "I told them you wouldn't accept it." I thought it was odd and it was the last I heard. Within a few days they appointed Danny Wilson, a great lad who is also heavily featured on these pages. Five years on I bumped into Dave and asked him what had happened. "You turned down the offer of a new contract, Ron," he said. Oh, really.

Looking back, I have nothing but fond memories of Sheffield Wednesday and I repeat my claim – those supporters are the best I ever managed for. We had great characters and a great side. The 1990/91 season was the sort that doesn't come around very often. Where on earth have 30 years gone?

Enjoy the book, and up the Owls.

PROLOGUE

To say the bus turned the corner into a sea of people would be a lie, because people had lined the streets throughout the entire journey. For the day at least, Sheffield was blue and white with the occasional spot of yellow. The Steel City belonged entirely to Sheffield Wednesday Football Club.

It was a day of unbridled celebration, when nothing else mattered. The Owls were saluting their people after 12 long months of trials and tribulations, ups and downs; all leading to this – a celebration of League Cup glory and Division One promotion in the same remarkable season. Club captain Nigel Pearson held the Rumbelows Cup like a baby, waving to the adoring support below. The crowds swelled mainly at Hillsborough and in the city centre, where the bus was heading for a civic reception with the who's who of the city. Throughout the journey boys had chased the bus as far as their legs would take them. The crowd chanted at the top of their lungs. "Atkinson's Barmy Army..."

The 1990/91 season had been an incredible journey for Sheffield Wednesday. Relegated the season before in circumstances that inflicted untold pain on anyone and everyone connected with the club, the expectation was that the side would fall apart. Key players had release clauses in their contracts and Atkinson's squad of internationals and highly-rated youngsters was one built for top-flight football, not for the second string. But it was the spirit shown on the streets of Sheffield that day, the togetherness and solidarity in full evidence, that made it a club worth sticking around for.

It was May 31, 1991, a warm but overcast day. And those players were riding that open-top bus not only as Rumbelows Cup winners, but as a First Division side once again. Although the story was a little complex behind the scenes, it was an image that not only celebrated the club's success, but offered a clear glimpse into an exciting future. In recent history clubs promoted from the second tier had gone on to challenge in the higher reaches of the First Division and Wednesday looked well set to do the same. They had a board willing to spend money to compete with those already there and a manager, despite a flurry of concerning headlines suggesting otherwise, who seemed ready to build a footballing dynasty.

The season before, plans made ahead of time to mark the end of the season had blown up in Wednesday's face when the remarkable events of May 5, 1990 conspired to relegate the club from a seemingly impossible position. Not this time. The Owls had dropped out of the top three for only one week in the entire campaign, but it was decided that a pen would not be put to another plan for celebration until the season was over. It meant the parade was organised with a little haste, so several first-team players could not be there; either having booked holidays, trips home or in the case of top goalscorer David Hirst, making his England debut in Australasia.

But those who were able to attend remember something truly special. They looked down on the crowds in awe. It was a Friday afternoon, but businesses across the city had closed or allowed the Owls fans among their workforce a few hours off. Roads were closed, literally bringing an entire city to a standstill to mark a truly incredible double achievement.

Among the players present was a lifelong Wednesdayite, Barnsley-born Peter Shirtliff, whose role alongside his skipper Pearson provided the muscle for those in front of him to thrive on their way to 103 goals in their 60 matches. For all the history-making moments across the course of the year, including lifting a major trophy at Wembley Stadium in front of 30,000 of his own people, it was on the open-top bus afternoon that the enormity of their achievements truly began to set in. The fact that the men on the top of the bus were being lauded and chanted about was bizarre to him, he said, given the folk below had played such a vital part.

"My God, there were some crowds there," he said with a knowing grin. "It was incredible, looking out at that lot. It made it that extra bit special that I had grown up a Wednesdayite and that I was a local lad. There were thousands and thousands of people and, to think some of the people there were my friends and family, it was a very special feeling. But those fans pulled us through that season. Whenever we were in a tough spot, they'd get louder. It's all a bit of a cliché, but it's very true. Standing up there looking at all those supporters celebrating, that's when it hit me...that we'd got promoted and won at Wembley. That's the first time it sunk in that we'd done what we'd done."

Pushing on into the city centre towards the town hall, the crowds got denser and denser. The nearby Peace Gardens, so-called six years earlier, were packed full of Wednesday fans desperate to greet their heroes. The full repertoire of songs were being delivered; street vendors made a killing on blue and white hats, blue and white flags and, yes, blue and white cuddly toys.

"The procession was incredible. The whole city was out," remembered Paul Williams, the striker who a year earlier hadn't even been a Sheffield Wednesday player, but in a few short months found a way to unlock the rabid potential of his strike partner David Hirst. "It wouldn't surprise me if there were one or two Sheffield United supporters who had crept out in blue and white that night because the whole of Sheffield was celebrating that we'd had this success. It was an incredibly momentous occasion, seeing for our own eyes what it meant to them, what it meant to the city. That's when you think: 'Wow, I am a part of a bigger thing.'

"The humble man who goes out to work from nine to five and who turns up god knows where in the country to support his team, it means the world to those guys. So much more than it does to us as players and I say that as someone who has been both a supporter and as someone who played. We're talking about supporters who have kids, their dads, their dad's dads having grown up with Sheffield Wednesday in their blood. This was a day that doesn't come around very often and we were the ones at the centre of that. It was incredibly humbling."

Once Wednesday's players had arrived at the town hall, champagne was offered and, as a team that didn't mind a drink from time to time, duly accepted. When they stepped out on to the balcony to address their public, noise levels rose to new heights. Lost in the shimmer of glory, certainly lost in the three decades that have passed, are memories of the times the 1990/91 season weren't so great; of the endless string of drawn games, the changing-room rows, the injuries, the fact that the league title hadn't quite been achieved. But nobody cared that day and they certainly don't three decades on. These were the sorts of days that Wednesday's supporters deserved.

"I remember a bloke climbing up the wall up the bricks of the town hall," said Danny Wilson. "We were up there and at first we thought he was joking. We were saying to one another: 'Isn't anybody going to pull him down?' And then all of a sudden he was beside us and we had to pull him up on to the balcony. I looked down at him and thought: 'Oh, my good grief.' That was what it meant to people. He was willing to scale a wall and risk breaking his bloody back just to wish us well. I'm not sure he'd have felt it, mind...He looked as though he might've had a couple."

The biggest cheer of the day came when Ron Atkinson took the microphone and reassured those present that, despite the newspaper headlines suggesting otherwise, he would be staying on to see Wednesday into the First Division. In his own words, he would be "barmy" to leave what he described as the best job in football and the supporters were the primary reason he would turn down the club, Aston Villa, that in many ways had his heart. To those up close and personal on the day, there was something amiss there. But that one is for later.

It had been a season of iconic moments; of 40-yard screamers, comedians on coach trips and beers in nightclubs. There were scrapes along the way; hospitalised fitness coaches, poor results and fights between players and staff, but they were outweighed five to one by savvy signings, raucous away days and famous nights at Hillsborough that have yet to be bettered all these years on.

This is the remarkable inside story of Sheffield Wednesday's iconic 1990/91 season.

A WOODEN SCOREBOARD

For six minutes, Sheffield Wednesday had got away with it. For six blissful, exciting, sun-baked minutes, the hearts and minds of Wednesday fans were filled with the sort of relief that only football can deliver. For six minutes, as far as they could tell, they were staying in the First Division and everything that followed would have been very, very different.

It was May 5, the last day of the First Division season, the first week of the long, hot summer of 1990 and at that time, the hottest matchday ever recorded at Hillsborough. An hour earlier, at the end of a long and winding, entertaining, but ultimately disappointing campaign, Wednesday were up against it – roared on by a crowd concerned but confident that their boys in blue and white would get the job done.

The Owls – striding out into the South Yorkshire sunshine in their striking blue and white stripes, with the instructions to "relax and enjoy" delivered by their charismatic coach Ron Atkinson ringing in their ears – needed only a point to stave off relegation. Luton Town, the only side who could send them down, were playing 32 miles away at Derby County's Baseball Ground. Anything less than a win for Town there and the Owls were safe regardless.

It was late on in the piece and, with a crackling radio signal the only way of knowing the scores elsewhere on the last day of a torrid season, all eyes at a packed Hillsborough stadium had for several minutes been glued not to the match before them, but to a small, but wholly-significant wooden scoreboard resting against the North Stand, designed to keep those present abreast of the scores from around the grounds that day. The Luton score was king. Wednesday were 3-0 down to Nottingham Forest.

It wasn't supposed to be this way. Six weeks earlier the Owls had made their way to the fated 40-point mark that was supposedly enough to secure safety and Atkinson, one of the most highly-rated managers in European football, had spoken of the need to finish the season with "a bit of swagger." A side featuring Carlton Palmer, Dalian Atkinson and David Hirst should not need any favours from Derby. A side containing Nigel Pearson, Peter Shirtliff, Chris Turner and Phil King should not live in hope of a Luton mishap. Not at that end of the table anyway.

These were respected First Division stars, many of them players of huge class. In Mancunian Republic of Ireland adoptee John Sheridan and Swedish full-back Roland Nilsson they had players heading to that summer's World Cup tournament. In Nigel Worthington and Trevor Francis, they had players of huge international experience. Sheffield Wednesday were one of the biggest clubs in the country. Relegation was unimaginable.

Having rallied back from a start of just four points in their first 11 league matches, in which they scored only two goals, Wednesday were playing good football and cruising. A 1-1 draw at Wimbledon seven matches earlier had propelled them to 13th place in the table and at 2-1 up at home to Tottenham on the last day of March, Wednesday were on their way to their fourth win in six.

A late dart for the outskirts of the top handful had not been considered out of the question and Atkinson – lovingly known as Big Ron in the football world – had said as much in the afternoon's programme notes: "I'm pleased to offer a warm welcome to Terry Venables and his Tottenham team for a game that has all the makings of a very entertaining fixture, what with Spurs seeking to maintain their push for a place in the top four, while our own goal is to finish the season with a flourish now that we've reached the 40-point milestone."

Wednesday lost 4-2 that afternoon thanks to two goals from Gary Lineker and a Paul Gascoigne-inspired second half laid on just months before his journey to Italia '90, Pavarotti, tears and superstardom beyond measure. The only way was up for the cheeky-chappie Geordie. The Owls, on the other hand, had been triggered into a spiral.

Atkinson should have known better. The late dart he spoke of was not out of the question for a squad of Wednesday's quality, of course, but only to those with no appreciation for what had by then long become widely known in blue and white circles as "the Wednesday Way" – the shorthand term for the club's ability to achieve defeat when only victory seemed possible. If there's a way to make things difficult, the theory suggested, then Sheffield Wednesday will find it. And they did. After Spurs came defeats to Southampton, Manchester City and Queens Park Rangers. The "finish-with-a-flourish" end-of-season swagger had crouched to a desperate, hurried limp and glances over shoulders at Luton were becoming a little more lingering with every passing fixture.

Despite shock Luton wins over fourth-placed Arsenal and much-fancied Crystal Palace – the latter thanks to an Iain Dowie goal so late that several news outlets reported that Luton had been relegated – a David Hirst double in Wednesday's 2-1 win over already-relegated Charlton on the penultimate day of the season meant that one point would be enough when Forest came to town. They'd made it tough. It was the Wednesday Way.

But on May 5, on those sweltering terraces, things somehow felt different. After all, all the Owls had to do was draw and even that was needed only in the event of a Luton win. Luton, who had won only one away league match in nearly 18 months, were packed with endeavour, but devoid of the sort of quality that Derby, and indeed Wednesday, had at their disposal. The Owls' guests, newly-crowned Rumbelows Cup winners Forest, had little to play for and some of their players had begun winding down for involvement in the World Cup a month or so later. There was a confidence in the Sheffield air that belied the seriousness of the circumstances.

"Luton hadn't won so much as a bloody corner away from home for months and months," Atkinson remembered. "We were quite confident of beating Forest and, to be honest, we'd played well in those last few weeks of the season. But after Tottenham we just couldn't put the thing in the net and we kept losing. We played at Man City, battered them and got beaten. We went to QPR, hit the woodwork about five times and got beaten. The thing is, the standard of play had been very high. Everybody could see that, I think."

It wasn't only through the home turnstiles at Hillsborough that the outcome of that afternoon was presumed to be destined to go in

Wednesday's favour either. On the Sunday before the final weekend Luton put on their player-of-the-season awards ceremony with celebrity fan and ITV Sport anchor Nick Owen – gearing up for a busy summer presenting the World Cup – playing host alongside their quietly-spoken Scottish manager, Jimmy Ryan.

"I spoke to Jim before we started and he told me he thought they would stay up," Owen said. "Well, I couldn't stop myself saying: 'You've got to be joking!' The thought of us winning at Derby and Wednesday losing was something that hadn't really been considered by so many Luton fans. But I remember looking at Jim and he looked so confident. I remember thinking he was crazy.

"We'd had such a wretched season. The Palace win the weekend before had come in the 90th minute and we lived to fight another day. I got home from that game, switched on *Sports Report* and they kept having to apologise for reporting that Luton had been relegated; the goal was scored so late. They thought we were down. And when we'd found out Wednesday had beaten Charlton, to be fair, so did we. We'd only won once that season away from home and there were 5,000 away fans who had travelled to Derby for what most of them thought would prove to be their last day out as a First Division side for at least another season."

At Hillsborough the crowd was building, and it was hot. Really, almost painfully hot. Some fans on the terraces were in tie-dye vests seemingly cast off from the set of a Wham! video. Others went shirtless, laying their shirts across the stadium's crash barriers. There was a tingle in the air. All present knew that there was much to play for, but the overriding feeling remained one of confidence. Then play began, players were sweat-drained within minutes of the kick-off and from the start, the ball bounced harder and bobbled further than usual; always, it seemed, away from the control of increasingly irritated Wednesday players.

The Owls had got into this scramble not through a lack of quality, but through a curious inability to score goals. The talented, fresh-faced, South Yorkshire-born forward Hirst – at 23 already a Wednesday icon after three promising seasons leading their line – was the club's top goalscorer with 14 league goals. His strike partner Dalian Atkinson, a lively Shropshire-born speedster with a burgeoning reputation, had

10. Their next-best sources of success were playing for the opposition because the Owls benefited from three own goals.

Down at Derby, Luton had scored early. Really early. And in the most unexpected fashion. As supporters were still settling into their seats and David Preece was preparing to float in a cross, the Hatters right-back Tim Breacker – who had scored only two goals in 200 league appearances for the club – decided that he was instead going to hit a second-minute free-kick from all of 35 yards. "My dad had written me a poem a few days before the game," he later remembered. "It was a bit like: 'You won't believe what you can do. Enjoy the game, don't worry about relegation and you'll be surprised what can happen.'

"That was in my mind; that's how I felt going into the game. Just give it our best shot. There were loads of supporters there; it was a fantastic atmosphere. David Preece stood over it, God rest his soul, and I just said to him: 'Do you know what? I fancy this.' He didn't argue with me; he literally just went: 'Go on then.' He knocked it to the side, I just hit it and it flew in. I don't think anyone believed it, least of all me – and I still don't believe it actually happened."

The news came through, those wooden Hillsborough scoreboards were altered and, as the minutes went on, the atmosphere at S6 went from one of hubris and expectation to bottom-belly nervousness. And almost immediately it filtered down to the players. All it would take was a Forest goal and a pair of final whistles for the unimaginable to become reality. Wednesday, one of the biggest clubs in the country, would be down in the Second Division for the first time in six seasons. All of a sudden, Wednesday were under pressure.

Early chances for the energetic Dalian Atkinson – no relation to his manager – and decorated old professional Francis came and went, the tension making itself plain as the latter scorned laconic midfield genius Sheridan for a misplaced pass after just a few minutes. Typically of the two managers – Forest were managed by the iconic Brian Clough – the early stages set the tone for an open, fluid match between two attractive footballing sides.

And then, the unthinkable. After so much talk of the threat of Stuart Pearce earlier in the week – Atkinson had discussed the possibility of placing an extra man on the goal-line in an attempt to keep out his thunderous free-kicks – the hard-man England international broke the deadlock early doors, crashing a low shot through a gap in the Wednesday wall and past the sprawling left hand of Owls keeper Turner. One nil. The atmosphere shifted further still. Anxiety hung heavily above Hillsborough.

A draw would do, Wednesday. A point was all they needed. At a team meeting at the plush Hallam Towers Hotel the day before, a handful of senior players had raised their eyebrows and then shrugged off surprise that Atkinson intended to set them up so openly, so gung-ho, against the counter-attacking wiles of Clough's Forest. In hushed tones, one quietly described it as "madness." But this was Atkinson, this was Wednesday and this was how they were going to do it.

"There was never an air of: 'We're going down,' simply because we felt we were playing well enough," remembered Turner, the Owls goalkeeper and lifelong Wednesdayite who knew Atkinson better than most, having played for him at Manchester United. "And we were. We were playing good football. We felt we had a good side and after that Wimbledon game, with the remaining fixtures, we felt we'd be all right.

"At the hotel the team meeting was all about us taking the game to Forest, attacking them. It was everything you shouldn't do against Forest in those days because they were a great counter-attacking team. But we went with it because Atkinson had this way of making you believe. And we were desperately unlucky on the day. We had all of the ball and the better attacks. They just had the attacks that got goals."

Left-back Phil King, a chirpy, self-described 'country-bumpkin' Bristolian brought to Hillsborough from Swindon earlier that season, remembers Big Ron's love of attacking football. "Looking back in those last few weeks, do you just set out to get the job done?" he said. "Plant two banks of five, get a couple of draws and get out of that season? I know in hindsight there is only one answer. The fact is that we should never have been faced with the situation we had against Forest. But he was never going to do that.

"It wasn't something Ron had in him and that's what made him so great. Maybe he'd have done that later in his career, but I think he felt we had the players to go out on a day like that, score early and win the game. He pumped his players up with confidence. And people often forget that Luton had an incredible run-in. We were really only ever one point away."

Down in Derbyshire, Luton put themselves two up through Kingsley Black's poked left-foot effort and, as news filtered into the Hillsborough terraces and was slapped on to that wee wooden scoreboard, quiet anxiety turned to belly-ache frustration, especially as Wednesday's woes in front of goal laid themselves bare. Hirst had rattled the post and had a rebound effort well saved by Forest goalkeeper Steve Sutton.

Worthington, a Northern Irish international with a left foot that could do a crossword, passed up the opportunity to rifle a shot across goal as he miscontrolled the ball on the firm Hillsborough pitch. Francis missed a header he'd have scored five times on another day and Hirst again misdirected an effort at the back post.

So lucky they were, then, that Derby had roared back with two quick-fire goals courtesy of Mark Wright and Paul Williams, later to become a coach at Wednesday. Half-time in matches across the country. Two-all at the Baseball Ground, 0-1 at Hillsborough. As it stood, Luton appeared to be running out of puff and going down. And despite all the missed chances and all the quiet spiralling, Wednesday were going to get away with it.

Amid the faux-dramatic footballing narrative ebbing and flowing between South Yorkshire and Derbyshire was the very human, very cold fact that the bulk of the visiting Forest side had returned to Hillsborough that hot May morning for the first time since the Hillsborough Stadium disaster a little more than a year before. It was an afternoon In April 1989 that has haunted visitors to the famous ground ever since, an FA Cup semi-final clash with Liverpool when 95 supporters – 22-year-old Tony Bland would become the 96th when his life-support machine was switched off in March 1993 – were crushed to death at the Leppings Lane end of the ground.

It had been suggested that Forest had requested to the FA that their visit to Hillsborough could be scheduled as late in the season as possible so as to allow ample time for the players and staff to prepare. A clearly-distracted Liverpool lost 2-0 there, to second-half goals from Hirst and Atkinson, in November; the match had been brought forward after remarkably being originally scheduled for the first anniversary of the disaster.

Brian Laws, the Forest right-back on both days who would manage Wednesday a quarter of a century later, remembered a cautious, lonely feeling in the Forest camp in the lead-up to the game. He had been just metres from the fences when the game was called off, later watching on with horror as bodies were pulled out of the stand. On May 5, 1990, the sun was shining as it had been on that fateful day; there was a big-game atmosphere, too. But the towering Leppings Lane end, as it would be for the entirety of the following season, was left empty; a harrowing reminder of what had happened just 385 days earlier.

"There was an awful lot of apprehension," Laws said. "It was almost like revisiting a ghost. It was something that had happened in our past that we didn't want to have to recall. The memories came back pretty vividly. It was in the warm-up that I think we noticed it most. The game had a lot of noise and the supporters played their part. But when we went out to the warm-up, it was only a quarter full. It was quiet. You can't help but take in the surroundings more. We actually warmed up on the Leppings Lane end. It was such a surreal and a really odd feeling. You didn't talk about that sort of thing back then, but there was a very sombre feeling among us.

"We would very, very rarely speak about matches in the lead-up. Cloughie would trust us to go out and get the job done. We were unique in that respect. But I remember him sitting us down that week and telling us that he wanted us individually to get our mindsets right and to play the game, not the occasion. We had to go out and show the public what we were about. He wanted to win the game. But it was tough. It was a physiological battle we had to overcome and Cloughie was pulling everything out of his hat he could to ensure our mindsets were right. These were unprecedented circumstances we were having to play under."

With Clough's rare pre-match meeting still fresh in the Forest players' minds, their unwavering attitude on their Hillsborough return was that, for all the emotion of the day, there was a football match to win. And as attack after attack from Wednesday span past the post, over the bar or into the arms of goalkeeper Sutton, Forest grew and grew in confidence. The counter-attacking attributes that Chris Turner had feared a couple of days earlier were homing to roost.

Moments after Dalian Atkinson had had a penalty shout turned down while rolling the ball agonisingly wide at the Kop End, Pearce scooped a cross to the head of Nigel Jemson. Pearson was unable to clear and the England international raced on to smash the ball past Turner and into the top corner of the Owls net. A stuttering Wednesday were 2-0 down and, although they continued to throw bodies forward – Sheridan had an effort saved, Carlton Palmer shot from distance and Atkinson again fired wide – all minds on the terraces remained fixed on events 32 miles away at Derby.

"Wednesday were playing with real fear," Laws said, remembering the atmosphere in the ground shifting wildly. "We sensed that and from that point we knew we would be able to get the job done – even though they were throwing everything at us. We knew what they had to do; we knew the pressure players at a club like Sheffield Wednesday are under. We had that at Forest.

"But as a footballer you sense it. You can smell fear. Before the match we felt they were going to be more worried about us than we were of them and that was pretty evident on the day. You could see that nothing went for them. There were little mistakes that players like that would rarely make and basic stuff just wasn't working for them."

It was at this point that *Match of the Day* highlights that evening cut away from flock-of-seagulls hair-dos and sunburnt faces of concern and to the dugout. "Well, whether the news has reached Ron Atkinson, I'm not sure," said commentator Martin Tyler as footage showed the Owls boss adjusting his sunglasses and wiping sweat from his brow. "But Luton are leading at Derby. I think he's heard."

As future Wednesday signing and teenage hot prospect Jemson added a Forest third from a counter-attack pieced together by the pace of substitute and former Owl Franz Carr, the game being played at Hillsborough descended into insignificance. The minutes whiled away and the sense of occasion evaporated into the May sunshine. As the desperate fizz of every Owls attack previously fell flat, the hopes and dreams of almost 30,000 supporters, players, staff and club employees fixed on a match elsewhere.

If the score stayed the same down there, the Owls were doomed. Eyes would flicker from time to time on the two club staff seated in the corner of the ground, tasked with keeping an ear to the ground elsewhere and updating the old, wooden scoreboard with the goings-on in Derbyshire.

"It was a horrible feeling," remembered dependable, man-mountain centre-half Peter Shirtliff, the boyhood Wednesdayite whom Big Ron had brought back from three years at Charlton Athletic ahead of that season. "It almost felt like we were drowning. We were playing okay, but nothing went for us and we were 3-0 down. When we realised Luton had scored, it was a feeling of helplessness. We bloody froze, didn't we?"

The tempo of the match slowed to a wander. Forest sat in, Wednesday had the ball and were allowed to pass it across the midfield, unable to pick the lock at the Kop End. With only a minute or two left, the ball drifted down the right through cultured Swedish international full-back Roland Nilsson, who narrowed down on the away defence. Over his shoulder, the man in the corner rose from his seat and headed towards the old wooden scoreboard with nearly 30,000 eyes fixed on his every step.

Nilsson pushed the ball inside to Hirst, who shimmied and turned, but got no joy out of two-goal Pearce, now marshalling the Forest defence. The forward rolled it to Sheridan, loitering with intent on the edge of the box, but not an eye in the ground saw his shot bundled tamely into the reach of Sutton. The man in the corner picked up a number. The Derby score read 3-2 to visiting Luton. Then, with one movement, pandemonium.

The change came. It was 3-3. With seconds to go, it seemed, Derby County had equalised. Luton would go down. Sheffield Wednesday had got away with it.

As the roar of relief rose and realisation made its way to pitch level, Brian Clough rose from his dugout to embrace his great friend and opposite number. Atkinson, nattily turned out as ever in his customary aviator sunglasses and a bright-yellow polo shirt chosen specifically for the day to exude confidence, shook his sun-kissed forehead with the look of a man fresh from a death-row pardon.

He stood tall, well in sight of the supporters in the South Stand behind him and clenched his fists. After a season of near misses, a late Derby County goal against Luton Town, it seemed, would keep his side in the First Division.

Wednesday's score seemed irrelevant. No matter the chances spurned by Dalian Atkinson, Trevor Francis and John Sheridan. No matter the margin that had seen a David Hirst shot bounce back from the Forest post. No matter a lacklustre defensive performance in which they had conceded three goals at home. Grown men cried tears of joy as news of that Derby goal surfaced. Fathers held sons and friends embraced. Up in the South Stand Press box, pages were hurriedly torn from notepads, the thinking cap on a new "top line" firmly pressed on. From the depths of despair just moments earlier Wednesday were staying up.

Local journalists who covered the Wednesday beat most weeks, Alan Biggs and Paul Thompson among them, allowed themselves half a moment of celebration at the reaction of the crowd. Like the season before, when the Owls had beaten Middlesbrough to stay up on the last day, they would be spending the summer looking forward to covering a First Division side again. Thompson, the long-time Wednesday correspondent at local newspaper *The Star*, followed the example of Big Ron in clenching his fist and began to prepare to switch his writing tone. From despair to relief.

A row or two behind him Biggs, a smart, moustached young reporter who dovetailed his work between the BBC and national newspapers, was covering the match for radio. His updates with goals from Hillsborough earlier in the day had set off scenes of jubilation for those with transistor radios in the away end at the Baseball Ground. His was a unique role in the process.

And unlike the thousands of supporters celebrating in the stands, and his friends in the print media, he knew that Derby County had not scored. The man in the corner had made a horrible mistake. Derby's goal had been disallowed. Luton were still winning 3-2 at the Baseball Ground.

Reality drifted in the breeze, time ticked on, confusion reigned. The final whistle blew. A stream of supporters made their way on to the pitch in hope of celebration and Wednesday players stood exhausted, hands on hips, completely oblivious of their divisional status. As the full-time whistle was blown at Derby, the truth made itself known pitchside and the face of Atkinson, so red with relief, drained to white. An announcement over the Hillsborough PA system confirmed the Wednesday agony. For six blissful, exciting, sun-baked minutes, Sheffield Wednesday players, staff and supporters thought they had got away with it.

They hadn't. They were relegated from the First Division.

Roland Nilsson, a classy defender who had been picked up for £375,000 from IFK Göteborg just months before, would head off to the World Cup with Sweden in the weeks that followed. But stretched out on the Hillsborough turf as reality hit, he was inconsolable. "We didn't play well enough," he remembered. "We didn't finish our chances and straight after the match, we just didn't know if we had made it. We were waiting on the result to come in from Derby. All of a sudden everything felt negative. You could hear it in the crowd and we realised something had happened. We were told on the speaker and that was it. We felt horrible."

Some supporters stayed in the stadium for up to an hour, shell-shocked by what had gone before. Again grown men cried, fathers held sons, friends embraced, although not with any hint of the joy that had gone before. One by one, players drifted off into a changing-room not filled with angry rants, but complete and total silence. Players remained in their kit, staring at the floor. Several sobbed.

Ron Atkinson, that larger-than-life personality who always knew what to say, walked into the changing-room and blanked everyone. Without saying a word, he turned around and wandered back out down the tunnel to complete his post-match media duties. Assistant manager Richie Barker and physio Alan Smith consoled the players and told them to get themselves changed. It was a feeling of absolute disbelief.

"Not a lot was said," remembered Turner. "It was dead quiet. In a situation like that, there's not a lot you can say. Big Ron could lose his temper and Big Ron could dig you out, but he was stunned. It was just a feeling of complete shell-shock. Richie Barker said a few words, that a team get relegated over 46 matches, not just for that one game. That was the reason we'd gone down, he said. But other than that, there was complete silence."

Interviewed in front of the South Stand, shoulders southwards, Atkinson looked a broken man, a million miles from the hearty persona that had set him on his way to national-treasure status. "Like the players I started the morning as a First Division manager," he said, his tone painting a picture of complete disappointment. "I'm now a Second Division manager.

"At the start of the season we were a rubbish side; we were really poor. But then we started to get over that and we looked as though we were going to get out of it. But we've taken three points from the last six games. That is incredible. You can pinpoint a number of reasons, but the biggest single reason is that we've not cashed-in on anything like our percentage of chances." As the interview drew to a close, two supporters over his shoulder shouted down messages of support to both their manager and their club. "That's what makes it worse," he said. "They're brilliant."

So confident they were that the relegation battle was not of their concern six weeks earlier, the Wednesday board had organised the end-of-season supporters' club player-of-the-season dinner to take place directly after the Forest match. After showering and changing in near silence, the players joined Atkinson and his staff and made their way up towards the hospitality rooms, nervous as to what would greet them. On the same day Sheffield United had been promoted to the First Division, and the power in the city had shifted dramatically in one afternoon. This, surely, would be a fan base angered by the events of the day.

"We felt sick," Atkinson remembered. "It's not something many of us had experienced in our career. I couldn't come to terms with it. We were waiting to head into this big room full of supporters; we stood there and we took a deep breath. A club like Sheffield Wednesday shouldn't get relegated and, although the supporters there are fantastic, you just dread to think how the reaction might be to us lot walking in among them. Well, I could not believe it. We walked in, they stood up and applauded us. I could have burst into tears."

It had taken Sheffield Wednesday 14 years to return to the First Division after their last relegation. Clubs of that size often take longer than others to recover from such a fall. As rumours of a money-spinning new super division at the top of English football began to drift into focus, the very reputation of the Owls as a major force in the city, let alone the national game, was at stake. Theirs was a side full of quality that would surely be difficult to hold together, it was argued in the local Press, and, even if they were able to do so, promotion from the Second Division at the first time of asking would be a difficult mission to accomplish.

The events of the next year at Sheffield Wednesday would be seismic, they surmised. How little they knew.

2

HOLIDAY BLUES

The morning after the day before, first-team players at Sheffield Wednesday climbed aboard a coach at Hillsborough with glum faces. Few had sore heads – they had been told not to drink too much at the supporters' dinner, for fear of being accused of enjoying themselves – and there was a feeling of genuine embarrassment among the party. Wednesday, barely 18 hours since their relegation to the Second Division had been confirmed on that stadium tannoy, were on their way to Manchester airport for a few beer-soaked days in Marbella.

If the supporters' dinner had been arranged in a wave of misguided hubris, a jolly boys' outing was on another level altogether. The Owls had been on a handful of end-of-season trips before, and the fact is that Ron Atkinson liked Marbella. More to the point, he liked Puerto Banús. And so did a host of other clubs. While some reached for the more traditional destinations enjoyed by a pack of thirsty young men – the week after the season in Magaluf was a notoriously popular spot for '90s footballers – there was something about the piano bars and moored super-yachts that Atkinson rather enjoyed.

Atkinson is not described by those closest to him at that time as anything like the champagne-guzzling 'Bojangles' character portrayed in the media. Although the then 51-year-old was savvy in using his profile to deflect attention from his players at times of struggle, and he from time to time enjoyed the celebrity that came with being Ron Atkinson, he was in fact a cup of tea man. Few can remember ever seeing him drunk and it is a bone of contention of many of his colleagues that such an image clouds his achievements as a manager. Not many have won major trophies with three English clubs, as he did.

Settled on the coach on their way across the Pennines, conversation was not exactly flowing among Wednesday players. They were a hard-working group of young professionals who felt they had let their club down, a feeling that punctured any half-hearted efforts from the usual suspects to get the usual levels of banter going. As senior man Chris Turner reached forward and picked up one of the several newspapers provided, the back page was dedicated to the relegation of his team. In a passage of sadomasochistic healing, he read every word of each one.

Once at the airport the players ordered jugs of beer and smiles began to creep on to faces again. The pain was still there, of course it was, but the players were beginning to enjoy themselves. There had been half a conversation between Atkinson and one or two senior players the night before about the possibility of cancelling the trip. The manager stamped it out in seconds.

"We went away," remembered social hub Carlton Palmer, signed from West Brom midway through the season before and widely regarded as one of the most talented midfield talents in the country. "You never go away when you're in a team that gets relegated, but Ron did that to look after us. He could see we were hurting and he wanted to keep us together."

Socially, this was as tight-knit a squad as you are likely to find in football, Palmer recalls in a Black Country accent so thick it could stir his Guinness. In John Sheridan, David Hirst and Phil King, the midfielder had partners in crime supremely talented on both the grass and in the bar. Other members of the squad liked a drink, too, and despite their unfortunate fate in the 1989/90 season they were an outfit who worked harder than they played, playing pretty damn hard all the same. Although not in the school of Manchester United and Arsenal atop the drinking culture hall of fame at that time, they knew how to see a pint off. The management knew that, and embraced it.

"I've never met a group of players like it," Palmer said. "It was a squad of huge characters. We'd pull each other out when we were under the cosh. Nobody was a prima donna; no-one was better than anyone else. It wasn't always a planned thing, but on a Saturday you'd be showering and you'd ask what the boys were doing. Nine times out of 10 we'd end up having a drink somewhere.

"We'd socialise, we were a tight-knit group and nobody would come between us. We'd go out, we'd drink all night and then, when we came in the next day, everybody would put a shift in to do what we had to do. It was an unbelievable time. It was the best time of my life. Not just in football, but in anything I've done."

The relegation season had been a freak, they told each other. They'd gone down with a record-high points tally. They'd be back. The consolation continued and rightly or wrongly, they flew off to Marbella with a spirit of redemption burning brighter than one of devastation. King remembers the trip well, with a devilish chuckle. Thirty years on he is the landlord of a pub in Swindon and, although only 23 at the time, he was not at all backward in coming forward when it came to enjoying a refreshment.

"We stayed in a hotel called the Andalucia Plaza, which is just over the dual carriageway, and then you'd walk over to Puerto Banús," he said. "Well, it was millionaires' paradise down there. I've no idea how our lot were allowed to wander about! It's gone a little bit more everyman now, but in those days it was just a beautiful little strip. You had Sinatra's on the corner and a few little bars; the Navy Bar was one. You'd knock on the door, a curtain would open and you'd go in.

"To be fair, it wasn't really designed for end-of-season trips for lads to go and have a good time like Magaluf or Benidorm or whatever. It was a bit up-market and going there as a player and as a team off the back of the relegation...it didn't feel right. We were all devastated. They had it booked and it was all paid for, but it just wasn't the same. But as the beers went down, things got a little easier. With the characters on the trip, it was difficult not to enjoy yourself."

Checked in, shirts on, over the dual carriageway and on to the strip, a pack of Sheffield Wednesday players turned past Sinatra's, a lively cocktail bar frequented by the somebodies and the could-be-somebodies, and looked for what Palmer described as a "starter bar". Outside, laughing and joking, clearly an hour or two further into the afternoon's delights, were Tim Breacker, Kingsley Black and friends. Completely unknown to anybody in the Owls party, Luton Town had made the trip to Marbella for their own end-of-season trip.

"Luton were celebrating and we were all glum," remembered King.

"It wasn't the nicest experience. A lot of our lads knew the players at Luton at the time; there was a crossover. You say hello, you offer your congratulations and commiserations and get on with it. I think Carlton got a little bit upset with one or two of them after a few beers, but nothing major at all. I think both sides were pretty wary of it and the Luton lads were good lads. We had a beer together early doors and then left each other to it, really."

But not everyone did leave them to it. Wednesday staff were also on the trip alongside the players, including Atkinson's much-loved and highly-respected right-hand man Richie Barker. He had joined them from the same post at Luton in controversial circumstances when Atkinson was initially parachuted in to save Wednesday from relegation in February 1989.

Luton, managed by Ray Harford, were celebrating their qualification for the League Cup final, and the opportunity to defend their 1988 win, when Barker answered a call from a South Yorkshire number. It was Atkinson, an old friend from their time at neighbouring clubs a decade or so earlier.

"I was old pals with Richie from when he was at Wolves and I was at West Brom," Atkinson remembered. "When I first went to Wednesday, I'd lined up that Lou Macari was going to come with me as my number two. I'd had Lou at Manchester United and he had done a good job managing Swindon. But Lou had whispers of some management jobs, he ended up going to West Ham and he called to tell me he wasn't going to come. All of a sudden I was short of an assistant.

"I rang Richie up, he was at Luton and they were in the final of the League Cup with Ray Harford. I rang up and he said: 'Oh, aye, I've got a great idea.' I asked who. He said: 'Me.' Well, I couldn't believe it. He was in the cup final! But he was adamant. We were bottom of the league and it struck me as an incredible decision. He just said: 'Well, I'd rather be there with you than here.' I tore his hand off. I'd never even given it a thought he might be interested."

Barker, the bad cop to Big Ron's good, was more of a disciplinarian, but was loved by his players. When the manager would concentrate on man management, getting the best out of those at his disposal, Richie would crack the whip on the training field when it was needed. The pair were great friends, spending hours upon hours discussing football in Atkinson's office over gallons of Yorkshire Tea. And it was towards the end of the Owls' doomed season, during one of these tea-stained chats, that Barker had shared an idea.

There was a lad at Luton, one of his old players, who would give Wednesday some of the experience and determination they needed. A midfield battler who had a little bit of everything. The 30-year-old was a little older than the sort of player Atkinson had a habit of buying, but he was a proven winner – having scored in Luton's 1988 Rumbelows Cup win over Arsenal. He was a full international and rumour had it, Barker said, he was looking for a move back north, closer to his family in Wigan and his wife's family in Chesterfield.

In the Marbella sun, Danny Wilson peeled away from his team-mates to share a quick beer with his Northern Ireland teammate Nigel Worthington. It was the second day on the trip and Wilson, one of the more mature members of the celebrating Luton side, rather enjoyed Puerto Banús' piano bars rather than the livelier spots. So too, it turned out, did Ron Atkinson and Richie Barker.

"It was a celebration for us, I suppose, staying up," Wilson remembered with a smile. "Staying up was a big deal for us. We were Luton, we weren't a big club and we were fighting against the odds all the time. We were enjoying ourselves. But it was a bit embarrassing bumping into the Wednesday lads, really. We'd just sent them down and next minute we were buying them a beer. Big Ron was there and he pulled me for a very loose chat.

"I opened up the conversation by offering my commiserations because I knew one or two of them, and obviously Nigel from the Northern Ireland team. It was a loose talk and I didn't think too much of it. We had a good time and, after a couple of weeks when I was back home, I had a phone call asking whether I fancied a go at Sheffield Wednesday.

"I never hesitated because of the size of the club. Luton weren't blessed with large amounts of money so any cash offered their way was always welcome. I knew Richie Barker, so he wasn't new. But I'd never even met Ron Atkinson before Marbella, so from that point of view it did come out of the blue. You'd hear things all the time, rumours and clubs sniffing around. You'd call it tapping-up in those days, but most of the time, when clubs had a word, it never came to anything."

Thirty years on, with a glint in his eye, Atkinson said he couldn't recall that "loose chat" ever having taken place. Sheffield Wednesday signed Danny Wilson a few weeks later.

***

By the time that the Wilson chinwag had or hadn't happened, Atkinson thoughts had switched towards the 1990/91 season not only in terms of recruitment, but in the motivation of his players. Marbella, a trip controversial though it may have seemed in the eyes of some supporters, was an opportunity to draw a line under the perils of relegation early, to stamp out any lingering ideas of departure in his key men and to pull closer together a squad that was in danger of drifting. On the second morning Big Ron pulled up a chair and placed a plastic wallet full of passports on the table beside him.

"He told us we were going to come back early, we were going to get fit and we were going to win the league. He said that anybody who didn't want to buy into it was welcome to collect their passport and fuck off," Palmer said, with immense seriousness. "Nobody said a word and so he said: 'I'm taking it from you that everybody is on board. Everybody go off and have a good time, do what you like, get in when you like. If anybody gets locked up, you're on your own.' And that was it. It planted a seed in us about the following season."

A good few days were had by all and passed largely without incident. Conversations flowed about summer plans, players relaxed and, as much as you can recover from such a shock relegation in a few days, the focus moved towards an immediate return to the First Division. If one or two players had reservations – and they did – they kept it quiet.

"We said on that trip that we had to bounce back from it," recalled Chris Turner. "We had a great bunch of lads, great players and we felt, if we stuck together, we would be all right. Everything could have so easily fallen to pieces after that. You see it at so many clubs. But it never felt as if that was going to happen. I think maybe Marbella helped in that regard, physically keeping the lads together that bit longer."

The decision of Atkinson and the club to go ahead with the trip had been a triumph, and an important milestone in what the manager had planned for the club's recovery. Within a month he and Trevor Francis would join Messrs Sheridan and Nilsson at the World Cup in Italy – not in a football capacity, but to act as studio pundits for ITV. Francis had played in Italy for Sampdoria four years earlier and spoke the lingo. Ron, well, Ron was Ron. Television audiences loved him.

The tournament proved to be a zeitgeist in the cultural standing of football in this country. The devastating Hillsborough Disaster – then so indelibly, shockingly and deviously linked with the so-called drunken behaviour of Liverpool supporters – came at the end of a long and painful decade for the sport. Heysel, the Bradford Fire and hooliganism had kept football in the spotlight for all the wrong reasons while Margaret Thatcher's Conservative government had revelled in the image of football supporters, using it as a tool to advance her image among European colleagues. Her role in the evil alteration of events at Sheffield Wednesday's home on April 15, 1989 ranges from complicit bystander to architect, depending on the account. In the media, football became a sort of sneering byword for the inconvenient anger of the working-class.

Heading into the World Cup, English clubs had been banned from European competition since the events of Heysel five years earlier proved to be the tragic final straw of two decades of football hooliganism abroad. Wednesday themselves were one of the clubs effectively punished, missing out on playing in the UEFA Cup in the 1986/87 season under Howard Wilkinson in a side including Kevin Pressman and Nigel Worthington. But a tide was turning.

Football had slowly gone from pariah territory to an area of semi-fashionable subculture. Fanzine culture had arrived, musicians were seen kicking balls and wearing colours in their music videos and football fandom was edging its way closer to becoming more socially acceptable among the middle classes, swollen in number – in some parts of the country at least – by a burgeoning economy.

Before the tournament UEFA president Lennart Johansson said the chances of English clubs being readmitted for the following season stood at only 10 per cent. Thanks to a tournament that saw England qualify for a semi-final for the first time since they won the thing, and more importantly thanks to a trouble-free tournament off the field, Manchester United and Aston Villa were invited back into the fold.

If acceptance in Europe was important for the future of the game, so, too, was acceptance at home. What it needed was something beautiful, something heartfelt, an icon. And when Paul Gascoigne shed tears in Turin, the country had their man. Set to the classical bars of Pavarotti's *Nessun Dorma*, the image of football was changed forever and, along with a post-Hillsborough-ordered Taylor Report that altered the face of football inside the stadia themselves, the sport slowly became theatre. Fashionable and money-spinning, BSkyB stepped up their plans to create a super-league which would eventually give birth to what we now know as the Premier League.

Within a few months, desperate to regain some sort of favour just weeks before her resignation, Margaret Thatcher posed for pictures with Gazza. Nick Hornby's novel *Fever Pitch* was released in 1992. The same year Channel 4's Sunday programme *Football Italia* became cultural iconography while the Premiership fired up its engines. Two years later England was incredibly named as the host of Euro '96, the centrepiece of a cultural whirlwind involving Frank Skinner and David Baddiel, Tony Blair and Oasis, but it all first shifted with Pavarotti. The BBC's coverage of Italia '90 changed football forever. Ron, albeit on the other side, played a cameo role.

On the field Sheridan's Republic of Ireland progressed to the quarter-finals, losing out narrowly to the hosts. He played only the final 12 minutes of their famous campaign as former Owls boss Jack Charlton searched for a moment of magic. His creative style was underused by the pragmatic coach, although Sheridan did meet the pope. In Group C Roland Nilsson played every minute of Sweden's sorry campaign. He played well, impressing one or two fluttering eyes at Old Trafford, even though they lost all three matches.

Nick Owen, one of the ITV Sport anchors that summer, remembers Atkinson, a great friend and sometime squash partner of his, as a man on and off the phone throughout. While his typically relaxed demeanour on-screen may not have let on, the Wednesday manager was fielding calls from all over; on transfers, on club matters and from current players. This was a man focused, hands-on and desperate to right some wrongs.

His favourite call that summer came from Owls secretary Graham Mackrell to confirm that despite the heartache of relegation, Wednesday had surpassed the number of season tickets sold ahead of the previous season by the middle of June. Atkinson proudly announced the fact to the studio. A few months later 20,000 fans attended an open day at Hillsborough so oversubscribed that police had to be called to assist with the crowds. This was a fan base behind the cause.

"He knew my affiliation with Luton, obviously," Owen said. "To be completely honest I found it all a little awkward at first, but he soon put the whole thing to bed with a joke or two. He told us, a room full of people at the studio, that Wednesday would be back at the first time of asking. And let me tell you, we believed him. Besides there was all this stuff with Swindon going on and it looked for some time as if Sheffield Wednesday would actually stay in the First Division. That was another sting in the tale, of course..."

***

If the phone call confirming a season ticket swell was Big Ron's favourite of the summer, there was certainly one he hadn't enjoyed receiving. For all the shock and all the heartache of that red-hot afternoon at Hillsborough just weeks before, there had remained a lingering feeling throughout the summer that Wednesday may just retain their First Division status after all – because of accusations of extraordinary misdemeanours at Swindon Town.

Swindon, playing a suitably attractive brand of football under the management of Spurs legend Ossie Ardiles, had finished fifth and swaggered their way into the Second Division play-off final, where they had beaten Sunderland 1-0 and were to be promoted to the big time alongside Wednesday's two greatest rivals – Leeds had won the division on goal difference from runners-up Sheffield United. Celebrations at Swindon, though, were decidedly tentative because of the black cloud hanging above their County Ground stadium, brought about by what had become known as "financial irregularities" at the club.

It had become clear in the final months of the season that something was afoot and the club were hit by a flurry of charges by both the FA and the Football League, some of which related to what appeared to be dodgy, off-the-field dealings as far back as 1985. In total Swindon were accused of 35 cases of making illegal payments to players. More eye-catching, however, were charges held against chairman Brian Hillier and their former manager, a certain Lou Macari, who stood accused of placing bets both for and against their own club.

With Hillier having failed to defend himself against a bet on Swindon to win the 1987 Third Division by calling it an insurance policy to stand against a hefty round of player bonuses, a host of further similar charges were made. To bet on your team to win is one thing, but to bet on them to lose is another altogether. Hillier had allegedly placed £6,500 on Newcastle to beat his side in a 1988 FA Cup match. Swindon, with a certain Phil King on the left-wing, lost 5-0.

"Swindon were a great set of lads and they were a great side who played very good football," King said. "For them to get promoted and then have it taken away from them like that was hard to watch. At that time I was sure a lot of clubs were making the sort of payments and doing the sort of things that Swindon were doing, but some clubs covered it up better and were a bit cleverer about things. You heard whispers on how some clubs were doing things and I don't think they were alone, put it that way."

The cases were to be heard in court on May 4, nine days ahead of the respective play-off first legs. A verdict would be found ahead of the play-offs and complications, it was hoped, would be averted. But the hearing was postponed to June on legal advice after Hillier, Macari and club secretary Vince Farrar were all charged by police for "intent to defraud the Inland Revenue by making payments without deducting tax or NI."

Farrar and Hillier were later found guilty, but Macari was cleared. The authorities watched on rather nervously as the play-off final was played ahead of the forthcoming legal circus. They were confident that Swindon had done wrong and planned to relegate them in the event of a guilty finding – in that eventuality and, if the Robins were to win, it would be down to the authorities to fill the space vacated by Wednesday in the top tier.

It would leave one of three options; allow Wednesday to keep their place, promote Newcastle United as the team who finished third in the Second Division table, or promote Sunderland as losing play-off finalists. After Swindon had pleaded guilty to all charges on June 7, debate raged as to who should get the nod. You can imagine how such a saga healed relations in the North-East. Atkinson attempted to use his media influence and World Cup screen time to launch something of a charm offensive to keep the Owls up and it was expected that they would. They had, after all, effectively finished six places higher than Newcastle and nine higher than Sunderland.

"I knew," said then-Sunderland chairman Bob Murray some years later. "Very few people know this, but before the game at Wembley I was pulled – very firmly – to one side by Bill Fox, the Football League chairman. He said that they wanted Sunderland to win because they didn't want to be forced to make the decision. I didn't even share that with the board, but I knew there was a very good chance we were going to be promoted to the First Division. The Swindon thing was such a big black mark. There were going to be severe consequences."

Severe consequences indeed. Swindon were relegated to the Third Division, although this was later reversed on appeal and they stayed in the second tier. There were fines aplenty and players had to be sold to balance the books. In July 1992 Hillier was jailed for 12 months for tax fraud. And on June 13, much to the bemusement of those watching on from Hillsborough and St. James' Park, Sunderland were promoted.

A dejected Atkinson was hauled on to ITV for his reaction to the news ahead of their evening match coverage. Sun-tanned and tormented, the Owls boss offered a spiky riposte with Ardiles sitting awkwardly in the studio alongside Nick Owen and England legend Jimmy Greaves, who was defiantly wearing a T-shirt donning the words: "Swindon supporters are innocent."

Atkinson said: "It's another body blow for our fans who have had to suffer and share the entrails of the Hillsborough Disaster. They've seen their team demoted from the First Division with the highest number of points, which any other year would've kept them up. And now this little ray of hope, because of the sad circumstances at Swindon, they've seen disappear in favour of a side that finished nine places below them. We always said we'd abide by any decision and we've got to do that, but to say I'm amazed is an understatement.

"An awful lot of people within the game, people whose opinions I respect, felt that, if there was anything going to be done, it should have been that Sheffield Wednesday should have remained a First Division side. We had more things going in our favour to stay in the First Division than the other teams to be promoted. There was never going to be a perfect answer. If we had stayed in, there were always going to be problems on Wearside. But quite honestly we think it would have saved an awful lot of complications and would in my opinion have been right and just to keep us in the First Division."

Biting back at his great friend Greaves once or twice, Atkinson bore the look of a man ready to go to war. Watching on from home, Sheffield Wednesday players felt ready to go with him. They hadn't even kicked a ball in pre-season yet.

3

THE SCALLYWAG

"Right, lads, I'm not having what happened last night," Ron Atkinson growled, standing hands on hips in front of a forlorn-looking Sheffield Wednesday squad. "I'm going to get rid of Sheridan. I'm sending him home and I'm going to sell him when we get back."

The Wednesday players, fresh from a quiet breakfast during which they whispered and worried about how their manager was going to play this one, took a sharp intake of breath. Arranged in front of their manager, sitting on plastic chairs like naughty schoolboys, one or two prepared to open their mouths in retort.

"You'd get rid of him, wouldn't you?" Atkinson interrupted, pointing at Danny Wilson, their newest recruit. "Well, boss," Wilson said in his dour Lancashire drawl. "I don't know about that..."

It had already been an eventful pre-season. Marbella, the World Cup and the Swindon debacle now safely in the rear-view mirror, Wednesday had touched down in Acqui Terme, a stunning north-west Italian city, for matches against local opposition in their attempt to sharpen up ahead of the season. Put up by their Italian hosts in a plush old mansion seemingly made entirely from marble, they arrived to find their opponents in their first match, Genoa, staying at the same venue.

"Pre-season is the most important time in the whole year," said defender Phil King. "You use that to get as fit as you humanly can in order to set yourself up for success in the season itself. We'd train and, make no mistake, we'd train very, very hard. But Ron was Ron and he knew what he had in us lot. So he'd be very easy come, easy go and let us go off and have a few drinks or whatever.

"We'd be getting back from training, having a bite to eat, heading up to our rooms and then coming down in jeans and a shirt ready to go for a few beers. And Genoa were playing chess in reception in their tracksuits. This is pre-season. They were in bed by eight o'clock, eating rice, chicken, beans, rest, plenty of water. We're finishing our beers and heading out and they're sitting there thinking: 'What the hell is going on here?'"

Wednesday had already played a couple of tune-up games on a trip to the south coast of England, well away from the pressures of fans and local media. An 8-0 win on a very part-time pitch against a very part-time Dawlish preceded a more competitive 3-0 win over Fourth Division Torquay United, in which Atkinson and Barker shuffled their pack with rolling subs. A gruelling pre-season had all started a few weeks earlier, back in Yorkshire and back at their Middlewood Road training ground. A side such as Wednesday, with *those* players, was expected to be picked apart by vultures in the top tier in the weeks after relegation.

David Hirst was understood to be on a scouting list at Manchester United, a list that had Roland Nilsson's name at the very top. Nigel Worthington and John Sheridan had release clauses in their contracts. Carlton Palmer and Nigel Pearson were quality First Division players and with the right word, could have left at any point. Wednesday, it was felt by those on the outside, would cash in and start again.

On the first day of training, which has since become the stuff of legend, Atkinson sat his players down on a pitch at Middlewood. "He mentioned the youth team, he mentioned the reserves and that he wanted everybody to win something and do well," remembered Chris Turner. "And he said he wanted us all to stay. He set these little goals at the start of the season. He made it exciting and we all looked at one another and wanted to be a part of it.

"It's gone down in history that he told us nobody was going anywhere, but the fact is that nobody wanted to. We were in it together. At the start of a season any club's aim is for a first team to do well and in our case the aim was to get promotion. We'd already spoken about that in Spain.

"But reserves? No. Youth team? No. He mentioned all of this. He wanted everybody involved and pushing in the same direction together. We had a big squad of players and everyone was included in what he wanted to achieve."

As expected, the club fielded inquiries as to the availability of their star men, but Atkinson, with club chairman Dave Richards and directors such as Cliff Woodward, held firm. They had a special squad of players, it was felt, and the mantra was simple; they were going to right the wrongs of relegation. There was much talk that summer about Worthington, an unflashy and dependable left-sided player who had quickly developed a telepathic partnership with King out wide.

A Northern Irish international and a calm, experienced voice in the changing-room, Worthington was a player the Owls couldn't contemplate losing. The papers, having got wind of his release clause, ran a number of stories about a possible move, with one even suggesting that he had issued Atkinson with a transfer request. With rumours rife, the much-loved fanzine *Just Another Wednesday* ran a photo of Worthington running down the wing, headlined: "You'll never catch me playing in Division Two!"

Worthington, lovingly known on the terraces as "Irish" and within the club as "Barney" after the Flintstones character, denies any notion of a transfer request to this day. There is even a suggestion that Big Ron, safe in the knowledge that the head of the then 28-year-old was screwed on too tightly to be fully turned, had allowed the stories to run on, in order to stave off any speculation around younger, more impressionable players.

"There was a lot of talk," Worthington recalled. "From my point of view, I'd been at Sheffield Wednesday for a long time and I was very happy. I'd had a great time there. Whatever was written and whatever was said, I just focused on being at Sheffield Wednesday. Until the manager comes to you and says that something is happening or that a bid had been accepted, you could be going to Real Madrid, but nothing is going to happen. I was focused on what was happening then and there."

"We had great lads, terrific lads," Atkinson said. "I was very lucky in my career to work with a lot of good lads and there are very few of the ones I managed that I wouldn't have a drink with now. But that bunch of lads at Sheffield Wednesday were brilliant, the very best. And there was interest, of course. I know for a fact we were getting calls from Manchester United for Roland Nilsson, for example. In the end we managed to fight them off and they went for a lad who did very well for them, a young Irish lad from Oldham called Denis Irwin. But Fergie really wanted Roland. I called the lads together and said: 'Look, we owe big time; we have to stick together and put the thing right this season.'"

Nilsson, identified for his exploits with Sweden and watched by Atkinson in a goalless World Cup qualifying match against England in September 1989, had been snapped up by December that year. A UEFA Cup winner with IFK Göteborg in 1987, he of the flowing blonde hair and chiselled jaw was a true Rolls Royce full-back; athletic, professional, strong in the tackle and calm in possession. In a previously stoic British football culture that had seen foreign players drip into the system in recent seasons, particularly from Scandinavia, Nilsson was a trailblazer for the game-changing influx that followed.

But his career at Sheffield Wednesday, which saw him grow into one of the club's ultimate icons, might easily have ended after six months. "My situation, playing in the national team, meant I didn't want to play in the Second Division," he remembered. "I wanted to play in the highest leagues because it was suggested that, if I played too low, I would lose my place for Sweden.

"That was one of the main reasons I might have wanted to go away to a team in the top flight. But Atkinson was very clear that he wanted to have a chance with this full team. He told me that I was a big, big part of that and he said that, if we could get the players to stay, we would all have a good year and go straight back up. He said we'd go from there."

A couple of weeks ahead of the World Cup Nilsson picked up the phone to Olle Nordin, the Swedish national team manager, for advice. It was a conversation that decided Nilsson's future and thankfully, it went Wednesday's way. "Olle said in an understanding way that, if I performed as I had done, it shouldn't be a problem. That was when I thought that the season would be good for me, to be part of both things at the same time. So I stayed."

Unknown to the squad and the club themselves, Atkinson himself had practised what he set out to preach. Since signing for Wednesday he had not relocated from the Midlands and was living – as he still does – in a sleepy Worcestershire village called Barnt Green, half an hour's drive from Birmingham. Atkinson is well-known in football circles to be an Aston Villa supporter and a short while after Wednesday's relegation he had received a knock on the door from his old friend Graham Taylor, then in charge at Villa Park.

Bobby Robson had already announced his intention to leave his post as England manager and the FA were keen to make an appointment public before the end of Italia '90. Terry Venables wanted it and had made his intentions clear, but was not included on the shortlist. Oldham manager Joe Royle, who had steered the unfashionable Lancashire club to two mazy cup runs, was being considered, as was former Everton boss Howard Kendall. Atkinson, sitting in his lounge in his slippers, was one of the first to find out they had gone for Taylor.

"I was offered the Villa job at the end of that season," Atkinson remembered. "Graham Taylor came to meet me and I just said: 'No' straightaway. I didn't feel as if I could leave a club that had just been relegated. None of the players knew this, but that helped me to get the message across, I think. I felt I was in the same boat as they were. It was up to us to put the record straight."

Taylor was offered the England job in June and was unveiled in late July, by which time Atkinson was well on with his pre-season with Wednesday. He said that he never regretted turning the opportunity down to speak to the club – *his club*. But as it turns out, it planted a seed. Czechoslovakian unknown Jozef Vengloš stepped into Taylor's shoes, becoming the first foreign manager to take on an English First Division job.

Back in Sheffield there was one outgoing deal to be done. Europe-bound Real Sociedad, who already had British players Kevin Richardson, formerly of Everton and Arsenal, and Liverpool icon John Aldridge in their ranks, had been over to Hillsborough early in the 1989/90 season to take a look at Franz Carr, the on-loan Forest speedster said to be available that summer. As it turned out, another bustling forward had taken their eye that day – Wednesday's Dalian Atkinson.

News of an imminent sale sparked a frisson of panic among supporters. Wednesday, a team relegated by their lack of firepower, were selling only one of two players to have contributed more than two league goals the previous season. Suspicion of the club's board – particularly chairman Richards, who had taken over from the popular Bert McGee in March 1990 – was rife. A son of a steelworker and a local businessman with an engineering firm, Richards had boasted in his early days that he remembered watching the likes of Derek Dooley and Albert Quixall at Hillsborough, but later admitted: "What I know of football can be written on the back of your hand." He later became an FA board member and the chairman of the Premier League. Go figure...

Wednesday had a new finance director in Bob Grierson and it was suspected that the Richards-led board had forced the dugout's hand in selling the man the players knew as "D-Boy" to make up for the losses run up by a recent shift in spending at the club. Wednesday were by this time £1.6m in debt and, alongside the recent signings of striker Atkinson for £450,000, Palmer for a whopping £750,000, Shirtliff for £500,000, King at £400,000, Nilsson for £375,000 and Sheridan at a further £500,000, their wage bill had risen from £1.4m a year at the end of the 1987/88 season to £2.2m by the summer of 1990. Had Hirst's exciting young strike partner been sold in a moment of financial withdrawal? It was a suggestion met with the fiercest rebuttal.

"Ron was under no pressure to sell Dalian," Richards wrote in the first programme notes of the season. "He's the man in charge. After we'd gone down, we had several offers for our players that would have cleared off the bank. But we didn't take them. We know that we have a damn good chance of going straight back to the First Division. There's no way in a million years that we are going to rush into big money trouble and go millions into the red. But we are being realistic. We are building for the future. We are looking forward to building a squad that is second to none. We're not going to hold Ron back in a way that would detract from winning the Second Division title."

Within seven years the club's debt would top £10m and by the turn of the century it would be closer to £16m. In the summer of 1990 Dalian Atkinson, who would go on to have a stellar career before his tragic and avoidable death at the age of 48 in 2016, was sold to Real Sociedad for an eye-watering £1.7m, of which £1m would be paid upfront. He became the first black player in Sociedad's history. It felt like a good deal all-round.

The year had seen the departures of Imre Varadi, Ian Knight and Craig Shakespeare as Atkinson sought to refresh a squad essentially built in the image of Howard Wilkinson. In a lower-profile departure, reserve-team man Tony Gregory was released and signed for former Owls player Jim McCalliog at Halifax Town as the Owls placed renewed focus on players coming in. Preston's talented Irish midfielder Brian Mooney was signed on loan with a view to a permanent deal, but suffered a serious knee injury and eventually left the club without making a first-team appearance.

With Wilson's £200,000 signing wrapped up within weeks of "the chat that didn't happen" in Spain, a goalscorer had been targeted. While Atkinson's pace had been an undoubted danger to rival sides, it was felt someone of a higher work ethic would be able to bring the best out of Hirst; someone to harry and stretch the defence while Hirst dropped in and found space in and around the penalty area. That someone was down at Charlton Athletic.

Peter Shirtliff, who had spent three successful seasons with the Addicks himself, knew before most others. "Big Ron pulled me aside one day at training and told me Dalian looked as if he was going," he remembered. "'What about Paul Williams?' he asked. Straightaway I said that he should go and get him. Straightaway. I had no doubt whatsoever. I told him he'd get more goals than Dalian, who was a great player by the way, but Paul was just what we needed. Ron had already made his mind up, I think. He usually had, but that might have just nailed the deal. He'd often ask us our opinion on things."

Charlton needed money. They had been playing at Crystal Palace's Selhurst Park since 1986 and were embroiled in a desperate, fan-led battle to return to a much-loved, but dilapidated Valley ground left behind after they had been unable to raise funds to pay for enhanced safety regulations set by the Bradford fire disaster. Athletic had been relegated with Wednesday the previous season as circumstances began to mount on top of them and Williams – not to be confused with the future Owls coach of the same name – was one of a handful of players known to be available for the right price. Charlton's top scorer in both of the previous seasons, he was signed by Wednesday for just under £700,000. A year later construction work on The Valley began. Charlton were back home by December 1992 and have remained there ever since.

The first thing you notice about Paul Williams is that he does not speak like your stereotypical footballer. Born as one of four children into a single-parent family in what he describes as a "really rough" East End estate, he left school at the age of 16 and became an accountant. Although he played football part-time and undertook trials at Tottenham Hotspur, Fulham and Leyton Orient, a career away from accounts looked a long way off until he was signed by Charlton from Woodford Town for £10,000 at the age of 21. Articulate, earnest and teetotal, he has a voice you imagine stands out in a rough-and-tumble, early-1990s football changing-room.

Not having been reared in a YTS or academy system had built him into an unorthodox player, he says, but one with unparalleled hunger to succeed. If Wednesday were after a hard-worker, a hard-worker they got. Fans, players and staff would take to him instantly. "It gave me an edge," Williams remembered of a left-field football upbringing. "I'd been out to work, I knew what it was like to get up at six o'clock in the morning and get home at seven o'clock at night; I'd known that world for a number of years. So when professionals around me used to complain about the training times or whatever, I didn't understand it. It was a luxury you don't have in the real world. It had given me a sense of hunger and a knowledge that, if I didn't do well, I knew what I was going back to. At the end of the day I came from a place where there wasn't a huge amount of expectation from friends and peers. I didn't have much to lose."

Within an hour of being told Wednesday were interested in him by the popular and softly-spoken Charlton manager Lennie Lawrence, another friend of Atkinson, Williams was in a car and heading for Barnt Green. Young and nervous, he remembers shaking with fear before getting out of the car to be greeted by one of football's great characters. A proud black man who had grown up in the perils of racism on a working-class 1980s estate, Williams knew all about the legend of Big Ron, particularly his trailblazing West Brom side that had Laurie Cunningham, Brendon Batson and Cyrille Regis in a historic all-black trio tagged with the rather "of-a-time" nickname of "The Three Degrees."

"I drove up to Ron's house and met his wife," Williams said of that first meeting. "I remember having this feeling of being very intimidated, almost like I was going to the headmaster for being in trouble. Not in a negative way, but just being in awe of this person I'd seen on the television and who had managed Manchester United.

"He had a reputation of unearthing good players and from a cultural perspective he had a great reputation for bringing on black players, so I saw him as a bit of an icon. I'd heard an awful lot about him and I was in total awe. But within two or three minutes of sitting down to talk to him, he immediately made me feel at ease. He is a great man manager and one of the greatest managers of all time in this country. A phenomenal human being and a great leader. Working for him was an absolute pleasure.

"I remember drinking tea with him and it struck me that he and his wife were both so well-tanned. I remember this very, very fine china that they gave me to drink my tea. It was like walking into a different world. He had a lasting impression of me and I don't have a negative thought about Ron. It was a great meeting and, if I'm honest, I came out feeling they could have given me half the money I was offered and I would've signed for Sheffield Wednesday."

While concern among supporters remained, it was felt within the club, and by the management staff in particular, that Williams and Wilson had enhanced a more well-rounded squad. Balanced though the squad was, there was one position that Atkinson had struggled to settle on; who should play in goal.

His former Manchester United man Chris Turner had finished between the sticks – thanks in part to a knee injury suffered the previous New Year's Day by former academy graduate and England under-21 stopper Kevin Pressman, by then 23 and four years on from an Owls debut under Howard Wilkinson. The two were locked in a fierce but friendly fight for supremacy. With the younger man fit and time ticking down, the pre-season battle was on.

Pressman, who would play more than 400 league matches for Wednesday in a 19-year career, believes the Owls' pre-season trip to Italy was one of many seminal career moments in that memorable campaign. "My wife was pregnant with my first child," he remembered. "I spoke to Ron and asked whether I could miss it. She was well overdue. He was honest with me and said: 'I'll tell you this, son, if you don't come with us, you don't start the season.' I sat with Joanne and spoke for a long, long time about what we wanted to do. It was what paid the bills, it was our living and I was young so we decided that I would go. When I came in and told him, Ron promised me that, at the first sign of Joanne going into labour, he would put me on the first flight home."

It was a sign of not only Atkinson's feted man-management skills, but of his absolute dedication to the season's preparation and to his honesty. Asked about the incident, Atkinson says his intention was to be honest with his young 'keeper; that, whatever the reasoning, a closer and prolonged look at Turner would have likely landed him the starting berth. He felt Pressman deserved to know that.

The long, hot summer of 1990 stretched way beyond South Yorkshire and into Europe as Wednesday lost 2-0 to a more committed Genoa in a half-hearted friendly in which substitutions were used intermittently because of the baking weather. Atkinson, keen to strike a tune out of his midfield, had told Palmer pre-match that Genoa had inquired about a possible transfer for him. In goal Pressman had made a couple of decent saves and despite the defeat, felt happy with his day's work on the squad's return to the plush old marble castle.

"There were no mobile phones back then," Pressman recalled. "We got back to the hotel and there was a message behind the desk to tell me my wife had gone into labour. Straightaway Ron got to it, true to his word. The next thing I knew, the Genoa manager had turned up at the hotel to pick me up. He took me to stay at his apartment closer to the airport and I was on the first plane out the next morning. I flew into Birmingham airport and raced up. I missed his birth by about two hours. And that is a big part of the reason, I believe, that I started the season ahead of Chris."

With Pressman home, the training camp continued and Wednesday went on to face Serie B side Cremonese, falling to a disappointing 3-0 defeat. But the events of a mid-trip evening, one that would prompt Atkinson's questioning of Sheridan's future, provided the lasting impact on Wednesday's 1990/91 season.

On arrival a few days earlier, the players had dragged their suitcases up the hill to their marble paradise to find dozens of beautiful women flouncing by the swimming pool and drifting in and out of a nearby bar, situated a stone's throw from their accommodation. It had been the final of a local beauty pageant, a number of the squad seem to remember, and though they packed up and left after the first night, a few had stayed on. It was at this moment, Atkinson thought, that it might be wise to set a curfew for his band of brothers. The focus had to be on the football.

But Wednesday were Wednesday – and Wednesday liked a drink. Atkinson and his staff embraced that. After the Genoa game and after Pressman's rapid departure, the players headed to the bar for a few relaxed pints. "We had a curfew of 11 o'clock, but the beer was cold and this bar was absolutely bouncing," said Phil King. "So it got to 10 to and we were all giving it to Nigel Pearson, asking him to go to the gaffer's room and get us some more time. We'd all had a good drink. He bounded back in like a hero. 'It's 12 o'clock lads; got us another hour,' he said. Then 12 o'clock came and of course we sent Pears over again. Well, the gaffer wasn't having it."

It was teetotaller Paul Williams' first experience of his fellow Owls players: "So I was on my best behaviour to an extent because I was meeting my teammates and coaches. All that was on my mind the entire trip was making sure I didn't do or say the wrong thing. I wanted to fit in. I was good friends with Carlton, who was good friends with Shez and so early on there was a little clique of players who hung out. We were given a curfew, told to go out, but we had to be back for that time. So we were getting close to that time, we were a little walk from the hotel and I said to Shez and those guys that we should really head back. One or two, including those two, decided to stay on a little bit. Most headed back and because I don't drink, I'd just about had enough and I went with them.

"I was rooming with Carlton and at about 12.30am, he came to the room to tell me there were people downstairs who wanted to get some autographs. I thought: 'Great, no problem!' I threw some shorts and a T-shirt on, went down into the lobby and signed some things. As I did that, Ron came bouncing through the door. There were me, Shez and Carlton downstairs. Richie followed him and Big Ron smashed through the foyer. He had gone into one, shouting and bawling and telling us we were past our curfew and that we had to go to bed."

Ron's memory of that night? "There were three players; Shez, Carlton and little Paul Williams. Richie and I were up watching a game on television, doing a bit of prep on something or other. And we heard some voices in the next room. Anyway I bounded in there to find those three and, let me tell you, I had a right go at them. Poor Paul Williams didn't drink, but the other two, bloody Laurel and Hardy, they'd lured him in, I think. Me and Shez ended up having this bit of a row. And I loved Shez.

"He was a right scallywag and I loved that. He ended up coming down to see me in my room. He was shouting and calling me all sorts. I couldn't be doing with him and we got into it a little bit. I almost threw him across the room. All I could hear as he was walking back along this corridor was all these lads with their doors ajar, sniggering their heads off."

Sheridan's teammates watched on with a bottle of grappa – a sort of brandy produced in Italy – for company. "It had all gone quiet and we were all sneaking up and down the corridor," remembered King. "We were all in our boxer shorts, hiding from Ron and Richie and passing this bottle of grappa to one another, giggling like kids. The next thing, we heard Big Ron coming through this corridor; it was an old-fashioned hotel with big corridors and massive ceilings. Ron had this thing that, if you'd been a bit naughty, he'd sort of slap you on the back of the head. Because he'd had a good drink, Shez stumbled a bit and started to take off his shirt. And then it went off. Mayhem.

"I remember me and Roland grabbing Ron and taking him back to his room. We were playing it down, you know, saying: 'You know what he's like gaffer; we've all had a drink, he was only having a laugh...' It all went silent and then all of a sudden we heard these feet outside. I opened the door and saw Shez. I whispered to him: 'What the hell are you doing?' He said: 'It's all right, Kingy, I'm just going to see the gaffer and apologise.' I said: 'Are you sure that's a good idea?' He waved me off and, dead quiet, he opened the door. And all of a sudden we heard this: 'Come on then, you bastard.' He was gunning for him again! We were all thinking: 'For fuck's sake, Shez...'"

Elsewhere Williams was panicking. "I was thinking they'd feel I was part of this naughty boys' clique. There were punches thrown, but I don't think any of them landed. Carlton and I were talking, thinking we would all be in trouble the next day." As his Owls teammates gathered for breakfast, Sheridan was sitting in his hotel room with his passport, which had been slid underneath his door by Richie Barker in a faux threat of exile. Atkinson stood in front of his squad, hands on hips, and singled out the new boy Wilson. "You'd get rid of him, wouldn't you?" "Well, boss," replied Wilson. "I don't know about that..."

The manager asked a couple of other senior players for their views and the squad rallied round their genius midfielder and good friend, unanimously voicing their opinion that he should remain a Wednesday player. Such was the unity building in the squad that not one player disagreed. Shez would stay. The manager agreed, but told his players that it was up to them to knock him back into shape; to abide by the management's rules and to ensure all future curfews were obeyed throughout the forthcoming season. The stakes, he reminded them, were too high not to. Sheffield Wednesday were in the Second Division and careers were on the line.

"I asked the question and I thought: 'I hope nobody agrees with that!'" Atkinson laughed, 30 years on. "But the lads all said he was the best player. They knew full well he was out of order, but he wasn't half a good player. Every one of them responded in that way and that was it. That was the moment I think that was a springboard for everything that followed. It pulled everyone together. It was very premeditated. I'd got up early and had a long think about it that morning. When people talk to me about Shez, they describe him as a good player.

"Let me tell you, he wasn't a good player. He was a great player. You would not know how good he was until you worked with him. My word, he was a scallywag and every now and then he did things that went against the grain on some rules we put in place. You always knew you were in danger of getting a word or two back from Shez. But I liked to have a few scallywags. If I was walking into a job or signing players and people would tell me: 'Oh, they're nice lads' – then no chance. I never wanted 'nice' – I wanted that bit of an edge. Not villains – I didn't like villains – but scallywags I liked."

The players and staff returned from training to find a sheepish Sheridan eating lunch in the hotel restaurant. "Sheridan, I want a word with you," Atkinson said, with the rest of the squad looking on and expecting the manager to hand out the bollocking of a lifetime. Dragged into a separate room, tension unbearable, Ron's face turned as the door closed behind them.

"Well, Sheridan," he said, building the suspense before launching into a comedic tone. "Bit of a crack, all that...We were all a bit pissed, weren't we?! I love all that, though, a bit of banter. You had a go at me, I had a go at you. That's what it's all about! Anyway I sat all the players down, told them I was going to send you home and asked what they thought. Can you believe two of the cheeky bastards wanted to get rid of you?! I asked them: 'Are you mad? He's our best player! The cheeky bastards, honestly...'"

4

YELLOWS

"You're a bit early, lads," smiled a polite member of the Suffolk Constabulary as the first raft of Sheffield Wednesday supporter coaches arrived at Portman Road. "We've had to get extra on for you lot – I wasn't even meant to be working today. Have a good season."

Extra police, extra space outside the ground for coaches, extra space for supporters in the stand behind the goal at the home of Ipswich Town as a proud Sheffield Wednesday prepared to get their 1990/91 campaign under way. It would prove to be a theme throughout the season. If the phone call that Ron Atkinson had received at ITV studios a few weeks earlier had left any doubt as to the commitment of Wednesday supporters heading into that first game, they were soon frazzled in the hot August sunshine. Wednesday had arrived in force.

The weather of the previous May had stayed on throughout the summer. UK temperatures in early August peaked at 37.1 degrees Celsius, beating the previous record set in the summer of 1911, and by August 25 – the first day of the football season – there was still absolutely no need for a jacket. Wednesdayites making the trip down to Ipswich that day waved to one another from cars and coaches with the sun beating down on blue and white flags billowing from closed windows. The A1 was theirs and the mood was good; one of excitement and optimism.

They were on their way to watch a Wednesday side that had returned from their time in Acqui Terme an even stronger unit and even more ready to pull in the same direction. Ron's psychology over the Sheridan shenanigans, so simple in hindsight, served to hammer home the spirit he sought to build in his teams. "Togetherness," he said in a radio interview leading into the Ipswich game, "is what will get us promoted this season. That's in the changing-room and on the terraces as well. We can win this division and we can do that in style. We've spoken about the need to right the wrongs of last season and we're confident we can achieve that. That's my message to Sheffield Wednesday supporters."

He later wrote in his programme notes for the season's first Hillsborough clash a week later: "This season our goal has to be nothing less than the Second Division championship – because that's the only prize that is good enough for our supporters. We owe it to you faithful fans who have stuck with us through all of the disappointments, not least the agony of that painful day at the end of last season."

Wednesday had played two further matches since their Italian sojourn; the first a Friday-night testimonial for long-serving and popular figure Lawrie Madden against Sheffield United and in the sort of dull, clinging breeze that only the hue of a hot summer evening under floodlights can provide. Madden, who was 34 and had an enthusiasm and commitment so clear that nobody mentioned he had played only seven of the 10 years usually required to be handed such an honour, had been told he could leave Wednesday in Peter Eustace's brief managerial reign before staying on under Atkinson as an example to the club's younger players. He'd certainly play his part.

Heading into the 1990/91 season as captain of the club's stacked reserve side, Madden had achieved a master's degree in leisure management from the University of Sheffield to follow up the BA degree he had earned from Manchester University as a junior with Arsenal back in 1977. Madden would go on to work in the media and for the PFA alongside consultancy gigs and, like Williams, it is fair to say that he was no lad-like footballer. Despite a certain image outside the walls of Hillsborough, it was a changing-room of all sorts.

"All the lads hope he gets the reward he deserves," John Sheridan wrote in the evening's commemorative programme. "We give old Lawrie a bit of stick because he's perhaps known as being a bit old-fashioned. I was only nine when he made his league debut and he would never win a prize as the club's best-dressed player! But he's a good pro and we've got a lot of time for him and wish him every success. He's earned it."

In front of more than 15,000 fans at Hillsborough Wednesday ran out 3-0 winners against their fierce rivals, who were preparing for a season in the First Division for the first time since 1976. It was a re-sult that ticked a lot of boxes, returning confidence and bragging rights to the blue half of the city while offering a genuine football test; firm friends Atkinson and Blades boss Dave "Harry" Bassett named full-strength sides for a game in which tackles were brutal.

Paul Williams poked home a first-half David Hirst shot saved by Blades keeper Simon Tracey before back-to-back goals just before the hour mark, Williams' second and a Peter Shirtliff header, sealed a mo-rale-boosting win. Williams later regarded the evening as one of the most important of his career; two goals in his first Hillsborough outing, especially against United, immediately connected him with the club's fans, going some way to allaying their fears about Dalian Atkinson's exit weeks earlier.

It was also the first experience of a Sheffield derby for Danny Wil-son, who went on to play in several more – including an iconic 1993 FA Cup semi-final – before managing derbies in the dugouts of both clubs. "No matter what kind of game it was, when Sheffield Wednesday played Sheffield United, you get a big crowd and you have to win that game," he said. "Lawrie got a fantastic turn-out. It was a great night for everybody and it set us on our way, I think. It put the fans in a good mood after what had been a tough time that summer. And it was a good way for me and Paul to be introduced to the fans."

Forty-eight hours later the feel-good factor grew further still when Wednesday won 8-1 at Crewe Alexandra, who would be relegated from the Third Division that season. Hirst, injured in the run-out against Cremonese, scored a classy hat-trick and there were goals for Nigel Pearson, John Sheridan, Trevor Francis, Nigel Worthington and re-serve forward Steve Bennett before Crewe scored a penalty generously awarded by a fairly sympathetic local referee.

So prepared, fine-tuned and brimming with confidence, the Wednes-day players were kicking off their season in a relaxed mood. Arriving at a well-to-do Suffolk hotel the day before, the squad were drifting down to their evening meal when fun-time left-back Phil King spotted a grand piano in the foyer. Unable to fight the voices in his head, he bashed his way through his finest Les Dawson impression, hammer-ing the keys to the hilarity of teammates and the horror of unknowing guests.

The squad ate and a couple of hours later, during a pre-match meeting with his backroom staff, jazz aficionado Big Ron heard the gentle tinkle of ivory and suggested they headed into the foyer for a more appreciative listen to the musician the hotel had provided. They pushed open the doors to find Roland Nilsson sitting at the piano, wearing his Owls tracksuit and playing classical music. While Ron, his physio Alan Smith and fitness coach Roger Spry stood open-mouthed, Richie Barker commented that the polar differences between the side's two full-backs – who remain firm friends to this day – had never been so clear.

In the afternoon sun the day after, late-coming Wednesday fans clicked their way through the turnstiles to the view of their players warming up. The nervous tingle of a first-day fixture was in the air, the crowd-controlling 1980s pens at Portman Road filling up a little uncomfortably. First-time father Kevin Pressman was battling the night-time disturbances of newly-born Thomas, later to become an academy goalkeeping coach at Derby County, but had been rewarded for a fine pre-season and his Italian commitment with the nod from Atkinson ahead of Chris Turner. The pair were great rivals professionally and got the best out of one another on the training field, but off the field there was an unspoken respect that prevented any unpleasantness.

"I've got on very well with every goalkeeper I've been with," said Turner. "It's different as a 'keeper; it's you or somebody else generally. Most of the time I played more than the other one thankfully, whether that be Gary Bailey, Barry Siddall, Kevin Pressman. It's never like: 'I don't like him because he's after my position.' Kevin and I got on very well. When you're not the one who starts the season, you either sulk and feel aggrieved or you go about getting your spot back.

"I was an experienced goalkeeper by then and it wasn't the first time I'd been put in that position. I knew what my options were. And there were only two. It helped that we had a proper reserve team that wanted to achieve something, but it was up to you to ensure that when your chance came – and all you could do is hope that for some reason it did – you grabbed it and kept the shirt thereafter. It was even more important to both of us because it was a Sheffield Wednesday shirt, of course."

As kick-off neared and the crowd behind the goal grew, the mood among Wednesday fans began to shift from excitement to concern.

The Ipswich policeman who had greeted the first raft of Wednesday-ites had mentioned that his superiors had planned for an inflated away following of 1,500 travelling supporters. But these were the days of standing terraces and pay-on-the-gate ticketing systems and in actual fact the figure was closer to 4,000, starting a crush that took the minds of many of those present to the tragic events 16 months previously.

Many supporters remember an initial reticence to help fans beginning to panic as the central pen at Portman Road grew busier, one reporting he saw a policeman using the full force of his baton to prevent a panicked youngster from climbing the fence. Once the potential issue was made clearer, however, the quick thinking of a Suffolk Constabulary on understandably high alert prevented any serious injuries, moving supporters into emptier pens and in some cases allowing them on to the fringes of the field of play.

Indeed a handful of over-exuberant Wednesday fans moved to sit by the advertising hoardings spilled on to the field after Williams' beautifully-taken opener after 28 minutes; a vital and nerve-settling first goal of the season for both player and club. Both supporters and police were later commended for their handling of the potentially-dangerous situation.

Hirst earned and missed a penalty a few minutes later, his effort cannoning back off the crossbar, and before long Wednesday had settled into a blistering pace Ipswich could barely deal with. Ipswich defender Neil Thompson, who would later go on to enjoy a long coaching career at Middlewood Road, hobbled off at 56 minutes. He remembered little about the fixture, other than Wednesday being "a bloody good side."

From the 4,000 behind the goal came a new war cry inspired by the now-iconic away strip chosen for the Owls by shirt manufacturers Umbro that year; the simple but effective bellow of "Yellows, yellows." It was bright and sun-yellow with minimalist sky-blue trim and, if Ron's similarly-coloured polo shirt a few months previously had missed the mark in terms of inspiring confidence, the same could not have been said for Wednesday's performances on the road the following season. The shirt was a thing of beauty and is regarded as one of the club's finest away strips by supporters to this day. They wore it well, playing with a style and bullishness rarely seen in the Second Division at that time.

By the time Peter Shirtliff had headed home Nigel Worthington's left-foot corner on the stroke of half-time there seemed to be little way back for Ipswich, swamped in numbers and quality all over the field. Remarkably 50 minutes had passed before they recorded their first shot at goal. Their 'keeper Craig Forrest made some good saves to deny Worthington and Sheridan, David Linighan – brother of Owls youth prospect Brian – headed one off the line and Wednesday remained in control throughout. Ipswich boss John Lyall later reflected that his players had been "in awe" of the Owls.

"I remember it was a stunning pitch, immaculate," said goalscorer Shirtliff. "And we arrived knowing we could really set a marker down and play on a pitch like that. As we were warming up, you soon noticed that it was going to be an amazing away following. Everywhere we went, we knew we were taking thousands and thousands and that they would be behind us. That's a powerful thing in football, especially then. It was good to get a goal and that was a target of me and Nigel, to contribute at that end of the pitch. It got us going."

It had been a successful opening gambit not only for Williams, but for Danny Wilson, whose endeavour on the right had played its part in the build-up to both goals. "The performance was magnificent," he said. "That was an indication of the way the season was going to go. I remember that first game vividly. On the coach on the way home I was telling them how exciting I was, saying: 'We have some good players here.'"

Three points, momentum rolling, job done. Or so you would think. With a tin or two of lager being thrown around the back of the bus and his players celebrating a handsome win, Atkinson leant back in his seat. "It was all right lads," he said, cutting into the party atmosphere like smiling cheese wire. "You played well. But there will be tougher tests this season, I promise you that. You're going to have to take your chances better." Under the surface, secretly, the promise of a league title to the supporters who had so keenly supported him over the summer lay heavily on the manager.

So to Hillsborough then – and a much-changed Hillsborough at that. In the wake of the disaster and the Taylor Report, published in January 1990, sweeping changes would have to be made to stadia up and down the country, with a particular focus on S6. Supporters shuffling into their normal spots for the visit of unfancied Hull City were again expectant and noticed a changing face to a stadium that had last seen major renovation work in the 1960s ahead of World Cup matches being hosted there in 1966, including a quarter-final.

Built in 1899 when the club was forced out of its previous Olive Road ground as a result of the rapid expansion of the city's railway service, its name was changed in 1914 from Owlerton Stadium – so-called after the area of Sheffield from where Wednesday in turn took their nickname – to take the name of the area's newly-formed Parliamentary constituency. To generation upon generation of Wednesday fans, it is the finest place on earth.

Gangways were widened, new fire doors and exits were installed at the cost of £150,000 and an emergency lighting facility was put in place for £10,000. The accounts included £30,000 spent on a new fire-alarm system, but most noticeable was the removal of the fences at the Kop and Leppings Lane ends of the ground, costing £70,000. In total £400,000 was spent. "We are delighted that the fences have gone and we think that the ground looks very good, but we implore our fans to stay off the pitch," said club secretary Graham Mackrell in the days leading into the Hull clash. "We are putting them on trust."

The moves, which Dave Richards made clear had been "imposed upon them" by the FA, were made as the mere starting-point of a plan to make the stadium all-seater by 1994, as per the ruling of the Taylor Report. It was vital work that later paved the way for Hillsborough to act as a host ground during the 1996 European Championships.

Hull arrived on the first day of September, having finished in 14th place the season before despite a long and uncomfortable flirtation with the drop zone. It had been a run slowly but surely turned around by no-frills new manager Stan Ternent, who was appointed in the November and who, by the summer, had spoken about continuing their late-season surge into promotion contention. A controversial rule change designed to restore the number of First Division clubs to 22 had decreed that Wednesday and their rivals were aiming for three automatic promotion places and four would qualify for the lottery of the play-offs.

For those looking at the likes of Wednesday from below, the rule change had made anywhere from mid-table upwards the land of opportunity. Hull had never played in the top division and it was a blow for them, then, to face Wednesday so early in the season. The Owls were in a different league in every sense of the word, except the one that really mattered, and in particular had a striker with a point to prove as big as his chiselled South Yorkshire grin.

David Hirst had been signed from nearby Barnsley for £250,000 in August 1986, Howard Wilkinson spotting raw goalscoring potential in a breakthrough season at Oakwell. Hirst was an England under-21 international and in his early years at Wednesday constant comparisons were made between him and his Young Lions strike partner, a Southampton forward called Alan Shearer. It was debated which of them would go on to have the most famous career. Like Shearer, Hirst's early years delivered huge promise, but were just a little short in terms of huge goal returns. This was his time to deliver.

Nigel Jemson, the Forest centre-forward who later signed for Wednesday to play upfront with Hirst, played for England under-21s alongside both Hirst and Shearer. "Now Shearer was an unbelievable footballer, I can't say anything against him obviously," Jemson said. "But I actually think that, if David Hirst had been clear of injuries, he'd have been better. He had power, he scored goals, he was quick, he was strong. One hell of a player." It's an opinion Jemson is not alone in holding.

By September 1990 a 22-year-old Hirst was Wednesday's main man up top and in the corridors of Hillsborough was well-known to be one of Atkinson's favourites, both in football terms and socially. He had everything you'd want in a striker; pace, power, a bullet-like shot and the sort of personality an entire club and supporters willingly could fall behind. Atkinson loved his streak of mischief and dry sense of humour, traits that in many ways held the changing-room together. In all his years as a manager, Atkinson said, only Dean Saunders made him laugh nearly as much as Hirst.

Only a twist of fate, literally, had prevented the two of them from working together earlier. "When I was at United, he was playing for Barnsley and he was the only player my chief scout at the time had ever recommended from the lower divisions," Atkinson said. "He told me about some kid playing for Barnsley, so I got in the car and went to watch him play at Leeds on a frosty, snowy day. After eight minutes he trod on the ball awkwardly and had to go off. He was out for weeks with that injury and soon afterwards Howard got him. I'd made the trip to Leeds to watch him play and it wasn't often I'd waste my time with those trips, let me tell you. So there was a reputation that he was a player. He was ahead of people. He was ahead of Shearer."

Atkinson wouldn't be the last United manager to show an interest in the Wednesday striker. Years later Alex Ferguson would show such a repeat interest in Hirst that Ron's successor Trevor Francis stopped taking his calls, which went down well. Over the years six separate United approaches were knocked back by the Owls on Hirst's journey to becoming their greatest striker in the modern era.

By September 1990 he had been Wednesday's top scorer in back-to-back seasons, hitting nine and a career-best 16 goals in those respective campaigns. On an afternoon that will be remembered evermore by those who witnessed it on the terraces, he claimed a quarter of that previous personal-best with four magnificent goals in an unflattering 5-1 win against a Hull side who simply could not cope with him. His goals showcased his full range of attributes; his first a sweetly-struck, swivelling volley past former Owls 'keeper Iain Hesford, his third starting with a turn on the halfway line and a pacey run that Hull defender David Mail might as well have sat down for.

As he turned away after completing his hat-trick, the Hillsborough crowd erupted. Having missed that opening-day spot-kick at Ipswich, this, it was now felt, would be David Hirst's season. It was the first time four goals had been scored by one Wednesday player in a match since Derek Dooley in 1952 and with closer inspection he might have been credited with all five, but nobody would take away Paul Williams' first league goal at Hillsborough. However much it seemed to take a devilish deflection off Hirst's hip on the way through to the back of the Hull net.

Wednesday had made an inquiry for former Atkinson favourite Cyrille Regis from Coventry City during the summer although it was not clear whether that would have been a transfer made alongside or in addition to Williams. The Hull win proved it to be a blessing if it was the former, with the Owls partnership quickly developing a telepathic understanding of how to play together; Williams stretching the defence while Hirst found space wherever he could, shooting on sight. With the delivery of King, Nilsson and Worthington and with the magic of Sheridan, they were a front two working in tandem and leaving Wednesday fans chattering with excitement. Williams and Hirst scored six between them in their first two matches. "Dalian's goals last season tended to be more individual ones," a grinning Hirst told reporters after the game. "This season I can see a lot of those like the one when Paul set me up for my fourth goal." Dalian who?

To this day, Hirst still regards Williams as his best partner up top, laughing when he explains their unspoken agreement that the London boy would do the hard work and he'd claim all the goals. Of the Hull game, he chuckled: "I still claim I got all five! But that's how good a strike partner I'd got; I let him have that one. It came off my hip and went in, so it might've been a rough one to claim. The way we'd started really got us going and I got a mixed variety of goals, which was a good sign. A couple of them today probably wouldn't be given for fouls.

"The experience of playing higher and doing okay allowed me that bit more confidence. We felt we should have been in the top division anyway and we wanted to show that in the performances we put in. And thankfully we did that. It was important to do that in front of the fans and really get the whole thing moving."

Williams' opening few weeks at Wednesday left him feeling as confident as he had been at any other point in his entire career. "It couldn't have gone any better for me in terms of the goals I scored," he said. "The way the fans responded to me, the way the players were with me... It was a dream opening for me. My first game at Ipswich and to score and to win the Hull game as we did was the best way to get into the good graces of supporters. My style of play was that I worked very hard and I think that was appreciated pretty early on.

"I came from London and my impression from outside was the people from Yorkshire revered people like me as southern softies. But my work ethic turned that around and ended up being something they admired. I worked very hard. That appreciation was so important to me and I managed to get that in a very short period of time. They knew that my heart was in the right place and that I hadn't come to Sheffield for the financial gratification. I wanted to make an impact and do the right things. It was a start I really needed."

In the season's third fixture, a trip to the big smoke for a clash with their old friends Charlton, Wednesday squeezed through by a goal to nil thanks to Sheridan's first of the season, a classy, dipping long-range volley past another ex-Owls keeper, Bob Bolder. But it was a win that came at a slight cost, with "Barney" Worthington tweaking a groin in the latter stages. The injury worsened in the week while on international duty with Northern Ireland and much-loved Wednesday physio Alan Smith, who played as big a part as any figure throughout the season, recommended that Worthington should not play in their following game, at home to fellow promotion-chasers Watford.

Atkinson, desperate to keep the now iconic King-Worthington partnership alive on the Owls left, ushered Worthington up the Hillsborough tunnel for a man-to-man chat that the local Press described as "a late fitness test." "It's when I open up my body to play it down the line, boss," said Worthington, who was in some pain, sheepishly, but truthfully. "I can't move my body quick enough to get into that position."

"Well, how's about this then, lad?" Atkinson smiled, placing his arm over Worthington's shoulders. "Don't do it. This afternoon all I want you to do whenever you get the ball is to look up, turn inside and give the ball to Sheridan. Got it? There's a good lad."

Worthington scored the second goal in a handsome 2-0 win.

Skipper Nigel Pearson had claimed the opener to add to the defenders' tally with Shirtliff's header at Ipswich and unlike the season before, Atkinson commented with some relief after the match, goals were finally coming from elsewhere on the field. A chart on the wall of his office, drawn up by Richie Barker, had set the squad targets; 45 goals combined from his strikers, 25 from his midfielders and 10 from everyone else. The chart also paved a game-by-game path through the season ahead; first safety, 50 points, and promotion, 90. Wednesday, having won their first four matches in some style, were ahead of schedule.

By now it was decided that a knee injury to on-loan Irish midfielder Brian Mooney required surgery, bringing his brief Wednesday career to an end, and reserve striker Dave Bennett was moved on to Swindon for £60,000. Atkinson subsequently put the feelers out for possible replacements, but it was so early in the season that even a contacts book as thorough as his couldn't prevent the search drawing a blank.

It wasn't for the lack of trying. Wednesday had posted a loss of £1.7m in their accounts in the previous year thanks to an ever-increasing outlay on players that had topped £5.5m. The matchday programme for the Watford game included a short article on the state of the club's finances, the first time a squad's cost had been outlined publicly. It was a move designed to articulate the idea that spiralling spending was a conscious by-product of the board's determination to achieve promotion at the first attempt.

Chairman Dave Richards, the article boasted, was willing to make more funds available for players during the season should Atkinson decide they were needed. These were communications well-received by supporters. The days of Bert McGee – circumspect or tight-fisted, depending on the viewpoint – were long gone.

Four days on from Watford came a dramatic and hard-fought 2-2 home draw with Newcastle United, Wednesday's first dropped points of the season. Paul Thompson, in *The Star*, described the outing as a "display of true grit" after back-up midfielder Steve McCall stepped up off the bench to send more than 30,000 supporters into raptures with a 90th-minute equaliser.

McCall, a club legend at Ipswich, from where he was signed in 1987, played an important role as a stand-in in what was his last full season of an Owls career littered with injuries. "I think the manager has got his team, but you always hope that, if injuries do crop up, then you'll be the one who gets in," he told Thompson. "I'm sure that scoring that winning goal won't harm my chances. I was happy just to get a game after being out for so long, but to score as well was superb."

The games kept coming and a confident and bullish passing display in a 4-2 win at Leicester was one of Atkinson's favourite victories of a season packed with them. In front of 6,000 travelling fans Hirst scored two and Williams one to continue their honeymoon love-in, and there was a first Wednesday goal for Danny Wilson. The Filbert Street win was the moment when Atkinson had full, unquestioned confidence in Wednesday's ability to achieve promotion playing football his way – not least because his talented opposite number, future Owls manager David Pleat, told him it was "easily" the best passing display he had ever seen in the second tier. So fine was the performance that Wednesday made a VHS recording available to buy in the club shop.

With only high-flying Oldham ahead of them, with the reserves winning and with smiles on faces all around the blue half of Sheffield, things looked rosy at Hillsborough when Third Division Brentford arrived the following midweek for the first leg of the first round in the League Cup – now known as the Rumbelows Cup after a change in sponsorship. For the seventh match in succession Atkinson named an unchanged side and, battling back from a goal down, Hirst and Pearson nudged them into the ascendancy in a 2-1 win.

"Our top priority this season is regaining our First Division status," Atkinson's programme notes that day read. "But, remembering that old adage about success breeding success, a good cup run would be welcome for the team and the supporters. And, with Wembley at the end of the trail, it offers the promise of vital income for the club if we can put together a few good results. Danny's goal at Leicester reminded me that he's been all the way in the League Cup, doing so twice with Luton. It would suit us all if he can complete a hat-trick with us this season. Well, you never know!"

Quite.

5

ONE IN A MILLION

Trevor Francis received a mountain of messages from friends, acquaintances and hangers-on after he was sacked as player-manager of QPR in November 1989. "So sorry, Trevor," was the general gist. "You'll bounce back." One of the most gifted players English football has ever produced, the classy forward was forever written into the history books after becoming the first million-pound player in his move from Birmingham to Brian Clough's Nottingham Forest a decade earlier.

An iconic headed winner in Forest's 1979 European Cup final win over Malmö entrenched him further into the annals of history, before he blazed a trail for British players by spending five successful years playing in Italy for Sampdoria and Atalanta. There's no question that Trevor Francis is a *bona fide* football legend.

So exciting it was then, even at the age of 35, that Francis arrived at Hillsborough in February 1990 after a short, typically to-the-point phone call from Atkinson. Like Hirst, the Owls boss had shown an interest in signing Francis during his time at Old Trafford, getting very close to making him his first United signing back in 1981 alongside Glenn Hoddle. Neither came off.

"I'm not going to bother saying sorry for what happened at QPR," Atkinson told Francis, calling his plush home in the grounds of Wentworth Golf Course. "Stop moping about. Get yourself up to Sheffield Wednesday and play for me. I want you in my team." Sheffield was a stunning city built on seven hills just like Rome, Atkinson told culture vulture Francis, before describing an imaginary line of new wine bars in the city. Agreeing that a move back into football was what he needed to snap out of his QPR heartbreak, the veteran signed for the Owls to add a touch of class and experience to a side that would ultimately go on to suffer that unexpected relegation.

Seven matches into Wednesday's near-perfect start to their bounce-back season, Francis' involvement had been limited to one start, in the League Cup outing with Brentford, and three substitute appearances as the Hirst-Williams partnership continued to flourish ahead of him. It was a source of quiet frustration for a player who found himself in such a position for the first time in a 20-year playing career and Atkinson's famous man-management skills came to the fore to keep those on the fringes of his squad motivated.

Indeed, Francis' cameo appearance against Brentford was the only change to Atkinson's preferred XI in the early weeks of the season. With Pressman between the sticks, Shirtliff and Pearson at the heart of defence and Nilsson and King either side, Wednesday had looked strong in defence. With Wilson and Worthington they had energy and endeavour out wide to complement the genius of Sheridan and the box-to-box qualities of Palmer. And then there were the front two. They'd won six and drawn one and Ron's attitude was simple: Why change?

"The older you get, the more desire you have to play," Francis later reflected. "When you're young, you think you will play forever. When you're older, you realise time is running out. I was okay about coming off the bench, but if I was the manager, I would have started me. I think I could have played from the start more often. There are players who can come on and struggle to get into the game, but I was recognised as a good sub and made some useful contributions."

Although Francis was to be used most regularly off the bench, Hirst credits the opportunity for both him and Williams to breathe in his experience and technical ability as a big part of the reason they had so much success. He had fond memories of the occasions when Atkinson played Francis on the left-wing and revealed a trick the pair had to give him the run on opposition defenders. "He was obviously coming to the end of his career when he arrived," Hirst remembered. "But it was great to work with him. He was a quiet person around the dressing-room, but, when he spoke, you listened.

"As a centre-forward he would just deliver it where you needed it. With him coming on for the last 10 or 15 minutes in games that you needed a little bit more, you'd have so much confidence. He told me early on that, if he went down the wing on his left foot, it would go to the near post and, if he cut back, it would go to the far post. All I had to do was to pay attention to what he was doing and invariably he'd put it where he said he'd put it."

On September 29 West Ham United arrived at Hillsborough as one of three unbeaten sides at the top of the Second Division. Under the tutelage of the highly thought-of Joe Royle, Oldham Athletic – who had enjoyed two incredible cup runs to the final of the League Cup and to the semi-final of the FA Cup the season before – had set the pace with 19 points from their seven league matches. Wednesday were a match behind them with 16 points from their six and West Ham, playing only their fifth season outside the top flight since 1958, had drawn four and won three to sit on 13 points. It was a three-way tussle that would last the season.

With club legend Billy Bonds at the wheel after Lou Macari's controversial exit – Macari was by now doing a little scouting work behind the scenes at Wednesday, having cleared his name in the Swindon fracas – the Hammers were playing a more direct style than their fans were accustomed to. Attempting to climb out of the Second Division at the second attempt following relegation in 1989, Bonds had assembled a talented side; the promise of Julian Dicks, Ian Bishop and Kevin Keen dovetailing nicely with the solid, physical strike partnership of Trevor Morley and Jimmy Quinn. This, it was felt, would be the Owls' first big test.

Any nervousness was settled when Hirst scored after 67 seconds, in what was his 150th game in senior football, and Wednesday – keen to make yet another early-season statement to the teams around them – set about turning it on. And they may well have done, were it not for a performance-of-the-season display by the Hammers' Czech goalkeeper Ludek Miklosko. By the time Dicks had levelled the scores with West Ham's only shot on target of the match, a 77th-minute effort that deflected off the legs of skipper Pearson, Miklosko had made nine saves.

The West Ham goalscorer admitted after the game that his side "could have been five down by half-time." Praising his 'keeper, Bonds said: "They outfought us, they outplayed us. If they'd got a second goal, we would have been dead and buried." Even more concerning than two dropped points, however, was an Achilles tendon injury suffered by eight-goal Hirst. "People forget that we had a few injuries across the course of that season," remembered Alan Smith, Wednesday's physio from 1984 until 1991 and a beating heart of life at Middlewood Road.

"Some were more serious than others and some players, with respect to that whole squad, made you a bit more nervous than others when they went down. Hirsty was one of those. Because of the way he played, he picked things up here and there that other players didn't. He was so whole-hearted and we'd have to work very hard to stop him from rushing himself back. He'd say to me: 'Do you know my problem, Smithy? I'm never fit enough to get injured!'"

But injured he was and Wednesday had to do without their main man for the best part of a month. Enter Francis, who stepped into the starting line-up for a rain-soaked trip to Brighton and claimed two effortless assists in a 4-0 win. Hundreds of Owls fans who made the midweek trip to the south coast removed their shirts and sang in the rain as Danny Wilson scored his 100th senior goal, the others going to Williams, Sheridan and Pearson.

At half-time, with boxing champion Chris Eubank paraded in front of his adopted home crowd a few weeks ahead of his WBO title win over Nigel Benn, the away support rang out with cries of: "There's only one Bomber Graham" in support of the Sheffield-based, Brendan Ingle-coached fighter, whom Eubank later admitted to having avoided at all costs throughout his career. The appearance was cut short and an apologetic entourage suffered a double-barrelled telling-off from Eubank. Chuckling Wednesdayites claimed a first-round knockout.

With a clash at Bristol Rovers scheduled three days later, Atkinson took the opportunity to keep his side together, enjoying a training camp in Oxford, his own stomping ground. A night in the local hostelries provided Wednesday players with a much-needed loosener after a manic start to the season, ahead of a gruelling few days overseen by enigmatic fitness coach Roger Spry. "It's not just a football thing," remembered Roland Nilsson on his initial shock reaction to the early-1990s drinking culture in British football.

"It's so deep in the British culture, to go to the pub. I come from a country where the drinking is done in another way. Not going out on weekdays, having some drinks on a Friday or a Saturday, but not really getting too drunk. For me it was a little bit strange, but at the same time

I knew that was the culture and that's how it was. I didn't drink as much as the other guys, but those who didn't drink lots – me and Paul and Trevor – would have some wine and enjoy the evening. It was fine."

Hair down, Wednesday went into a unique clash at Rovers – played at their temporary home of Bath City's Twerton Park – high in confidence and with renewed vigour. On a sodden surface not fit for second-tier football and at a small ground with an even further reduced capacity because of an earlier fire to one of the stands, this was a long way from European Cup finals and Saturdays at the San Siro for Trevor Francis. But the 36-year-old, 52-cap England international was the star man, netting the only goal – his first for the Owls – and earning praise from all around the club. Among those lauding Francis was Paul Thompson, who had to borrow the car phone of club secretary Graham Mackrell to ring through his report for *The Star*. So torrid were the conditions that his phone had been broken. A sixth consecutive away win equalled a club record.

With Nilsson playing for Sweden against Germany three days later, Lawrie Madden stepped in as a utility right-back for the second leg of a Rumbelows Cup tie against Brentford that Wednesday again won 2-1 with the rejuvenated Francis scoring after only 11 minutes and claiming another man-of-the-match gong. Pearson netted six minutes later and, although the Owls battled through with a healthy 4-2 aggregate scoreline, they were made to work hard for it and events that day led Atkinson, in the corridor outside the Griffin Park changing-rooms, to tell Spry that he had something special going at Wednesday.

"Brentford were bang up for it and they took us on the hop, got in between us and disrupted us," he said. "And to be fair, those were the games early on where I knew we had something. If there was any doubt that these lads were expecting to rock up in the Second Division and pass their way through the league, it was those games that showed they were able to pull their socks up and give it some. They were tough matches."

It was about this time that Big Ron was linked with a shock return to the First Division with Everton. Former Wednesday player Colin Harvey was floundering after three years in the role and, with the Toffees attempting to shift themselves out of a hangover from unprecedented mid-1980s success, it was felt that they needed a manager of huge personality to turn over a tired squad. Although his title rival Royle, a former Everton player, was the clear favourite for the job, the *Daily Mirror* in particular seemed hot on links between Liverpool-born Atkinson and the Goodison Park dugout. Crystal Palace boss Steve Coppell was also a name heavily mentioned. All three were sounded out; but a phone call from Everton to Dave Richards was, it was reported, one of few words.

Thirty years on, Atkinson remembers little of the approach and maintains that the closest he came to taking up the Everton job came in 1998 after his second stint with Wednesday and before Walter Smith gave a U-turn on an agreement with Wednesday to take up the Goodison Park role. As it happened in 1990, Atkinson signed a new contract with Wednesday at the end of October, a couple of weeks before Howard Kendall made a shock return for his second of three spells with the club. To top the merry-go-round off, Colin Harvey was appointed as Kendall's assistant manager.

***

Part of the package that had enticed Francis to sign for Wednesday was the opportunity to learn from an experienced boss such as Atkinson on his eventual route back to management. But after stepping into Hirst's place in the side and scoring in back-to-back games, and ahead of a home clash with Plymouth Argyle, the city in which he was born and raised, it was clear that he still had plenty to offer on the pitch. The match, now forever known as "the Francis game," would hammer the point home.

Such was their celebrity, Francis and Atkinson would most regularly fill the attention of national column inches and grab air space as Wednesday coverage reduced following their drop into the second tier. In an appearance on immortal football magazine show *Saint and Greavsie* ahead of the clash, Francis was asked of his new role as third fiddle in the Owls' attack behind Hirst and Williams and said: "I have no complaints because they are excellent players. David Hirst is an excellent player. He has a great left foot, he's strong, he is good in the air and over 30 yards he's the quickest in the club. He's only young and, if he keeps on going, he can go all the way – I'm talking about full international honours." High praise indeed.

Plymouth, a very direct and hard-working side built by Dave Kemp, were entrenched in the Second Division and had full honours in the "dark arts" of the game, designed to nullify the technical quality of players such as Francis by whatever means necessary. On the day they might as well not have bothered as the veteran ran the game, creating all three goals – two for Sheridan and one for the now free-scoring Wilson. Taken off at the 77-minute mark, he received what physio Smith still regards as the loudest standing ovation ever awarded at Hillsborough. "If I could turn back the clock and make Trevor 26 again, we'd have it sewn up by Christmas," Atkinson laughed.

Atkinson now remembers the performance as one of the finest he ever saw from one of his players: "He's a Plymouth boy. He's the most famous Plymouthonian since Sir Francis Drake; that's what I always told him. One of the things I remember most keenly about him is during team talks we'd have. Whenever I was giving him a team talk, I'd try to keep them short, sharp and snappy. You do that, you do that. And then I'd ask if anybody had any questions. Trevor always had one.

"I remember ahead of one game, Trevor stuck his hand up and said: 'Ron, when the ball goes into their penalty box, where do you want me to go?' I said: 'Trevor, I played 500 games for Oxford United and I scored 14 goals. You used to score 14 goals in a month. You've played for your country, scored in a European Cup final and got bought for a million quid. When the ball goes in their penalty box, you go wherever you've been going for the last 20 years!' I told Ron Greenwood this story and he said: 'Trevor asked me the same question. And he got the same answer.'

"For somebody of such immense talent, he'd need reassuring all the time. We paid him an okay wage, but we made sure we incentivised everything. He'd got a reputation of being a bit injury-prone. Well, I tell you what...he wasn't half available for games! I actually marked him on his debut. I always told him he only had one kick all game. It was the equaliser, mind! Players are funny. He's a great lad, Trevor."

A class act though he undoubtedly was, many players remember that Francis' age, experiences in the game and different way of looking at life set him slightly apart from the majority of the changing-room. One player remembers a prank after training turning nasty when the newspaper Francis had brought in was set on fire and felt that, while in the main part there was a great deal of respect there, he was harshly dealt with by his teammates from time to time. Although Francis largely kept himself to himself, there was something of a divide between him and the larger-than-life teammates – an issue that would show its teeth some years later after he had taken over from Atkinson as manager.

Paul Williams spoke honestly on his relationship with Francis, who, he says, he learned a huge amount from in their time together. On their early-days commutes to Sheffield from the south, Williams and Danny Wilson would often pick Francis up en route and the young striker would hang on every word, desperate to pick up what advice he could. But he'd turned down a move to Francis' QPR a year earlier, in doing so scuppering a double transfer with his Charlton colleague John Humphrey. It was apparent, Williams felt, that the older man held a grudge against him from the start of their time together.

"It wasn't the right move for me at the time," Williams remembers on the mooted QPR switch, which would have meant both he and Humphrey moving across London in a million-pound deal. "I had an awful lot of admiration for Trevor, he was a hero in many respects and he achieved a great deal, but I came away from a meeting at his house feeling that it wasn't the right thing to do at the time. Completely different from how I felt leaving Ron's house the following summer. I'd only had one proper season under my belt at Charlton and felt that I needed another one before I went anywhere. I wanted to establish myself and had made good friends. It just wasn't the right thing for me.

"I didn't take it personally, but I'm not quite sure that the same could be said for him. Deep down I get it; you go to someone, you want someone and you don't get them. That can be tough and it can bruise your ego a little. I declined the opportunity and I think it was taken in a personal manner. Trevor took that personally and it was always there between us, I think. It was definitely evident after Atkinson had left and he took over. I only lasted a few months under Trevor and I ended up moving through mutual agreement. It just wasn't the right environment for me under those circumstances and I told him I wanted to get back to London." In September 1992 Williams moved to Crystal Palace in a swap deal involving Mark Bright.

John Harkes, a talented but largely unknown USA international who had returned to Wednesday after a trial with the club earlier that year, had huge respect for what the legendary forward had achieved in the game, but remembered a similarly difficult clash of personalities. Again when Francis took the reins from Atkinson some months later, Harkes claims the new boss refused to honour an agreement about the terms of a new contract after a stellar first season.

"I had a photo of me posing with Trevor Francis when I was 10 or 11 years old," Harkes said. "My Aunt Ethel, my dad's sister, used to work for Detroit Express, where he played for a little while in the late '70s. So I went to visit her and I made sure I got the photo on the field with him at the end of the game. It was a big deal to have Trevor Francis play in America. I showed it to him one day and he was confused by it.

"It was an interesting relationship. He didn't disrespect me being a US international; I just think he looked at them as a lower-class national team. Whenever it came around to international games, he'd tell me it wasn't too important and that I didn't have to go. I always felt as if I had to keep earning respect from Trevor; he never looked at me as someone who had accomplished a lot or that I deserved that respect. He may have a different perspective, I guess."

***

The night before a Wednesday XI including Sheffield resident and former England captain Emlyn Hughes played at Stocksbridge Park Steels to formally open the use of a £20,000 floodlight system, the club held their annual meeting at Cutlers' Hall in the city centre. As is often the case when results on the pitch are favourable, the meeting went swimmingly and lasted only 40 minutes. The exciting takeaway line was that Atkinson had hinted further player reinforcements would be made to ensure the Owls' title challenge.

But frustration reared its head when an unfancied Port Vale held Wednesday to a 1-1 Hillsborough draw on October 20, with Williams the scorer, before a dramatic 89th-minute header from Carlton Palmer, his first goal for the club, earned a draw by the same scoreline at South Yorkshire rivals Barnsley three days later. The night before Palmer had gone to the room of his midfield partner John Sheridan for advice on breaking a 19-month duck for the Owls. Sheridan, typically lyrical, told him: "Get in the box more, you nugget."

Ankle better, Hirst had replaced Francis in the Port Vale match as Atkinson went searching for a winner before taking the place of the 36-year-old in the clash at his former club. Although he was a regular off the bench, it would be more than a month until Francis would start another game. Back-to-back draws signalled a slowing of the blue and white machine, but confirmed a 12-game unbeaten run, two matches off the club record of 14 from way back in 1899. Wednesday were in second place as they headed off to London to face Millwall and were hoping to gain on Oldham, who were three points ahead of Wednesday on 31, having played a game more. West Ham, a point behind the Owls, were hot on their heels.

Millwall were fourth and, although it seemed Wednesday would breeze through to within a single match of the club record when a fit and firing Hirst put them 2-0 up in 16 minutes, the bottom fell out of their world when their leader Pearson was taken off at half-time with a groin issue and Roland Nilsson twisted his knee awkwardly in the South London turf. Wednesday's eventual 4-2 defeat was not the worst news of the day. The Sweden international had ruptured his cruciate ligaments.

"Straightaway I knew we were in trouble," said physio Alan Smith, who soon found himself working with the Swedish FA in looking after Nilsson's recovery, as per the agreement in his contract. "He rotated on the halfway line, twisted around and his body weight went the other way. I can see him now signalling to us and I remember this feeling of dread. When I was running on the pitch, I had a pretty good idea of what was going to greet me and when I was testing him, I knew right away. We got the stretcher and got him off. It's a horrible feeling, that."

A similar sense of foreboding had reached Nilsson and, while the club's initial public communication suggested he would be out of action until Christmas, in-house they knew it would be much longer. Atkinson set about looking for reinforcements at the back, a right-back who could cover at centre-half, and he didn't want rival clubs to know how desperate they might be. The news soon got out.

"Roland was one of the best professionals I played with in my entire career," remembered Danny Wilson. "He was absolutely extraordinary, such an athlete. He looked after himself very well and he and Trevor Francis were so far in front of us, having played in Sweden and Italy.

They had different experiences from the clubs they'd come from with diets and all that. Roland was the ultimate example of that and I loved playing with him. He was a very intelligent player as well and so, when he did get injured, you think to yourself: 'We've lost a player there.'"

Even after all this time, the pain in Nilsson's voice is evident when he remembers the injury: "I knew straightaway. He got on the inside of me and I was in high speed trying to shift my body weight over as my boot got caught in the grass. I just felt my knee pop out and something had crashed inside of it. I knew right away it was something very serious and that I would be out for a long time."

Wednesday, so comfortable up to half-time in that Millwall defeat, had looked all at sea after the enforced departures of two of their most dependable players. A reshuffle had caused chaos and all of a sudden they were three matches without a win. With no quick-fix transfer available, and with only four days until their Rumbelows Cup second-round tie at Swindon, Big Ron would have to try something different.

Luckily he had something up his sleeve.

6

"WHAT HAVE WE LEARNED?"

In the mid-1870s, nearly 4,000 miles from a then 10-year-old football club that would come to be known as Sheffield Wednesday, a huge, family-run company based in Paisley, Scotland, set off on plans to expand their thread and weaving empire into a far-flung, but burgeoning economy – the United States of America. The firm, known then as the Clark Thread Company, opened up two factories just a short, 20-minute drive from the Statue of Liberty and set about taking over the monopoly of the industry in what was then still a relatively young country and the freest and most exciting economic climate in the world.

The geography was favourable, business boomed and the company expanded, soon to be joined by other British firms wanting to get in on the dollar goldrush. Textiles, lino, the manufacturing of railroad tracks; before long there was a lot going on in the town and company bosses preferred to employ people from back home. People they trusted. It meant that the town of Kearny, New Jersey, had a decidedly Caledonian accent.

The expansion of mainly Scotland-based firms in Kearny boomed and by the 1960s a census listed somewhere in the region of 21,000 residents – more than half the town's population – as "Scottish American." A wander through the town centre would take in traditional British pubs, butchers and a fish-and-chip shop in which a teenage John Harkes, the son of Scottish parents, battered haddock to pay for his football boots.

Stroll on any longer and you would see dozens of first-generation British immigrants playing not baseball, basketball or American football, but what those outside the town called "soccer." Several would play in the country's top leagues. To this day Kearny is nicknamed "Soccer Town" by Stateside sports fans.

In January 1990 Ron Atkinson was sitting with his feet up on the desk of his Hillsborough office when he took one of his many calls a day. This time it was his old friend Ian St John on the other end of the phone; the legendary Liverpool goalscorer and one half of *Saint and Greavsie*, the show on which Atkinson was a regular guest. It transpired that St John's son Ian had been working with a club in the US and that he had a couple of players worth taking a look at.

Harkes travelled to South Yorkshire with fellow Kearny resident Tony Meola, a stocky goalkeeper who would go on to win 100 caps for the US national team. The pair were looking forward to representing their country at Italia '90 ahead of their country hosting the World Cup four years later, but this was almost a decade before the inception of the MLS and well before the days of Brad Friedel, Landon Donovan and Clint Dempsey. Scandinavian players had begun to entrench themselves in the British leagues, but there was still a mountain of snobbery attached to US players.

"Usually you take these things with a pinch of salt, but you sit up and take notice when the Saint calls you," Atkinson remembered. "He was a good judge of a player. Where Harkesy was different was that his old man was Scottish and, even though football in America was a completely different sport altogether at the time, he used to go to some little Irish bar and watch British football. He was ingrained in our culture and way of playing through his father. He wasn't away with the fairies, running in penalty shoot-outs...He knew what proper football was."

The fortnight went on and, although neither Meola nor Harkes were spectacular in training, Atkinson went to the trouble of organising an unpublicised, behind-closed-doors clash against his old club West Brom to give the pair a chance to show what they could offer. Minds had already been made up about Meola, who appeared to have his gloves on backwards and had Pressman, Turner and highly-rated youngster Marlon Beresford in his way. Harkes was doing merely okay, before a single moment late on in the West Brom kickabout convinced Atkinson there was something there.

"He was playing out on the right-hand side," Atkinson remembered, "and right at the end, he went right up to the byline and put in a great cross. Curving, sharp, right where you'd want it. I turned to Richie straightaway and said: 'I like that.' I had visions of Hirsty getting on the end of those; it was the sort of service he loved. I called it a 'German' cross – it was how they used to do it, fast as you like. But there's no doubt that moment kept him on board. If I'd left early or I'd been looking the other way, it may not have happened for him. I'm glad it did."

It was only at the club's 150th anniversary celebration 27 years later that Atkinson told Harkes just how fleeting his career with Wednesday might have been. Harkes had otherwise assumed it was because of goals he had scored in training. On the back of that cross the pair were invited to stay on until the end of the season. Meola shocked Atkinson by telling him he would go on to look for opportunities in Europe – "Juventus? You'd be better off at Fray Bentos, lad," the manager told him – and somewhat more surprisingly Harkes, ambitious and desperate for his big chance, also politely declined, intending to return to the US to prepare for the World Cup a few months later. Atkinson couldn't believe his ears.

"We'd set up a real run of games for us to get some chemistry together and that was so important for me at that time," said Harkes on the run-up to the USA's first World Cup in 40 years. "Well, Ron thought I was mad. Looking back, maybe I was. He was giving an American an opportunity to play football at a high level here, which was unprecedented, but I had belief in myself that I could make it work at both ends. As it happened, he was out there with ITV covering it, so he had kept an eye on me. We spoke after the World Cup – I had done fairly well there and the US team had done okay – and I was invited on trial again, which was great."

Harkes was in his second stint at Wednesday at the start of the 1990/91 season when Atkinson offered him low-wage terms on a three-year contract that would be revisited if he had had a good first campaign. St John's son, Ian junior, looked over the contract on offer. And although Harkes insisted that Wednesday felt like a good fit, St John organised trials with Blackburn and Celtic in search of a better offer. What he didn't know was that the clubs all spoke to each other, so all knew exactly what Harkes had been offered by Wednesday.

"Both clubs offered me the same salary and neither felt right for me in the same way Wednesday did," Harkes said. "I remember finishing training at Blackburn and asking whether any of the lads would be going for lunch, like I'd gotten used to in Sheffield. I was told it was something they didn't really do. So I circled back again and I was on a train with a duffle bag, on my way back to Sheffield Wednesday with my tail firmly between my legs. I arrived at training, straight from Scotland, and Ron invited me into his office. There was dead silence, he looked at me slowly from across the table and said: 'Well, son...What have we learned?' I felt like a little kid."

Such was the undeveloped nature of US soccer at the time, a transfer agreement was struck not with a club – Harkes was playing with the Albany Capitals – but with the US Soccer Federation, for a fee of £70,000. He played initially with Frank Barlow's reserve side, his first appearance coming in a wet 1-1 draw in front of a few hundred supporters at Nottingham Forest. "He made me earn it," Harkes recalled. "I worked so hard, I played in three more reserve matches and did well. And then we signed and I was there. But he definitely made me work for it."

A classy technical player with an eye for goal, Harkes had played on the left of midfield to good effect in the World Cup, earning praise for his job in marking Milan superstar Roberto Donadoni, but usually played as a ball-playing central midfielder for the US. Atkinson saw him as a right-winger. The idea had been to use the American international sparingly as he adapted to his surroundings, introducing him to the first team as the fixture schedule got more manic towards Christmas. But injury to Nilsson changed everything.

***

Wednesday had another right-back. Darren Wood was a highly-rated, committed and experienced player who had made more than 150 appearances for two big clubs, first Middlesbrough and then Chelsea, from whom he joined Wednesday in 1989. A broken leg had robbed him of a fair crack of the whip at Hillsborough and by the time his opportunity had come along, a red card in a reserve match meant that he was banned for three matches. Back issues materialised and he retired midway through the season. Now the owner of a range of butcher shops across the north of England, he politely declined the invitation to contribute to this book, describing his brief time at Hillsborough as one of the most difficult periods of his life.

With the feelers out for a new man, Atkinson began peering around the training ground for answers after Nilsson's injury. Lawrie Madden could fill in, but it was feared that he would be unable to cope with the week-on-week rigours of first-team football at 35 years of age, let alone contribute to the attack in the way Atkinson and Barker had encouraged Nilsson and King to. Barker, Barlow and Atkinson mulled the matter over tea in the manager's office, where a lightning bolt arrived the day before Wednesday's Rumbelows Cup third-round clash with Swindon on October 30 – the same day the Swedish international would travel home for knee surgery.

"Harkesy," the manager called out during a training session. "Have you ever played at right-back?" The American – who, in his own words, "puffed his chest out and threw his head back" – said: "Yes, boss, of course I have." And so it was done. Wednesday managed to push through the final stages of his dual-passport application and John Harkes made his debut in English football the next day. "Is that true?" asked a suspicious Nigel Pearson as the two walked off the training pitch. "Have you played right-back?"

"No," came the honest reply.

"He was a real joker, but he meant that," remembered Danny Wilson of his early memories of Harkes. "A proper American, full of bullshit at times. He'd talk a load of rubbish, but he'd do it on purpose and we loved it. He came in and wasn't one to sit back or let people speak first. He took the opportunity to make himself a central part of the team and he did really, really well. Harkesy was a great acquisition. He was fresh and bright and fit. He was just what we needed."

Harkes, later to become a successful coach with championship-winning USL side Greenville Triumph, said: "I'm adaptable. I've always had that since I was a kid, not just in football, but in life. Heading into any environment, I think: 'I can do that easily.' I was a quick learner and watching Roland play there...I always remembered he was a great defender, but also that he was a pioneer of the early days of wing-backs, very cultured in that way. That's how I wanted to go about it. I had to add in the defensive qualities.

"One thing that Ron knew he was getting from me was that I had a pride in not letting anybody beat me on the field. It didn't matter what position on the field or in training I was, I had a thing about not letting people beat me. He thought I could fill in at right-back and do a good job. So I did."

Madden came in at centre-half for Pearson, whose groin injury proved not to be so severe, and under the lights at S6 the makeshift back-four kept a clean sheet. Unfortunately for Wednesday, so did Swindon – thanks to a classy performance from Sheffield-born Fraser Digby, who had been at Manchester United under Atkinson and had acted as an understudy to Chris Turner. Harkes impressed, setting up attacks with regularity and himself forcing a good save from Digby in the second half.

Although Wednesday were now four games without a win going into November, the goalless draw with Swindon was far from ideal preparation for the visit of table-topping Oldham Athletic to Hillsborough. Joe Royle's side, unbeaten after 14 league matches and famed for an awkward and controversial plastic pitch as well as a well-drilled side high in quality and high on confidence from their cup heroics the season before, were by now seen by many as the champions-elect. Atkinson went as far as to say Oldham were "certain to get promotion" in his programme notes.

If they were mind games on behalf of the Owls boss towards his great pal Royle, they weren't the only ones. The same programme notes revealed Wednesday were well aware of an Oldham figure – Phil Black – watching the majority of their games during the season, with Atkinson even cheekily describing him as "a rotund figure." With the managerial opening at Everton at that time still unfilled, he also chose an opportune moment just a couple of days before the match to rule himself out of the running and hint at Royle's suitability. He wasn't daft, but the tactics seemed to fall flat, at least after 20 minutes of a match 34,845 supporters attended – the highest Second Division crowd in more than two years.

The Latics raced into a 2-0 lead thanks to goals from Nick Henry and David Currie. King, one of a handful to have suffered a dip in form in Wednesday's lean run, received a torrid time from onrushing Oldham right-back Paul Warhurst, who in turn would sign for the Owls the following year. It was here, in front of a frustrated crowd, that Wednesday's promotion mettle would be tested and they responded well, Palmer showing his newly-found confidence in front of goal when he rattled the crossbar of John Hallworth.

Hallworth made a handful of fine saves to deny first Wilson and then Hirst as the Owls pressed the issue. In the words of Nigel Worthington, Wednesday "battered" Oldham. "We got better as we went on," he remembered. "With the crowd as they were, it had a real sense of occasion about it and, once we'd settled down, we were able to get control of the match. If we'd scored a little earlier, it was a game we would've won."

On the hour mark Sheridan slotted in a penalty after Hirst had been fouled clean through on goal and, with the crowd roaring them on, Wednesday forced save after save from Hallworth. The equaliser came eight minutes from time after Sheridan again stepped up to convert the penalty he earned himself, leaving Royle to describe the clash as "a great advert for Second Division football."

"Nobody could begrudge us the point we salvaged," Atkinson reflected. "But the final scoreline could have been emphatically in our favour. The crowd served to emphasise the enormous potential that still exists at Hillsborough and how dearly I would like us to be able to enjoy that tremendous atmosphere more often. The game lived up to the occasion and I rate it among the best half-dozen I have been involved in during my career."

Wednesday were now winless in five, but had put on a display that felt like a win for all involved. Except Phil King. A beating heart of the dressing-room, the charismatic and popular left-back was by his own admission going through a difficult spell in the side. Having struggled to combat the pace and directness of Warhurst against Oldham, he took time out the following day to prepare himself for a match he'd been looking forward to since the 0-0 Rumbelows Cup draw with Swindon.

King had joined Wednesday from Swindon three years earlier and most of his friends and family supported the Robins. So, having organised a fistful of tickets to the County Ground reply for some of his nearest and dearest, this would be the match he felt he could come roaring back with, against a side that had lost five times at home and were susceptible to the dangers of attacking full-backs. That was until he took a casual look at the teamsheet at Middlewood Road. Without a word, and knowing full well what the match meant to King, Ron Atkinson had dropped him for the first time. With King watching Steve McCall fill in at left-back from the stands, Wednesday won 1-0 to book their place in the last 16 thanks to Nigel Pearson's header after 10 minutes.

King, who described being dropped at the time as an "all-time embarrassment," was furious. "I remember speaking to Carlton at the training ground," King said, "and saying: 'That fat bastard, he's dropped me for Swindon; I've got all my family coming!' Carlton was old mates with Ron and knew him better than any of us. I was ready to go and have it out with him in his office, but Carlton stopped me, which was very wise because I'm not sure what I would have said. I was fizzing.

"Carlton told me he was just looking for a reaction out of me, that he'd done the same to him before. And the following game I was back in. Without saying a word, Ron sent me such a strong message – that I had to buck my ideas up and be more consistent. It worked. I was a better player from there. It was his way of saying he wasn't too happy with me, to sort myself out. That's the way he was."

King's stint on the sidelines continued four days later at mid-table Blackburn and, after a wasteful Wednesday had put in 33 crosses to Rovers' one in a smash-and-grab 1-0 defeat, Atkinson unleashed a rollocking on his players that was heard by delighted home supporters on their way out of Ewood Park. Despite picking up just three points from their last five league games, Wednesday were still third in the table, but had fallen five behind West Ham and nine back from Oldham.

Middlesbrough, a surprise package in fourth place, were two points behind the Owls and the Rovers defeat was the first time in the season that Wednesday had fallen below the two-points-per-game marker that had been set out by Richie Barker at the start of the season – a marker he and Atkinson felt would ensure that they won the title.

With the required message sent, he surmised, Atkinson returned to his favourite side – apart from the obvious omission of Nilsson, who had by now returned to Sheffield and was beginning his rehabilitation work with Alan Smith. Wednesday enjoyed a break from their league commitments when they made the short trip to Elland Road for a testimonial match for long-serving fans' favourite Mel Sterland, by now at Leeds after a brief stint at Rangers.

With the Wednesday international contingent elsewhere, the late former Leeds maverick Frank Worthington had been drafted in to play for the Owls in the friendly affair and Francis netted a hat-trick to remind Atkinson of his goalscoring touch. While they had missed a number of chances at Ewood Park, the relaxed setting meant that Wednesday won 7-2 against a side led by their old boss Howard Wilkinson. As you might expect from a Mel Sterland party, felicitations continued long into the night at the Queens Hotel for those who enjoyed that sort of thing. A born-again Phil King, usually a man at the epicentre of such an occasion, headed back to Sheffield for an early night.

He may have had one eye on Wednesday's next game, which was yet another meeting with Ossie Ardiles' Swindon. Relaxed and rejuvenated, Wednesday ran out 2-1 winners to improve their recent run despite another fine performance from the Robins' 'keeper Digby. Williams and Pearson netted the goals before a late consolation from Alan McLoughlin – into an empty net after Kevin Pressman had been injured seconds earlier – cost the Owls what would have been a well-deserved clean sheet.

Facing reporters afterwards, Richie Barker responded to suggestions that the stuttering Owls were too fancy, too ambitious with their style of play to go the long haul in a division more direct than they were used to. "Ron has his way of playing and we're not going to budge on that," Barker said. "We have the players to play a certain way and we intend to win the championship in style. That doesn't change because of a bad run of games. Many of our players are internationals and have had to contend with midweek games when many others have not. That takes a toll, but the fact is that they are international players and our fans deserve to see a certain style of play. We won't be budging on that."

7

QUE SERA, SERA...

Sheffield Wednesday fans have always taken great pride in being an individual bunch. And somewhere along the way in the 1990/91 season, when other sets of supporters were hitting the headlines for throwing dangerous missiles towards opposition supporters, the Owls faithful – by now known as "Atkinson's Barmy Army" – were raising eyebrows by throwing items of a different kind between themselves. Cuddly toys.

Although it is now difficult to pinpoint exactly how or when the strange phenomenon started, it had reached epidemic proportions by the time that the Owls arrived for an ill-tempered match at West Bromwich Albion. Some believe the trend took its inspiration from Manchester City's famous inflatable banana craze, which took on a life of its own after the signing of former Owls forward Imre Varadi – a surname that apparently sounds similar to "banana" when pronounced in Mancunian timbre.

Whatever the reasons behind it, one soft toy turned to two and before long the sight of dozens of them being thrown around Wednesday away ends was a common sight, offering bobbies around the country the impossible task of preventing them from being thrown from time to time at opposition players loitering on the touchline for too long. Many Wednesdayites remember the soft-toy craze kicking into fifth gear at the Hawthorns with a constant shower of Disney characters falling from the cold Midlands sky. And while the away end was filled with good cheer, the reception offered to the Wednesday players elsewhere was anything but soft.

In three-and-a-half years in his first stint at West Brom, Ron Atkinson had led the Midlands side to three European campaigns by playing good, attractive football, having assembled a squad of the calibre that they were unlikely to see again. By the time he had returned in 1987, via a five-year tenure at Manchester United, they were a different club altogether and Atkinson had been given the task of keeping them in the Second Division. He succeeded, having brought in Andy Gray and Brian Talbot to fuse alongside youngsters such as future Owls defender David Burrows and a certain Carlton Palmer.

But the return spell did not last long because Atletico Madrid came out of left field to appoint him. He was on a £40,000 salary at the Hawthorns, but the Spanish side offered him a quarter-of-a-million a year. Although he loved West Brom and their supporters, he grew frustrated at the Hawthorns. Money was so tight that Atkinson agreed to do an after-dinner speech at a national hotel chain on the premise that the club could use their facilities for away matches. Spain was the land of opportunity and, looking to rebuild his reputation as a top manager after his shock Old Trafford sacking, he was begrudged a move to the sun by few in the game. The few, of course, included West Brom fans, who felt he had unfairly abandoned them for a second time.

The reception Wednesday players and staff received when stepping off the bus was not reserved only for their manager. Palmer had made the switch to Wednesday from the cash-strapped Baggies two years earlier and was also targeted with some of the vilest abuse you can imagine. The line had been spun by the West Brom PR machine that the young midfielder had asked for a transfer request in order to grease the wheels of a move to Hillsborough. In actual fact he was one of three players involved in a flash sale designed to pay some outstanding debts, taking the advice of World Cup winner and then-Baggies youth coach Nobby Stiles to reject Ken Bates' Chelsea and re-join Big Ron up north.

"It was tough, that," Palmer remembered. "I got so much abuse. You can imagine the things that were being said to me. West Brom were a club that I owed a lot to and cared a lot about; I still do, and to be honest it affected me. On some level I was expecting it, but I really hoped it would at least be a mixed response. It really wasn't and I played shite."

With his long legs and gangly body, Palmer was recognised as one of the brightest prospects in English football and had been capped by England B. His later association with Graham Taylor's failings as England manager meant that he was unfairly slapped with a reputation with those who don't remember his quality, that he was something of a "football donkey." But not in Sheffield. His relationship with the enigmatic John Sheridan remains one of the finest midfield partnerships the country has seen; the perfect foil for a creative hub plucked out of Brian Clough's reserves at Nottingham Forest for a bargain fee. The pair were right at the centre of not only Wednesday's on-field success, but many of their off-field escapades as well. To this day they remain firm friends.

"We're very close," Palmer said. "We had a great understanding and teams couldn't work us out. Teams turned up throughout our time together and set up with their runner on me. It never worked that way. Shez would always take the runner, which meant that I was left with the one who couldn't run and couldn't get around the football pitch. That freed me up and it was always a major problem for them.

"Other teams constantly underestimated Shez's ability to get around the pitch. He wasn't just a technically gifted player; he was also brilliant at getting round to pick up gaps and pick up runners. That left me with a player who couldn't keep up with me. You'd end up with Andy Townsend or whoever trying to catch me. That would open up space and we were able to dictate to teams."

But not that afternoon. Incredibly rarely, and by his own admission, Palmer wilted in the atmosphere and at half-time, despite dominating the majority of the play, Wednesday were 1-0 down to a side just three points from the relegation places. Atkinson made a bee-line to the player he'd worked with at that very ground. "He told me I was playing shite," Palmer remembers. "And he had a point."

Other Wednesday players remember Ron's handling of Palmer sometimes coming across as favouritism. Few minded, though; after all, Palmer was unique. The 6ft 2in battler was not just a bundle of energy on the field, but off it, too. He would enjoy "four or five" pints of Guinness the night before a game and required a tot of brandy on his way out to play to settle the nerves.

"I would always come out of the dressing-room last and insist on being the last one on the field," he said. "I would wander into the lounge in the main stand at Hillsborough, past the surprised sponsors and suited executives, jog to the bar where the staff had lined up my drink, swig it down, joke with them: 'See you again in 90 minutes when I come in to collect my man-of-the-match award' and run out on to the pitch. Big Ron never had a problem with it. Nobody had a problem with it as long as I did my job on the pitch. What you do off the pitch is immaterial in my view as long as you perform on it. It was a psychological need."

West Brom had nicked a goal, largely against the run of play through England captain Bryan Robson's brother Gary, and the wounds of Blackburn, where Wednesday had failed to hit home their dominance, were seeping apart again as Harkes, Hirst and Williams all went close. But with four minutes to go, just as the West Brom support dared to start singing: "Judas, what's the score?" at the frustrated Owls manager, former Birmingham icon Trevor Francis rounded Baggies' goalkeeper Mel Rees to equalise and the atmosphere quietened. When Peter Shirtliff nodded home to win the game three minutes later, there was barely an Albion supporter in the ground.

"It's 2-1 lads," Atkinson chuckled to himself under his breath, keeping his emotions under wraps but for a trademark double fist-clench. Outside the ground a club employee and Wednesday fan known as "Bobbo" – who would regularly drive Atkinson to and from Sheffield from his home in the Midlands – grabbed the manager in a tight embrace. "Who writes your scripts?" he asked.

Making their way back to their coaches through the smog of engine fumes in the Hawthorns car-park, Wednesday supporters joined in a hopeful chorus of "Que sera, sera," looking ahead to their Rumbelows Cup last 16 tie with First Division Derby County four days later and hinting at a possible final booking. "Whatever will be, will be," they sang. "We're going to Wembley..." The Derby clash would be a tight Hillsborough affair in which David Hirst broke a rare, seven-game goal drought with his 10th of the season in a 1-1 draw. The fun would come at the Baseball Ground in yet another replay.

Although it didn't really show in his performances, Hirst struggled throughout the campaign with knee and ankle injuries. "There were times in the season when I didn't feel particularly fit," he reflected. "But I was never concerned about any goal droughts or anything like that. I wasn't that sort of player anyway; I wasn't a worrier, but there were always going to be chances in a team like that. So I always felt one would be along soon. If there's one thing I would say, it is that there was always a tendency at that time to push players out on to the field when maybe they weren't ready. I was one of those who just wanted to play; I played with a broken ankle later in my career. I just wanted to go out there and score goals.

"But Ron had the team he wanted and he would do what he could to get you out there, with little words here and there, despite what Smithy had told him. I obviously struggled with injuries all the time I was at Sheffield Wednesday and I look at the sort of environment they have in football now, when everyone is better looked after, and wonder. That's not to say anything against Ron or anyone else; it was always my decision to go out there. Looking back, I cut a lot of corners."

***

It was at the start of December that a curious transfer rumour arrived as Ron Atkinson sought to beef up his options ahead of a busy second-half push. "Ron Wants Robbo" screamed the *Daily Mirror* headline ahead of the clash with Notts County, a side sitting in seventh place and slowly manoeuvring themselves into the promotion conversation. The Robbo in question of course was not Baggies' goalscorer Gary, but the main man himself, Bryan – who Atkinson had taken to Manchester United for a British record fee of £1.5m nine years earlier, but had been out for six months after two Achilles tendon operations.

Alex Ferguson was rumoured to be ready to start a squad revolution at Old Trafford, the report said, and the futures of the likes of Robson were under consideration. It was suggested that Wednesday would provide the 90-cap England man with the opportunity to take on a coaching role while continuing to play. Although Dave Richards had promised cash to burn in the Owls' pursuit of a return to the top division, it would have been an extraordinary move. To this day Atkinson regards Robson as United's greatest player – not just of his era, but of all time.

"All being well, I have no intention of leaving United," the report quoted Robson as saying. "At the end of the day it will be down to the boss whether he wants to keep me." Atkinson still does not remember making an inquiry as to Robson's availability. A well-placed ploy between two friends to force Ferguson into showing his hand on the future of the man known as Captain Marvel, while showing Wednesday's ambition in the national media? Perhaps.

Owls supporters arriving a minute or two late to the Notts County clash may well have had to double-take as their beloved side passed the ball around confidently wearing not their blue and white strip, but in yellow. Both County's home and away strip, the referee had ruled, clashed with the traditional blue and white of the Owls. When it was suggested that Wednesday should hand their away strip over to County, skipper Nigel Pearson voiced his displeasure at the idea that another set of players would have the opportunity to wear the Wednesday badge. So yellow it was.

County were the division's surprise package, a term coined by Atkinson himself in the fixture's programme notes. Managed by Sheffield-born future Blades icon Neil Warnock, celebrating his 42nd birthday no less, they had been on a handsome run that had enabled them to rise to seventh in the table with a good squad, containing cultured midfielder Mark Draper, England under-21 international and Craig Short, Dean Yates and future Owls forward Tommy Johnson. They were a side making their way in the second tier for the first time in six seasons, having been promoted the year before. Typical of Warnock's want, they were tough, uncompromising and desperate to break up the footballing monopoly at the top of the table.

But there was no birthday party for Warnock. Wednesday dominated the first half after Trevor Francis was brought down inside 90 seconds for Sheridan to stroke home yet another penalty before Hirst added another in his newly dusted-off scoring boots on the stroke of half-time. Boyhood Blade Warnock, managing competitively at Hillsborough for the first time, flew into a furious interval rant, later made famous in reels of documentary footage. The opportunity was slipping, the young manager said, for his under-appreciated players to make a name for themselves in front of 23,000 supporters. It did the job, as his players recovered to draw 2-2.

"I didn't know him from Adam," Atkinson remembered of a first meeting with Warnock that left an impression on him. "He came on the scene and he'd got a reputation for what he'd done at Scarborough and all that. Joe Royle is a big pal of mine and he knew him. Let me tell you, from what he'd told me about Warnock, they weren't the best of mates. We played them at Hillsborough and I had Trevor playing on the right-wing. He went flying through and this big centre-half, Craig Short, came out of the middle and clipped him. I didn't think he'd done it deliberately; it was just a late tackle.

"Well, Neil came over and started ranting and raving. He said to Short: 'I've told you, you kick that Francis...you missed a chance there.' I couldn't believe it. I said: 'Oi, you. Get back in your dugout. Big Joe has told me about you. Keep your mouth shut.' We'd been 2-0 up and they came back to draw it, and they deserved to. We'd been lucky to be leading like that. They had a bloody good team. After the game he came running down the tunnel after me, saying: 'What did Joe say? What's all this?' Well, I turned round and said: 'Why don't you...?' You can guess the rest. He got dog's abuse."

The Owls had dropped two more points and, with West Ham and Oldham winning elsewhere, had lost more lost ground in the title race. The Hammers, still unbeaten, were looking imperious, particularly at home, and goal-happy Oldham won their next three fixtures – all on their artificial pitch – 6-1 against Brighton, 4-1 against Wolves and 5-3 against Plymouth.

By now the memories of that long, hot summer were becoming more and more distant as the weather set about balancing itself out for 1990. With rabid snow storms scheduled in the north on December 7, Wednesday players and staff set off early that morning to Bristol, moving their scheduled departure forward several hours so as to avoid any potential drama. Supporters hard at work but looking forward to a match at Bristol City the next day, of course, didn't have that luxury.

Despite a raging blizzard further up the country there was no snow whatsoever at City's Ashton Gate ground. The issue for fans hoping to attend the match was battling through the conditions up north. Most bus companies issued refunds to frustrated supporters and the hardy souls who attempted the trip ended up marooned somewhere in Derbyshire. Two buses of supporters jumped out of their transport to have a snowball fight with a group of Sunderland fans attempting in vain to make their way to a 3-3 draw at Tottenham. After the coach drivers had turned back, Danny Wilson's third goal of the season earned a disappointing point for Wednesday in a 1-1 draw.

One Wednesday supporter did manage to navigate his way to Bristol after setting off from his Swinton home at 8am, fighting train cancellations, delays and ignoring weather warnings to forge onwards. His Bristol train from Sheffield cancelled, he headed down to London, where he boarded the underground. He then eventually settled on to a train to Bristol that would have got him to the ground on time had it not been stationary for more than an hour when it got to Swindon after the train in front reported a wobbly bridge. Having set off nine hours earlier, Fred Ronksley arrived at Ashton Gate to watch the referee blow his final whistle, turned around and began planning his route home.

8

"GO HOME, YANK"

All of a sudden Sheffield Wednesday were nine points adrift of table-topping West Ham and just one point ahead of Colin Todd's Middlesbrough in fourth. It was still early days, of course, but things were not quite going to plan for Atkinson's Barmy Army. The pressure was on and many Owls supporters began to look gratefully at the third automatic promotion place which opened up just months before. Besides, they had the excitement of the cup in their lives and a last-16 replay at Derby County to look forward to.

Walking on to their Middlewood Road training ground the day before, John Sheridan sidled up beside John Harkes to pass on a word or two of wisdom. The former Leeds United playmaker, whose mood would switch from happy-go-lucky to grumpy to mischievous and back depending on the scoreline and situation he found himself in, was not usually one for profound speeches or moments of emotion, but there was something that had caught his attention. "Harkesy, you can play, lad," he said. "Don't let anybody tell you otherwise."

Harkes had been parachuted into English football ahead of schedule and was filling in for the great Roland Nilsson in a position foreign to him. And although he had put in nine solid back-to-back performances and despite his go-get-'em outlook, it had not always been a breezy start for him. Any suspicion attached to the suitability of American soccer stars within the game itself was extended 10-fold on the opposition terraces. To the media Harkes' nationality had become something of a novelty. He was, after all, only the ninth US player in history to make the transition to Europe, and the first at this level in the UK.

"There was a lot of cat-calling and chants," Harkes remembered. "'Go home, Yank!' and joke accents, that kind of stuff. The British culture was, to a degree, not all that accepting to a lot of foreigners back in those days. Every country had a stereotype and it's tough to imagine it today, but in terms of foreign players there were just me and Roly in the Wednesday team.

"And two were a lot in those days. But if you show you can play, eventually they will accept you. You have to be thick-skinned; you have to be able to take a few shouts here and there. There are tough places in English football. You go to Millwall and they let you know. So you have to have strong self-belief, take all the shit that is thrown at you and fight through it. That resilience was a big challenge; fighting day-to-day, week-to-week, trying to get acceptance around the league."

The moment that changed Harkes' life, and in some ways the course of Sheffield Wednesday's season, arrived after half-an-hour of the Derby clash. It came courtesy of a perfectly imperfect ball from Nigel Worthington on the Owls left, hit first time in order to recycle possession, arms half-hanging to his side like C3PO. His lofted, left-footed, curling pass across the field was a yard behind the American, who checked it forward into space with one exquisite touch. Another touch followed, edging Harkes closer to Peter Shilton's penalty box. And then, just for a second, the whole world stopped.

"I was crying out for the ball," Harkes remembered. "The gaffer had told me that he wanted me to take the freedom to get into the spaces further forward and create, but that we were away from home and I wasn't to do it too early. I had to protect the centre-backs as well. Kingy and Worthy had been knocking the ball around the left and, by the time it worked its way across to me, I had crept eight or nine yards over the midfield line.

"I was in acres of space. I remember feeling as if I was in so much space. My first instinct, even when the ball was coming over, was to catch it on the half-volley and push it forward. As soon as I took the second touch, I knew I was hitting it. Absolutely no doubt in my mind. It didn't matter that it was 40 yards out. Nobody was stepping out to me and I thought: 'Take your chance while you can'. So I did."

John Harkes' 40-yard wonder goal against Derby County is simultaneously an utter masterpiece and material taken from the throwaway script of a movie; the unknown American, out to achieve his dream – to beat the British at their own game, against all odds – hits one from 40 yards past the 125-cap England veteran goalkeeper Peter Shilton, to the adoration of his teammates and the acceptance of a football public. It was his first goal in English football. You could not write it. But if you did, it would go straight to DVD. "It was pre-planned," Atkinson told reporters after the game with a glint in his eye. "We always say: 'When you are 30 or 40 yards out against the world's best goalkeeper, have a shot.'"

After the game, Harkes had a brief post-match discussion with Shilton and asked the England legend for his gloves. "I got a short answer of about two words and the second was 'off,'" Harkes laughed. "He did congratulate me, though – I'll give him that and that shows a lot for his character. He was the most-capped international player at that time and his fingertips could not have been any closer to that ball. He was a quality goalkeeper and to score like that was amazing. That goal changed my life. Without a doubt it was the number-one most influential and positive change in my life I could ever have hoped for. Without a doubt."

Williams scored in the opening minutes of the second half, his sixth for his new club, and aside from one or two hairy moments, not least when Gary Micklewhite put the Rams to within a goal of parity, Wednesday dominated. Derby had finished fifth in the First Division two seasons previously and had some players out, but there was still quality throughout the side; ahead of a 42-year-old Shilton was Mark Wright, the England centre-half who had starred in Italy that summer, a young Dean Saunders, England B-capped Mike Forsyth and Mick Harford.

The serendipity of beating that team at that ground, which had been so intrinsically linked to their last-day relegation heartbreak a few months earlier, was not lost on Wednesday's players or staff. It was their first win at the Baseball Ground since 1938.

It might have been more, with late chances for Wilson and Palmer going begging, and Derby went on to suffer relegation themselves that season. But the fact remained that Second Division Wednesday had outstripped their top-tier opponents to remind the national media of their quality. No longer were the newspaper inches and radio waves reserved for only Atkinson and Francis. There was interest in the blue and white wizards once more.

Not one to rest on the glory of a first qualification for the League Cup quarter-finals in six seasons, Atkinson again set about strengthening a squad that was losing ground in the league. Three days after their Derby heroics, an Ipswich side so smoothly put to the sword on the first day of the season arrived at Hillsborough and were 2-0 up within 21 minutes. Phil King was again the fall man in Big Ron's 25th-minute reshuffle that paid dividends, as some Francis magic and a Pearson volley earned the consolation of yet another point at home.

"We firmly believe that we are the best footballing side in this division, but, if we keep dropping home points like this, we are in danger of missing out," said an angry skipper after the game. Atkinson described the opening half-hour as the worst he had ever seen from his side, his misery compounded when Nigel Worthington suffered a nasty knee injury that kept him out of action for a month.

Thanks to back-to-back replays in the Rumbelows Cup, Wednesday had played 26 matches in 116 days since the start of the season, at an average of one every four-and-a-half days. In the league at least, they were looking leggy. With Worthington shuffled back to left-back and Francis brought in to play on the left-wing, King remained out of the side for yet another midweek cup match, a 3-3 Zenith Data Systems Cup match against Barnsley.

Despite a classy Hirst hat-trick against his former club, Wednesday went out on penalties and the following weekend, at second-bottom Oxford, they recovered from going a goal down to lead 2-1 before conceding sloppily from a free-kick to draw yet again. Eight back from leaders Oldham' but only two ahead of Boro, Wednesday were looking over their shoulders.

In search of a much-needed boost, Atkinson dug deeper into his black book of contacts. He felt he needed someone with huge experience, someone who he knew could come in and do a job. A huge-money signing was not on the agenda, but Dave Richards had said over and over that cash was there to give the manager the bump the club needed. Two names cropped up that he felt would fulfil two roles – Viv Anderson and Norman Whiteside.

It's a popular misconception that Atkinson had managed Anderson before. The first black man to play for England at senior level back in 1978, the popular right-back had become Alex Ferguson's first signing after Ron's departure nine years later, but suffered injuries and struggled to make his way back into the first-team reckoning after the purchase of Denis Irwin – rather than Roland Nilsson – earlier that year. Ferguson's interest in the Swedish international was so well-known that national newspapers jumped to speculation that a cash-plus-Anderson deal was being negotiated. In actual fact Atkinson picked up the phone to the Manchester United boss with the words: "Now, Alex, we're not going to speak about Roland, but..."

Whiteside was a player Atkinson *had* managed. Another experienced competitor with a proud international distinction, and still the youngest player to play at a World Cup at 17 years and 41 days old, the Northern Irishman had enjoyed some of the best years of his career as a prodigious talent at Manchester United, where Big Ron had given him his senior debut. Atkinson had tried to sign him when he left Old Trafford in 1989, but he had moved on to Everton, where injuries continued to be a scourge of Whiteside's young career.

Atkinson had won two FA Cups with the powerful midfielder and, knowing that Whiteside's big personality, winning mentality and love for a pint would fit in well with those already at the club, he set about inquiring as to his availability. The Owls boss was told that Irish international forward Kevin Sheedy was available, but showed no interest.

The need for a clear-out at Everton was well-known and, while Howard Kendall had by now already gone about making changes, Atkinson saw an opportunity. Whiteside had starred for Everton the season before, scoring 13 times in 35 appearances. But the hard-line fitness sessions of the Toffees coach and former Owls captain Mick Lyons took a toll and his knee blew up. With only a handful of reserve games under his belt after subsequent surgery, Wednesday bid £100,000 for the man who had had the world at his feet just a decade or so earlier.

Atkinson felt he could save his old friend's career, but he could not. Any potential deal fell through when it became obvious that his injury problems were worse than hoped and Norman Whiteside, once with the world at his feet, retired from the game six months later at the age of just 26.

***

Christmas was a busy time on and off the field for the Owls, who were given no respite from a gruelling schedule when old foes Wolverhampton Wanderers arrived on Boxing Day. The Owls had beaten them in an FA Cup third-round match that January, but were to be wary of a Wolves side in sixth, seven points back on Wednesday, and of England international striker Steve Bull, who before the game had talked up his side's chances of a promotion push. Wolves boss Graham Turner was no stranger to those in the home dugout either, having worked alongside Richie Barker at Molineux for three years.

Some 30,000 Wednesday fans who were getting soaked in miserable, monsoon weather had their mood improved as their side raced into a 2-0 lead inside 22 minutes thanks to goals from Steve McCall, stepping in on the left-wing in place of the injured Worthington, and a well-finished team goal for Palmer. Then came the turning-point; a sliding tackle from Harkes who slipped on the sodden Hillsborough turf and collided with Rob Dennison.

With the entire ground expecting nothing more than a stern lecture by referee James Ashworth, Harkes was sent off after 54 minutes to resounding boos from the Wednesday faithful. Paul Cook, a Scouse midfielder three decades later heavily linked with the Wednesday manager's job, scored with 20 minutes to go before Bull equalised 15 minutes later. In 11 days, John Harkes had felt the most soaring highs and the most bitter lows that football has to offer.

"There's not a lot I can say because you can get yourself in trouble," Wolves boss Turner said after the match, "but both sides have reason for complaint. I do sympathise with the player who was sent off." In his post-match talk with reporters that lasted all of 90 seconds, Atkinson was less measured. "I did not enjoy that game one bit," he said. "It was spoiled by something not appertaining to the players on the pitch."

Another draw meant that Wednesday lost more ground on the teams ahead of them and, with Middlesbrough claiming three points in a 1-0 win at Portman Road, Bull's equaliser had pushed Wednesday out of the coveted top three for the first time that season by virtue of goal difference. The Owls remained unbeaten at home, but had drawn seven of their 11 games at Hillsborough, developing a curious habit of either falling behind to slow, turgid starts or letting leads slip. They were one match from the halfway stage and there was no need to panic, of course. But for the first time local reporters, including Paul Thompson from *The Star*, began to surmise that after their blistering start, promotion was no certainty.

Another painful statistic fell in the goals conceded column – not across the entire season, but in recent times. Having kicked off the campaign by letting in only one goal in their first four matches, suddenly Wednesday were leaking at the back and had not kept a clean sheet in their last 10 games and only two in their last 16. With one match to go to the halfway stage, they had shipped 26 league goals – twice as many as West Ham at the top. Something, Atkinson felt, had to change.

When the teamsheet was pinned up for the December 29 home clash with relegation-threatened Portsmouth, Kevin Pressman gave it a cursory look. There had been no indication from Atkinson or any of his staff that he was about to lose his place. On a second glance he saw the name of Chris Turner. The Wednesday manager knew that a goalkeeper is only a fraction of the problem when it comes to a team's poor defensive record, but felt the side needed experience between the sticks. In Turner, he had a trusted lieutenant who had been a fine goalkeeper, occasionally on the verge of an England call-up. Several players remember having the feeling that Pressman had lost a degree of confidence, particularly in the Boxing Day capitulation. The young 'keeper was furious.

"There was no conversation or forewarning or anything. He just left me out," Pressman remembered. "Jack Charlton taught me as a kid that you should always knock on a door and ask. So I went to see Ron in his office. He told me I wasn't playing well enough and that he wanted to make a change, so that was it. I had to knuckle down and get my place back. But if or when that change comes, nobody knows. Life can be tough as a goalkeeper. When a manager wants to make a change, it's not always easy to do that with the outfield players because it disrupts things.

"Changing a goalkeeper is a more subtle move. Looking back now, I can see why he did it because Chris was an excellent goalkeeper. I was desperate to play. In terms of preparation I was ultra-professional; I

always prepared myself for games very, very well, whether I was playing or not. But there was no hiding that I was hugely upset at the time.
Absolutely devastated."

Pressman, who was just 23 at the time, appreciates that he did not
handle himself at all well in the weeks that followed, in his own words
"moping around" the training ground and making it clear to everyone
that he felt the decision was unwarranted. Instead of engaging in confrontation, Atkinson remembered completely ignoring him, as he had
done months earlier when Pressman was out for six months with that
career-threatening knee injury. Now a goalkeeping coach, he looks
back fondly on his relationship with Atkinson, as every first-team player interviewed for this book does, but admits that their time together
was complex.

"Throughout all those months injured, Ron never spoke to me once,"
Pressman said. "He'd pass me in the corridor. He told me early doors
that he didn't have time to be running around after injured players and
that I'd be working with Alan Smith. And that was fine; I understood
that. Then when my leg was out of plaster, he called me in and sent me
and the wife to Cyprus for the week, entirely on the club.

"He'd been to the powers-that-be to sort it out and he didn't have to
do that. When I was cleared fit, I popped my head round the door of
his office and it was like I'd never been away. He had a way of doing
things."

The beneficiary of Atkinson's decision, Turner, had seen things differently. With Wednesday conceding goals more regularly as the season had gone on, he stepped up his efforts in training and sent signals
that, should the time come, he was ready. Atkinson had signed Turner
from Sunderland in his time at Manchester United and made him his
number one ahead of Gary Bailey. And with the rough and tumble of a
promotion battle on the horizon, he felt that his added years would do
the team good.

"As a player you always feel you should be in the team. We were conceding goals and I had to be ready," Turner remembered. "Alan Hodgkinson was the goalkeeping coach in those days and I used to have chats
with him quite often, about keeping myself sharp mentally as well as
physically. I was doing extra bits and bobs in the week to make sure
that, if the call came, I was ready. It's hard as a goalkeeper when you're

not playing, I won't lie. But I was an experienced player by that time and I'd been on both sides of the challenge, so I knew I had to keep going.

"That's football. You're out in the cold for a length of time and you come back in and things turn; it's up to you to prove your worth. The way I looked at it, I got my reward for all that time slogging away when I was out of the team, doing extra sessions here and there. Kevin was a young lad and he was desperate to play. He thought he should be playing, but he wasn't and he was frustrated. To be fair he threw his toys out of the pram and Ron didn't pick him again."

Although Wednesday were far from their best, Turner's return did signal a return to winning ways at Hillsborough, if not a clean sheet, with a huge slice of good fortune. Owls past and future Mark Chamberlain and Guy Whittingham threatened Turner's goal on a number of occasions, to blow any cobwebs from his gloves, before Whittingham equalised on the hour after Hirst's fifth-minute opener. And then came the big moment.

With 20 minutes left and the Wednesday crowd roaring their heroes on for a winner, Nigel Pearson dived towards a loose ball at the feet of legendary Pompey goalkeeper Alan Knight, who leapt downwards in his attempt to clear the danger. The impact broke his hand. A few minutes later Hirst worked a clever one-two with Francis to roll the ball past the agony-stricken stopper to claim his second goal and claim his place as the top scorer in the country. Knight had to go off and in the days of two substitutes, forward Colin Clarke took his place in goal. Portsmouth came out in support of Pearson, saying he had every right to go for the ball and that there was no malice attached to his challenge on Knight.

"We had a little luck," Hirst told reporters after Wednesday's 2-1 win. "Perhaps this could be the turning-point. I feel pretty certain that my second goal would have been saved had their 'keeper not broken his hand; he got to the ball and then seemed to pull away instinctively." Atkinson, usually a darling of the media with a well-trained warm and personable approach to journalists, took exception to the line of questioning of one national reporter, who suggested his side were underachieving.

"Our better performances have been unrewarded, so perhaps we deserved the result," he said. "Portsmouth were encouraged because they hadn't been killed off. There's been some brilliant entertainment at Hillsborough this season. And if you blokes don't like it, don't fucking come."

In a passionate, tub-thumping speech in the home changing-room the manager hammered home the fact that seasons can be turned on moments such as the Knight injury, that the near misses and poor performances were behind them and that those periods were sent to test good teams. Middlesbrough, their New Year's Day opponents, had lost 3-0 at mid-table Bristol City and Oldham and West Ham had drawn with Millwall and Port Vale respectively. Despite the understandable frustration with their draws, Wednesday had been regularly picking up points and were back to three in front of the chasing pack. They finally had some momentum heading into '91.

9
___

'91

A lot had changed at Sheffield Wednesday in the 11 months in which Ron Atkinson had been at the wheel. New faces, new routines, a new way of looking at the life of a footballer. Under Howard Wilkinson, and by extension during the short reign of Peter Eustace, things had been regimented, structured and organised. Training was similar most days, involving a lot of running and work on shape.

Legend has it that one Sheffield Wednesday player counted the number of times a whistle was blown in a single Wilkinson training session, and the tally topped out at well over 100. A lifelong Wednesdayite who transformed the modern history of the club, Wilkinson forever has a seat at the very top table of Hillsborough legend. But football management takes all sorts. Atkinson's approach was so very different.

Often, Wednesday's players would head out on to the training ground to see Richie Barker marking out intricate drills before Atkinson would bowl up, divide them into teams of six and play small-sided matches for two hours. The Owls manager thrived on a buoyant, happy changing-room of players who would go to war for one another and felt that, by keeping things light at Middlewood Road, the performances elsewhere would benefit. Plus, having driven all that way, he'd rather fancied a kickabout himself. By now 51, the joy of ball on boot had not left him and the sight of Big Ron – still Oxford United's record appearance holder – being clattered by one of his own players was not a rare sight.

"Ron played," remembered a chuckling Chris Turner, since a successful manager in his own right. "He'd play every day. And everybody loved not to be on Big Ron's side. He'd come out in a thick jumper and a woolly hat perched on the top of his head, he'd spin a ball out in front of us and tell Richie to get us into teams. This is before big games! Richie's face could be a picture, I tell you. The thing is that Ron loved playing and we loved not being on his team. Whoever was playing against him would work so much harder to get him beaten and wind him up! The banter was fantastic.

"Ron was a player's manager in that he created an atmosphere that was fun to play and train in. Richie was the organiser and did a lot on set-plays and shape, but Ron picked the players, picked the team and told us how we were playing. He wasn't one of those who would change too much, he wasn't all that analytical as they are today, he knew his players inside out and he knew what they could do individually and as a collective.

You'd be surprised how many managers don't. It was clever. Ron would get someone in who could pass, one who could run and tackle. Upfront he'd have one with pace and one who could hold it up. Out wide he'd have lots of pace and lots of legs down the flanks. And he'd have centre-halves who could defend. He'd make up that jigsaw and you'd go out and play.

"It was the same when I played under him at Manchester United. The game doesn't change; it's about getting players to do a job on the field of play. And that's what he did. There were no drawing-boards, Xs and Ys, red pens across a board. He just told you exactly how we wanted to play, that he had got this team together to play that way and that was why we were there. Training was pretty much the same most days, eight-on-eight games, lots of banter and the lads enjoying training. He created this scenario where we'd run through brick walls for one another. They were great days."

Alongside Atkinson, Barker and the supremely talented physio Alan Smith came a more left-field appointment at that time. Roger Spry, then 41, arrived at the start of Atkinson's reign almost a year previously after the Owls boss had heard of his extraordinary methods from the iconic former Manchester City and Crystal Palace manager Malcolm Allison.

Allison had worked with Spry during his time in charge of the Kuwait national team and Vitória Setúbal and interestingly, during his time with the Portuguese side, Spry had mentored the son of the club's goalkeeping coach who was then an aspiring youngster. Three decades on, Spry and José Mourinho remain firm friends.

Atkinson spent some time tracking Spry down. Although from the same neck of the woods as the Midlands-based Atkinson, with a thick accent as proof, he had barely worked in England and had forged a road less travelled, learning Portuguese and working first in Brazil and then all over the world. Doing some consultancy work for a few clubs down south, Spry got the call from Atkinson and in a couple of days was putting the Wednesday players through their paces on Hillsborough Park in the shadow of their famous stadium.

"Ron asked me to come along to do a few days with them initially," Spry remembered. "He'd never seen me work; he'd only heard things. After the first session on the first morning he came over and said: 'Okay, that's enough.' Well, I thought that was that! But he loved what we were doing and he offered me a contract there and then." Sheffield Wednesday were one of the first clubs to employ a full-time fitness coach.

"I was always fascinated with South American football," Spry said of a coaching education less travelled. "I had a friend who ran a soccer camp over in Seattle and I'd go over to help him out. They'd have some Brazilian coaches come up and it really caught my attention. All the coaching in the UK and Northern Europe was based on running and strength and size and power.

"In Brazil, South America and Portugal it was all based on dance-like movements. Instead of beating a player by running past them, you'd beat them by throwing a shape, taking them off-balance and taking them the other way. I spoke to one of the coaches and told them how fascinated I was, and they set me up with a family member who was the vice-president of Fluminese. On my first day, Mario Zagallo was there. It was incredible."

Spry, who had done karate since he was in his teens, noticed players studying what looked like martial arts as part of their training. In one session the entire Fluminense squad were stripped to their waist and, to the beat of live drummers, began performing an Afro-South American martial art known as capoeira. As soon as he saw it Spry, now a staff coach at FIFA who went on to work alongside Bobby Robson, Arsène

Wenger, Gérard Houllier and countless others, decided to incorporate it into his sessions.

Although it was a little more subtle, a few years later the likes of John Sheridan, Carlton Palmer and Nigel Pearson were effectively learning dance moves based on a Brazilian martial art in their Sheffield Wednesday training sessions. It was decades ahead of its time.

"You'd have some moaning at first," said Spry. "Shez would moan at certain things I was doing and I'd ask: 'What do you think of Zico and Socrates? This is what they do every day.' At first a few of them thought I was some lunatic, but all of a sudden they started realising they were feeling sharper. And because we were doing exercises based on dance stuff, the hamstring tears, the groin strains, the injuries that tear a season apart normally...that stuff was heavily reduced."

After the relegation Atkinson had the core of the squad back in early in his attempt to ensure they were the fittest set of players in the Second Division. His players could pass the ball around most teams, he knew that, but he wanted to ensure they weren't beaten for fitness. Despite his new-age approach to coaching Spry had the face and old-school demeanour of a man whose pint you'd rather not spill.

A world-renowned champion at mugendo, a martial art similar to MMA in style, in his grumpier moods players would be in the air before he even told them to jump. Atkinson would joke that after the side's less impressive performances, he and Richie would take a couple of days off and "feed them to Roger."

For much of pre-season Spry was given full autonomy on conditioning. The difference was that traditional fitness training in English football was based on athletics – Wilkinson would often have his players running around pitches for hours at a time – but Spry kept a ball involved throughout. Players enjoyed it. "Carlton came up to me one day and asked when we were going to be doing the aerobic stuff," Spry said. "We did some tests and they were all as fit as they'd ever been in their career. They all bought into it very, very quickly."

Spry is now seen as one of the forefathers of modern sports science. World-renowned fitness guru Tony Strudwick, who joined Wednesday's staff in 2019 after working with Manchester United and England among others, said: "He was a pioneer. The things he was doing back then really influence the way things are done by me and lots of people in the industry and we're now using a lot of the things that he brought over from South America decades ago.

At that time there was a lot of static stretching and Roger was a pioneer in the sense of dynamic flexibility. He was the one who took that on and pushed sports science towards dynamic movement and to try to incorporate strength, rhythm and co-ordination. He had some game-changing ideas."

Frank Barlow, a coach brought in by Eustace tasked mainly to look after the reserve side, was a very popular and central figure in the club who would often assist the first team with training. A former Sheffield United player who had managed Chesterfield and Scunthorpe, he later became Danny Wilson's hugely-respected assistant manager at Bramall Lane.

"It was great working with the lot of them, absolutely brilliant," Barlow remembered. "Ron had this personality that was always, always positive. And that rubbed off on the whole club; matches, day-to-day training, with the players and with the staff. The people who think he was a big-time Charlie or that he took an easy approach to tactics or delivery are absolutely bang wrong. He took the game very, very seriously and his knowledge was extensive.

"The thing that impressed me immediately in one of our first meetings was his knowledge; he knew all the top players, he knew all the foreign players, all the league players and the non-league players as well. Vast, vast knowledge like I'd never seen before. People didn't think Ron was all that involved on the training field and that he left Richie to all that, but he was. It was an enlightening time to work as a coach at that club. We all learned an awful lot from Ron on so many things.

"Then there was Richie, an incredible coach. Alan was an incredible physio on that side of things, Alan Hodgkinson was an excellent goalkeeper coach. Then there was Roger, who was a hard man. From time to time there was confrontation. You've got a lot of competitive blokes in one place and there would always be a little discussion about things. You've got to accept and deal with that, and Ron helped with that. It ran like clockwork."

It is a memory Atkinson himself holds dearly. "I liked a very close-knit staff," he said. "I liked to be able to know my staff inside out to the point when, if anyone disagreed with something or had an idea, we could get it out in the open and have a proper talk about it. I had a routine. We'd finish training, I'd have a pot of tea brought to my office and we'd all go in there and sit down and talk. I'd tell them: 'Say what you like in here, but once the decision is made, it stays in here; that's the decision. I don't mind if you don't agree with it, but that's the decision.' I wanted staff who were all pulling in the same way and I was lucky in that respect. When I first went to Man United I had to change the whole staff around. I didn't need to do that at Wednesday."

The year of 1991 kicked off with a big game, a trip to Middlesbrough's Ayresome Park. Colin Todd's safety-first outfit had been enjoying a fine season and had been the only side to break the monopoly of the top three since the earliest rounds of the season, albeit on goal difference and only for one week. A win over Boro, Atkinson surmised to the Press in the days leading up to the match, would put healthy breathing-space between the two sides and allow Wednesday to relax a little more. They wanted to play their football, he said.

The issue was that conditions were continuing to make that difficult. Swirling wind and rain in the North-East would serve to test the character of the Owls, but they had miles in their legs and because of the hard work of Spry and Co. felt equipped to rough it out when required. Middlesbrough started brightly with Tony Mowbray forcing Chris Turner into a fine save before Nigel Pearson blocked a firm strike by Paul Kerr from outside the box.

But when David Hirst scored Wednesday's first goal of 1991 with a well-taken finish after 34 minutes, the Owls took control. Pearson had an effort of his own hacked off the line, Paul Williams went close and Steve McCall shot over the bar. A combination of all three landed the knockout blow when McCall's swinging corner found the head of Pearson, who nodded down for Williams to hook home. Two-nil. Three points. Breathing space.

"Those two goals gave me a lot of confidence," remembered Williams. "It felt like a very big game for us at that time and there had been a question mark at that time as to who was going to play and who wasn't going to play in terms of the final. Trevor was so influential in terms of what he contributed when he did play and was making a real case for himself. It felt at the time as if those two goals were really big for me."

"We knew this was one of the big games in this division this season," Atkinson said afterwards. "We have made life a lot easier for ourselves and a lot more difficult for one of our major competitors and played better than you might expect in such atrocious conditions." Todd was equally forthcoming with praise, conceding that Wednesday had taken control of the match. "They're probably the best side in the division," he said.

With Middlesbrough out of the way, the start of the year offered Wednesday the opportunity to build up a head of steam; on paper at least. Cup draws had been kind although both were away; first to near-by Third Division Mansfield in the third round of the FA Cup with struggling First Division side Coventry City later standing in the way of a first League Cup semi-final for the Owls.

Their FA Cup progress at Mansfield was solid, but unspectacular; a second of the season for Shirtliff adding to Barker's wall chart before Stags player-manager George Foster bizarrely stuck out a hand to deny Palmer's Hirst-bound cross and gift the Owls a second-half penalty that Sheridan put away with little fuss. A sheepish and embarrassed Foster later bemoaned "a moment of madness" in a short talk with reporters.

It was at this point that the reinforcements Atkinson had been work-ing so hard on finally began to come through. Viv Anderson, he of 30 England caps and two European Cup winners' medals, joined his old teammates Trevor Francis and Danny Wilson – from Forest – and Chris Turner from Manchester United. He had turned down a widely-reported move to Leicester City in order to sign on at Hillsborough and, although there were concerns about his fitness, given a lack of match action in recent months, Atkinson felt that Anderson was just what his squad needed; experience and versatility to cover two posi-tions, centre-half and in the Nilsson-shaped hole at right-back.

"Everyone thinks I'd had him at United, but the fact is that our time didn't cross over," Atkinson remembered of Anderson's signing. "That said, I knew he was a great lad, one of those who just comes with the reputation he'd earned. I thought it was ideal. We'd had in mind an out-an-out right-back when we'd set out really, but Viv gave us cover at centre-half as well. That was something I didn't have a great deal of at the time although Lawrie would come in and do a job for Pears and Shirty.

"The shame was that he'd played for United in the League Cup so he couldn't play in that, but it didn't matter a jot to me. We wanted to get him across. He had such a good attitude, the perfect type of lad. He'd had both Cloughie and Fergie as managers so he knew his way around and he ended up staying there for some time. It was very straightforward. I rang Fergie straight off the bat and it was one of the easier ones you do. He was in and out of the team up there and a little bit frustrated, so we took him on and the rest is history."

Ferguson originally wanted a fee for Anderson, who was the sort of name few Second Division clubs could have attracted, let alone afforded. But Atkinson talked him around and, partly as a favour to his player, the Scot let him go for free, having been told that a transfer fee was out of the question until Wednesday had moved players on. Unknown to the Manchester United boss, they were in the process of selling out-of-favour forward Steve Whitton to Ipswich for £150,000 and could have easily paid a similar fee. It was one of a handful of occasions when Wednesday wound up Alex Ferguson in the transfer market in the next few years.

"I wasn't playing because I'd been injured," Anderson recalled. "Then one day Alex grabbed me after training to ask whether I would want to go to Sheffield Wednesday. It was done quite quickly; they could have got a fee for me, but they didn't want one. Ron took me there and then. I'd never come across Ron until I'd signed for Wednesday.

"Sheffield wasn't too far, I lived in Manchester and, wherever I went, I didn't want to move the family all over, so it was quite convenient for me at that time of life, a 45-minute or hour commute. They had some decent players, too. I knew a fair few of them, including little Danny. He had come to Forest as a youngster and we were big pals. We are still today."

Atkinson, safe in the knowledge that his new man was a consummate professional, would often give him days off training to cut down on the grind of a commute to and from Manchester. Unlike some of his younger players, he said, he trusted Anderson to put in the hours away from the training ground and do everything he needed to do to be prepared ahead of a match. Atkinson had a unique way of pumping up a slightly-bruised confidence, too, settling debates among rowing players by asking them how many European Cup medals they had earned.

Then, with a shrug and a wink, he would ask Anderson to act as judge in the argument.

"I had a point to prove," admitted Anderson, who was 34 when he arrived at Wednesday. "I'd gone from Arsenal to Manchester United, at which point I'd only missed three games in four years. I went to United and got injured early on; I dislocated my knee and a few different bits and bobs. To be fair, it was a calamity of injuries at Man United and I just wanted to get back playing and prove to people I wasn't too old, I guess.

"I could have stayed at Man United; Alex gave me the opportunity to stick around and say: 'I'm going to prove you wrong, boss... I'm staying here, getting fit and will get in your first team,' but I thought it was a good time to try getting fit, knowing I had a good chance of playing every week as opposed to being in and out at United."

Anderson made his Wednesday debut on January 12 at rock-bottom Hull City, who had shipped an eye-watering 63 goals in the league alone by that point and looked certainties for relegation. Stan Ternent, just months on from his proclamation that his side fancied a shot at promotion, had been sacked days earlier and caretaker boss Tom Wilson first took charge of a farcical 5-2 FA Cup defeat at home to Notts County.

But Wednesday fans, fearing a new-manager bounce, found themselves relieved as the Owls ran out 1-0 winners thanks to Williams' first-half goal. The game was perhaps more memorable to Owls fans for an incident in which a linesman was showered with teddies after signalling for a close-call offside. Not a classic.

A frustrating 0-0 draw with relegation-threatened Charlton Athletic the following weekend – the first time they had failed to score at Hillsborough that season – meant that after switching his goalkeepers, Atkinson's side had conceded one in five. While they were ticking along and picking up points, matters at the other end of the field were suddenly just a little jittery. They stood firm to their principles – playing on the deck, the good, attractive football that Big Ron had said their fans deserved – but for a long while they rarely did things simply. The Wednesday Way.

At this time Francis, still a magnet for headlines in the national newspapers, was linked with managerial roles at Hull and Birmingham City. The Birmingham link in particular was of interest to the media, given Francis' legendary status with the Midlands club – then in Division Three and marooned in mid-table under Dave Mackay. The million-pound man was keen to get back into management, Atkinson knew that, but there was little movement. Hull were flailing; Birmingham were ambitious, but a little broken. Francis would wait for his chance, it was decided – which eventually came at Birmingham just a few years later.

***

Elsewhere, something exciting was building. The early rounds of the Rumbelows Cup had been a battle for Wednesday and Brentford and Swindon proved themselves to be tough customers, more than able to mix it with the Owls pass masters. But something had been sparked by the manner of their replay win at Derby. Perhaps it was Harkes' goal, the felling of First Division opposition or the fact that the national Press were talking about Wednesday once more.

Perhaps it was the feeling that, having drawn Coventry, they would end up in the semi-finals – one built not on emotion, but on probability. Wednesday had never been to the last four of the League Cup since its inception 30 years previously, and both supporters and players remember a gear change heading into the clash at Highfield Road.

Until then all focus had been on the title charge. Any cup heroics would be nothing more than a pleasant bonus. The chorus of *Que sera, sera* heading out of the Hawthorns had been a little bathed in irony, after all, but a quarter-final is a quarter-final and, having swatted aside Mansfield, Wednesday had drawn old friends Millwall in the FA Cup fourth round. On their day Sheffield Wednesday were a match for anyone, regardless of what they still believed to be a false second-tier status. And everybody knew it.

"It wasn't something we spoke too much about," said Nigel Worthington. "Back then we knew we were playing twice a week, every week. But that is just how it was back then. You just set up for every game, nothing like it has become with prioritising things and cups being devalued as they have in the modern game. The League Cup was a big deal."

Peter Shirtliff remembers Wednesday quite simply just wanting to win every game they could. "If you look at the teams we were putting out, we didn't have what you might consider a weakened team all season," he said. "It might have cost us in the long run when you look back, I don't know. But that's how you did it in those days and to be fair you couldn't have told any of us that we weren't playing the next game, whether that was against Manchester United or whoever. We had momentum and we would've played five times a week if there were that many games. The signings helped in that way."

A player on the fringes of the squad got things going for the Owls, under the lights in their wonderful yellow kit. Steve McCall made 19 appearances in the 1990/91 season, six of those from the bench, but was proving to be a vital squad member, covering injuries, loss of form and bans on both sides of midfield and, from time to time, at left-back. Called into action with Worthington pushed back into defence because of Harkes' suspension and Anderson's unavailability, his darting run after 10 minutes drew a foul from Sky Blues' skipper Trevor Peake, setting up what had become a famously dangerous situation for Wednesday – a set-piece.

For once Sheridan's floated ball in was a poor one, but Hirst was able to curl his foot around it at the by-line to find Pearson, who twisted and turned and poked the ball past Steve Ogrizovic for the only goal of the game. Centre-half Pearson, a colossus at both ends of the field in a clear man-of-the-match display, now had four goals in seven League Cup matches that season, three of them winners. It was a cup run with his name stamped all over it.

Atkinson, seeking to keep his players' feet on the ground, told them afterwards that he was dissatisfied with the performance. But the win sparked pandemonium in the Wednesday end, who headed off into the cold late-January evening with dreams of Wembley. A week earlier Leeds United had entered the next round by virtue of a 4-1 win over struggling Aston Villa and ties between Chelsea and Tottenham and Southampton and Manchester United had gone to replays that night. Scrambling around radios in coaches and cars, the Owls fans discovered that Chelsea had overcome Spurs 3-0, with Manchester United squeezing past the Saints 3-2. Wednesday would play Chelsea over two legs in the Rumbelows Cup semi-finals.

Drifting out of Highfield Road, again to the defiant strains of *Que sera, sera*, a coachful of Worksop Owls argued as to their evening plans.

As is often the case with a bus full of supporters leaving an away match, there was a debate as to whether the driver would break up the journey for the passengers to enjoy a celebratory pint en route. "This only happens so often. We've got to enjoy it," argued the 50 per cent keen on extending the night, while the others argued it was late, it was a Wednesday night and they had work in the morning. If a stop was made, they said with arms folded, they would stay on the bus.

The ruling was made that there would be no detour and that the bus would stop on sight of the first bar they saw, which turned out to be a shadowy place just outside Coventry with its windows blacked out. As the bus pulled up, those who had campaigned for a direct route to Sheffield tutted, folded their arms and closed their eyes for some much-needed shut-eye. "Lads," said the doorman to those queuing for entry. "Just to let you know, we've an event on this evening. It's a quid in and the barmaids are topless."

Rumour has it that a coach has never emptied so quickly.

10

THE RALLYING CRY

D ressed in a thick, blue sweatshirt with a woolly hat daintily perched on top of his head, Ron Atkinson opened his body up to find a pass. As was usual practice during their many small-sided games in training, the Sheffield Wednesday manager had strapped on his boots to take part and was loving life, pushing the ball about when he could and revelling in the banter. "I'm 51 years old, lads," he would chuckle. "If you can't beat me, you've no chance." The Owls were preparing for their FA Cup fourth-round clash with Millwall and Atkinson had an audience with members of the Press invited to watch the session.

The reporters were expecting to be ushered into Atkinson's office for one of his regular catch-ups and, if they were surprised to be standing watching training in the late January chill, they were even more taken aback to be desperately trying to take down the manager's every word in their notepads as he peddled and panted his way through the session. "What do you want to ask me then, lads?" he said before laying on a pass down the wing to Danny Wilson. It took a moment or two before the frozen reporters suddenly realised that they were in a Press conference.

"Ron was tremendous fun," remembered Alan Biggs, who has worked in television, radio and in newspapers for 40 years covering sport, mainly football, across South Yorkshire. "He broke the mould of everything Sheffield Wednesday had been before; his background, the flamboyance, his extrovert nature. It completely changed the mood of the place. He was a master at mood-setting and he could control it like a thermostat, bringing it up or down.

"I got on famously well with him, as did all of the journalists at that time and he was so aware of everything. On his first morning I'd been invited on to the *Today* programme on BBC and he'd listened to it. After his first Press conference the local reporters among us were invited to meet him afterwards and he already knew everybody's name.

"He said we'd be welcome to speak to him at any time and gave us his number – which is unthinkable today – but he also said that we were welcome to come down any day around 1pm and he'd give us five minutes. I was in awe of him at first; I couldn't believe I was walking into an office to talk to Ron Atkinson, but you could establish a relationship with him.

"He was good value in that he knew what you wanted and most of the time he'd already prepared what the story was. He'd snap his fingers and say: 'Well, here's your line' and give you a quote about something – and sure enough it was always a good tale. He'd give one line to one reporter and another line to another, so we all had our own stories. So clever."

If Atkinson had the club and Press under a spell, his handle on the changing-room was one that he need not have worried about. Wednesday's side was packed with leaders he could trust, the addition of Viv Anderson and experienced midfielder Steve MacKenzie – once the most expensive teenager in world football after a 1979 move from Crystal Palace to Manchester City – adding to a side that had heeded his words in pre-season about righting the wrongs of the previous campaign.

Beers were never far from reach of course, although not to the same extent as some of the other teams around the league, and Wednesday were encouraged to play as hard as they trained. Players were never late to training and after late nights in Sheffield several players remember black plastic bin bags being handed around the changing-room at Middlewood Road, to be worn under training gear and designed to sweat any hangovers out of the system.

"He treated us like men," Chris Turner remembers. "It's a little bit overstated, I think, the drinking culture in that side at that time, but not by too much. Some of the lads had families by then, so a lot of the time it was left to the younger lads, but when we went out, we went out all together; wives, girlfriends, the lot. And we had some big nights, I can tell you! Some of those guys could really drink."

"It was heavy," remembered John Harkes, name-checking Carlton Palmer, John Sheridan and David Hirst as the Three Musketeers when it came to enjoying themselves. "It was really shocking for me at first to be honest, a big shock. In my first couple of weeks after I had signed, we got together for dinner about two days before a match. That's how close we all were.

"It was a little Italian place just down from the Hallam Towers Hotel where I was staying. I thought: 'Oh, we'll get together before a match, a bit of bonding a couple of days out, a chat about the other team.' I got there and, well, the pints were flowing!

"As an American, we're so health-conscious. I was thinking: 'What are we doing? We've got a game in two days!' The lads were just throwing them back. I couldn't believe it. Two or three pints down, I was like: 'Whoa, I've got to slow down here.' It was so different. That whole culture, the British football thing, your Georgie Bests drinking all night… and they were still able to go out and play. I never really wanted to adapt that culture, but you could see that was there in that old school way. Our guys were drinkers, but they knew when to have fun and they knew when to work hard."

The play hard, work hard mentality was watched over by club captain Nigel Pearson, whom Atkinson has often described as the best captain he ever had. A leader in every sense of the word, Pearson had struck up a fearsome partnership with Peter Shirtliff; every club in the country sought a tall, strong, unflashy defender deep in both voice and character, but Wednesday had two. Standing together at the heart of defence, they had the look and demeanour of a pair of nightclub bouncers and, by the time that Wednesday went to Millwall, had kicked every opposition striker to the curb in the past month, overseeing five consecutive clean sheets.

It was an effortless partnership, Shirtliff remembered: "I didn't know Pears at all before I signed. We had some practice games in training and Nigel pulled me over and said that he liked to play on the right. I told him I wasn't bothered which side I played on, so I played on the left. It was that simple and we just gelled straightaway. We both became better players as a result of playing together. It really was a great partnership.

"We understood everything about one another's game, we bounced off each other well and we got goals. Nigel just kept scoring; I got a few. There were 20-odd goals from centre-half, which wasn't bad. I loved playing with him."

Barnsley-born Shirtliff, a boyhood Wednesdayite, had left Wilkinson's Owls for a three-year spell at Charlton before Atkinson nipped in ahead of Leeds United to bring him back ahead of the previous season. The £500,000 fee looked a bargain by January 1990, but it was a transfer that might not have taken place if Atkinson had got his way and brought Paul McGrath to Wednesday in the summer of 1989. McGrath was another player Atkinson had managed at Manchester United and, having got wind of the Irish international's intention to retire amid continued struggles with a knee injury, he hatched a plan.

"He'd been given some advice to cash in some insurance money and give it all up," Atkinson remembered. "It was only right at the last minute he decided not to when he spoke to the PFA, who spooked him. Alex Ferguson wanted £400,000. I rang him up and told him I'd give him £100,000 for McGrath and, if he does this, that and the other, we'd build it up and they'd get their full fee.

"They were mulling it over and two days later I got a phone call from Graham Taylor at the Villa. He said: 'Tell me what you know about Paul McGrath.' That's how things used to work; you'd have pals in the game that you knew and trusted and you'd get their opinions. Graham knew I'd had Paul at United so he asked the question. Well, I levelled with him and said we'd approached United for Paul.

"I told Graham about Paul's injuries, but that he was a terrific player and that we'd offered this deal for him. His drinking hadn't really been a problem while I'd been there. Graham needed a centre-half, went in and paid £400,000 straightaway. He went down to Villa and ended up being the biggest legend they ever had. If I'd stumped up the full fee, I'm sure he'd have signed for us.

"When the money got that high, I didn't hesitate to bring in Shirty. I couldn't be paying £400,000 for someone with a suspect injury record. My centre-halves had to be durable. I knew Shirty wanted to come back this way so I spoke to some people down there who were very complimentary, saying he'd be a seven or eight out of 10 every week and that he'd hardly miss a game. A good lad, good age. Everything was right.

He was a very good player, little or no trouble, a good professional. It ended up being a brilliant signing."

Roland Nilsson, whose continuing comeback from knee surgery meant that he would not make a return trip to the scene of the crime all those weeks before, remembered feeling an aura of leadership around Pearson from his very first session with the club: "One of the first things I'd say about Nigel was that he was competitive. He wanted to win every single match, whether that was in the league or the cup or in training. He was desperate not to lose. And he was a very strong leader at things around the training, talking to the team after training sessions and before matches.

"He was always there, pushing and helping. He was excellent and, when things weren't maybe as good as they should be, he made sure that everybody knew that. If you weren't doing your job – and it wasn't only him – you were soon told about it. Of course he said a lot of positive things as well, but you heard him the most when we maybe didn't play quite as well as we might have."

One of those dressing-downs came in the bowels of The Den after Wednesday had led three times in a thrilling cup tie, only to draw 4-4. Highly-rated young Millwall forward Teddy Sheringham, who scored 34 times in a remarkable season, cannoned a first-minute ball into Turner with George Stephenson there to tap in on the goal-line, but then an astonishing game of cat and mouse brought goals for Francis, Hirst, Pearson and a first Owls strike four minutes from time for Anderson. Alex Rae, who had scored the Lions' third equaliser, turned home another Sheringham shot that had been saved to take the tie to a replay at Hillsborough, which Wednesday won 2-0 in front of 25,000 supporters thanks to Anderson and Hirst again.

The match programme for the home leg was a 28-page rallying cry for the future from both dugout and boardroom. Atkinson, now proudly embracing the "Barmy Army" notion of Wednesday, devoted his programme notes to geeing up a home support he felt had been unduly nervous in the grit and gristle of the promotion race. Although Wednesday were 10 points behind Oldham at the top of the table, they had a game in hand and were four clear of Notts County in fourth.

"It has to be said," he wrote, "that if our fans want us to achieve what they want us to achieve (and the more success the better), it's important to recognise that they can play their part by seeking to give us that same level of vocal support that we get in away matches. Our travelling fans have been fantastic and I'd like us to enjoy the same kind of sustained backing at Hillsborough." Not many managers would get away with such a thinly-veiled criticism.

There were big movements on the stadium front, too. The club announced that, after the £700,000 safety improvements undertaken in the summer, they would press on with further recommendations, including plans to make the stadium all-seater. The Leppings Lane end had remained an empty, haunting reminder of the events of April 15, 1989, and remained so throughout the season.

Having already made sweeping safety and aesthetic changes, secretary Graham Mackrell reiterated the club's commitment towards a £300,000 scheme that would replace all turnstiles and convert the lower enclosure, the scene of the tragedy, into a 2,200-seater facility. The plans also included the extension of the Leppings Lane roof.

Coming some 21 months after the disaster, the announcement drew a line through any notion that the stand would be bulldozed and rebuilt and Wednesday hoped the changes would allow them to host FA Cup semi-finals again as they had so often before. Hillsborough was chosen to host a 1992 semi-final between Sunderland and Norwich and then a 1997 replay tie between Middlesbrough and Chesterfield, although Old Trafford and Villa Park became the go-to venues before all semi-finals reverted to Wembley in 2008.

"The empty terrace has been a constant reminder of the tragedy and, although it will never be forgotten, we do need to press on," Mackrell wrote in the Millwall programme. "That is not a callous remark. It is a truthful one. It is an emotive subject, but we are conscious of the feelings expressed by players and supporters who want to see something done with that end of the ground. The work will not be dependent on the status of the team.

"The aim of the board is for Hillsborough to be restored as an FA Cup semi-final venue and I'm confident that we can achieve that. Such aspirations couldn't be considered until the Leppings Lane end was dealt with. I believe Hillsborough is already one of the country's better grounds and it is our ambition to maintain and improve it – but not at the expense of the playing side."

Looking back, several Wednesday players welcomed the news, which they were told in a meeting ahead of time. While the impact of the disaster on those in the changing-room largely went undiscussed, players were later able to admit that it took a toll. Several remember a feeling of dread whenever a ball was kicked into the vacant Leppings Lane end, the echoing structure a constant reminder of the tragedy. Many of them were at the ground that day, including 20-year-old centre-half Jon Newsome, who in 1991 was making a name for himself in Frank Barlow's all-conquering second string. In 1989 he was Wednesday's head apprentice, in charge of the ball-boys.

"For three days before the semi-final we would be at the ground, cleaning the dressing-rooms, grouting the tiles, minting the place out," he recalled. "Then on the day we were running around after the Forest and Liverpool players, making pots of tea, changing their studs, whatever they wanted. I used to sit at the end of the tunnel in case anything was needed, so either team or anyone at the club could grab me. The match kicked off and all of a sudden I was told to go and get the two young lads who were ball-boying at the Leppings Lane end.

"I got to that end and I just felt sick. You could see people's faces purple and crushed against the fences. From a distance you think it's a bit of trouble, but I remember telling the lads that people were dying in there. Within a few minutes we were kicking the hoardings down and carrying people to the corner where the ambulances were.

"I wouldn't like to say it affected the football club too much on the pitch, but individually there are some scars, certainly. It was horrific what happened. I can close my eyes now and remember the first game back at Hillsborough; West Ham at home. It was a really eerie, horrible evening. The Leppings Lane end was empty, unused; you couldn't look at it. It never becomes the norm and it's not nice to say, but like most things in life, you do get used to it a bit."

Chris Turner, a lifelong Wednesdayite and the first-team goalkeeper at that time, had claimed a pair of tickets from the club and was sitting with his young son just metres from the tragedy in the top tier of the Leppings Lane end. As the player closest to the stand whenever Wednesday were kicking towards the Kop end, the experience of playing at Hillsborough weighed heavily on his shoulders in the following months. Thirty years on, despite having played, managed and worked as a pundit at hundreds of matches at the ground since, arriving at Hillsborough remains an emotional experience.

"Even when I go to the ground today, it's the first thing I look at and think of," he said, his voice breaking slightly. "Now can you imagine having to play there, especially so soon afterwards? That's the worst I ever felt on a football pitch. It makes my stomach turn, that feeling of running out to play there for the first time. Every time I ran out of that tunnel it was the first thing on my mind, every single time. And we had to play there every other week.

"You don't realise how much it affects you at the time. Your mind drifts to it from time to time and I get cold shivers just thinking about anything to do with that afternoon. I walk in and look there straightaway at that stand. You can't help but picture what happened, what was outside, the panic. I was there with my 10-year-old son. It was horrific.

"I can't tell you how awful that was, waiting for a ball to be thrown back, having to look up at the tunnel. We were above on the day so we couldn't quite see what was happening below until people started climbing up after the kick-off. It was just absolutely terrifying. Then we started hearing about the deaths. It affects you as a person.

"As a young player I used to go behind the Leppings Lane end and smash the ball against the wall at different angles, catching it off the wall. The tunnel where so many people died, I used to run through there in fitness training. As an apprentice we used to have to clean that stand, paint it, take a wheelbarrow down that tunnel when you were helping the groundsman. I used to stand on Leppings Lane in the early days of following Wednesday with my mum and dad. That stand was a part of me."

Cold though Mackrell's words might have read on paper, with the two-year anniversary fast approaching, it was important the club did all they could to begin to heal the scars described by Newsome.

***

On the field the Owls were busy looking forward to a February 10 trip to Chelsea, but performances took a turn. With Shirtliff missing with a virus, Palmer filled in at centre-half alongside Pearson and Wednesday missed his legs in midfield at Watford, who were in the relegation zone, but went into half-time with a shock 2-0 lead. Atkinson delivered a famous speech at the break, choosing not to dust off the hairdryer, but to demand a good result from his players clearly and calmly. And it worked as Wednesday claimed yet another home point.

Having roared back in a pulsating start to the second half through Harkes, the introduction of Trevor Francis with 20 minutes remaining proved to be a game-changing move as Paul Williams stretched full-length to direct a header past a young David James in the Hornets' goal.

There was something a little Wednesday about the fact that with 7,000 visitors' tickets sold for their February 10 trip to Chelsea, their first semi-final in any competition since they were runners-up in a famous 1966 FA Cup final, the match was postponed after what was yet another bite of a horror winter.

It left a two-week gap in the fixture schedule and, with Anderson now safely through the door, reserve-team skipper Lawrie Madden had been allowed out on loan to Leicester City for a month and England under-21 striker Gordon Watson was signed from what had quickly become Atkinson's favourite talent pool down at Charlton Athletic. Nicknamed "Flash" after the comic-book character Flash Gordon, he had the big, bold personality to match, bounding through the door with a confidence belying his 19 years after being signed for £250,000 plus add-ons.

Watson now describes his spell at Wednesday as the best time of his life, admitting: "I loved it. I was this cocky lad from London coming up to have a go at this massive club. I just wanted to kick the arse out of it. You've got to think, I was a talented boy, there were a lot of people talking about me back then and I'm walking into a changing-room with Carlton Palmer, David Hirst, John Sheridan, Trevor Francis. But I wasn't the sort to be getting shy; I wanted to get among all the banter, everything. It took me a couple of days and I was right in it.

"Wednesday used to train at Charlton when they came down to play the London clubs. And when I was a young boy, I used to stay on to do extra training sessions, whether that was running or doing finishing or whatever it might have been. So when I was coming in off the training field they'd be coming in or finishing up and I'd be running around grabbing towels for them or getting whatever they might need.

Sheffield Newspapers

The Star

Green'Un

Saturday, May 5, 1990   No 32,087   20p

BLADES GLORY — OWLS DOWN

Goal—happy United go up in style

Wednesday relegated in horror show

THAT sinking feeling: Ron Atkinson pictured at Hillsborough this afternoon as the Owls went out of Division One

BARCLAYS LEAGUE Division One

GLORY, GLORY FOR UNITED ... GLOOM AND DOOM FOR WEDNESDAY.

United made sure of promotion to the First Division with a champagne-style 5-2 victory at Leicester. Wednesday crashed 3-0 at home to Forest and were relegated as Luton pulled off an incredible 3-2 victory at Derby.

A goal down at Leicester in nine minutes United put on an unstoppable first half show at Leicester. Mills put the home team in front but then Paul Wood, Brian Deane, Tony Agana and Wilf Rostron smashed four goals past the former Wednesday keeper Martin Hodge to put the team at the gates of the First Division.

In injury-time of the first half Leicester pulled one back but United, hanging on to what they had got, defied Leicester in a tight second half to sweep through to promotion in front of 8,000 ecstatic followers. Leicester played the whole of the second half without Hodge, playing defender Marc North in goal.

Leeds pipped United for the championship with a 1-0 success at Bournemouth while Newcastle went down 4-1 in their North-East derby at Middlesbrough.

Left: The cover of the Green 'Un on the day that Wednesday were relegated from the First Division – and to make things worse, city rivals United were promoted in their place

Below: A lone Liverpool fan sobs amongst the wreckage of the Hillsborough Disaster in 1989. A total of 96 fans tragically lost their lives, leading to big changes in safety and stadia – but the day left scars, some of which have not healed even to this day

Sheffield Newspapers

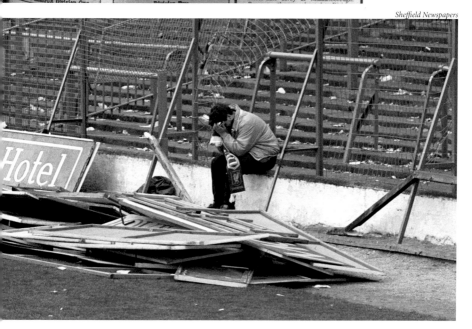

Despair on the Hillsborough terraces after relegation to Division Two was confirmed with defeat to Forest. For six glorious minutes, Wednesday fans thought they had got away with i

Rarely seen without his trademark aviators, Ron Atkinson held half a city in the palm of his hand. His charismatic way gave him a cult-like relationship with Owls supporters

The much-loved Richie Barker was a central cog in the Sheffield Wednesday wheel. Ron assistant manager, he was hugely respecte among the players and sadly died in 2020

Steve Ellis

Left: Trevor Francis was a superstar in the twilight of his playing career when he was at Wednesday, garnering a quiet respect in an otherwise boisterous changing room. Atkinson used him sparingly but to incredible effect

Right: You had to go back all the way to the 1950s to find the last time a Sheffield Wednesday player scored four goals in a match before David Hirst got his stellar season underway in a 5-1 win over Hull City at Hillsborough. He could have been credited with all five, too Paul Williams' strike deflected off his hip!

Steve Ellis

Nigel Worthington was one of the more understated players but his partnership with Phil King is one of the finest in Owls history

Wembley hero John Sheridan won doubters over to write his name in folklore and become a modern-day Wednesday legend

The 'Roly Royce' of a classy team, Swede Roland Nilsson could have easily moved to Manchester United in the summer of 1990

Carlton Palmer, dressed here in the season' iconic yellow kit, was the beating heart of Wednesday - both on and off the field

wasn't often those two spilled much! The celebrations after Wednesday's Rumbelows Cup
mi-final second leg at S6 are the stuff of legend. Thousands of players and spectators
ke regard the evening as the greatest-ever Hillsborough atmosphere

wasn't just about the first team. Wednesday made their first and only appearance in the
A Youth Cup final that season, beating Ryan Giggs and Manchester United at the seminal stage. Ryan Jones - pictured holding the matchball - was the star of the show

A special weekend calls for special memorabilia, and Wednesday fans bought momentos by the bucketload from Wembley

The Owls wore one-off shirts in their Leag Cup final at Wembley, with the Asda spon and special embroidery under the badge

Steve

Above: Nigel Pearson was not the most technically-gifted payer in the Wednesday side, bu he was one of the greatest leaders in the club's history and man-of-the-match in the Leag Cup final. Right: Celebration time after the Owls' Wembley win over Manchester United

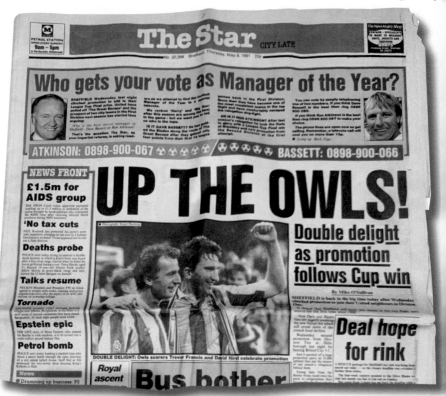

The headline says it all as The Star, Sheffield's daily 'paper, report Wednesday's promotion back to the top flight after a classy 3-1 win over Bristol City - they did the job in style

Hillsborough was a hive of activity throughout the 1990/91 season. The atmosphere for the second leg of their Rumbelows Cup semi-final is still regarded as one of the best ever

"You fast-forward two or three years and I'm playing with them. I wasn't going to let that pass me by, was I?"

With both Anderson and MacKenzie, Watson was another name added to the list of cuptied newcomers and watched on as Wednesday made the trip to Cambridge United in the fifth round. Although United were Third Division opposition, they had a firm reputation for upsets after claiming second-tier scalps in the previous two rounds. John Taylor, an in-form striker who had scored nine goals in the FA Cup that season, including both in the 2-0 win over Middlesbrough in the previous round, said in the build-up to the game: "We've seen off two of the top Second Division sides in Wolves and Middlesbrough so we must have a good chance against another one, especially as they let in four against Millwall. I fancy us against anybody at home." Bullish stuff, but hardly surprising given their run of seven consecutive wins and a fearsome forward pairing of Taylor and a 21-year-old Dion Dublin.

Their manager John Beck had taken over in January with a unique management style that later earned him the nickname "Dracula" in corners of the football Press because he was perceived as sucking the life out of the game. He placed dozens of signs with the words "Simplicity is genius" on the walls of their Abbey Stadium; from the players' bar to the back of toilet doors.

Obsessed with percentage football and parachuting long balls into dangerous areas, legend has it he would regularly punch his players in the stomach if they failed to carry out his actions and once fined his goalkeeper a week's wages for playing a goal-kick to his right-back. He would turn the showers cold if his team lost and in many ways, he invented the dark arts of football management. Three decades on, Beck is now a coach educator for the FA at St. George's Park. Go figure.

"Every single thing you've heard from that time was true," Dublin said in 2019. "We were a horrible team to play against. Playing at the Abbey Stadium was so uncomfortable for other teams. We used to put loads of sugar in their tea and give them no hot water at all. We put the warm-up balls in the bath so they would be soaking wet. This all got around the other clubs so it was very much a case of: 'Oh, no, it's Cambridge United this weekend.' They did not like us because we were horrible."

Fancy-dan Sheffield Wednesday were going to the Abbey with their internationals and their fancy manager and their aspirations. They arrived to sugary tea, they endured broken showers and they lost 4-0. Looking back on the tie, Ron Atkinson chuckled on what he described as a "weird one." He added: "Everyone knew we could play a bit and teams were starting to try different things to disrupt it, so when we got down there, we went to have a look.

"The middle of the pitch was spotless, but when we had a look in the corners the grass was up to your knees. That's the way they played; they used to hit every ball into the corner and run on to them. When we played them, well, we played a passing move the length of the pitch, about 18 one-touch passes. We rolled it across the goal-line and it just bounced up. They went up the other end, a goal-kick right up to Dion Dublin and he flicked it in. It went on in that fashion and that was us out of the cup."

Back at Middlewood Road the search for players went on. Just as Harkes and Tony Meola had wandered over from the US on the recommendation of Ian St John all those months earlier, Roger Spry had contacts in Portugal who had uncovered a free-agent striker apparently set for big things. Short, stocky, pacey and built like a bull, Angola-born Manuel Saavedra spent two weeks training with the Owls and taking extra sessions as the Wednesday coaching staff put him through his paces to test the water.

Could this be the bargain to push Hirst, Williams, Francis and Watson to the next level? Naturally Spry had taken him under his wing and, doing some crossing and heading practice after hours one afternoon, the fitness coach – whose football involvement was limited to schoolboy trials with Wolves – was helping out, partly as a translator and partly as an extra defender for Saavedra to navigate.

Spry remembered, wincing: "This cross was miles off where we'd asked them to put it, so I went to catch the ball, relaxed as you like. Well, this lad was desperate to impress, so he came full force trying to get the ball and smashed me in the face with his head at about 100 miles per hour. I knew straightaway something was seriously wrong. Alan Smith saw me and ran over; Nigel Worthington was there holding me in position.

"Alan ran to the car-park and drove his car on to the pitch. I fractured my cheekbone, broke my jaw, my face was a right bloody mess. Alan told me afterwards he was worried that, if I moved my head, my eyeball would fall out because all the bone structure in my face had caved in. I had a five-hour operation and they wired all my face together. I was out of action for months. To this day my lip on the side where the issue was is completely numb. It destroyed all the nerves in my face."

Needless to say Wednesday passed on Saavedra, who went back to enjoy a successful career in his homeland. The Owls would be without their highly-respected coach for several weeks, a blow as they prepared for two League Cup semi-finals in four days. As it turns out, when it comes to South American martial arts against a flying Portuguese, the Portuguese wins every time.

"YOU WON'T DO IT THIS TIME..."

T he transformation of Chelsea Football Club from proud-but-middling London club to the footballing superpower they are today was still in its early stages in February 1991. The club had made a return to the top tier of English football only the previous season and more than half of their previous 15 had been spent in Division Two. But under controversial businessman Ken Bates – who years later failed in a short-lived bid to buy Sheffield Wednesday – they were building rapidly towards everything that would fall for them in the coming decades.

With their February 10 date postponed, 7,000 Wednesday supporters shuffled into Stamford Bridge a fortnight later high in expectation, singing loudly above the home supporters – some of whom wore "Chelsea at Wembley 1991" T-shirts that some argued was typical of the over-inflated attitude of the club at the time. The stadium itself had seen better days and several fans remembered that it was crumbling at the corners.

Club-produced radio was pushed into the ears of home and away supporters alike pre-match, peddling the notion that Chelsea were the club of the future and that Bates was "building a dynasty." In terms of "controlling the narrative" from a PR perspective, they were a football club ahead of their time.

Having finished fifth the season before after their promotion in 1988/89, the Blues had talked themselves up as title contenders to the likes of Arsenal and Liverpool but, after opening with a run of just three wins in their opening 11 matches, they were languishing in mid-table, bereft of an FA Cup run after suffering the humiliation of a 3-1 home defeat to Second Division Oxford United in the third round. Sheffield

Wednesday were not a proposition to be taken lightly, but, the Chelsea camp admitted, a similar "upset" was unfathomable.

"To save our season we've got to get a decent win over Wednesday at home and finish the job at Hillsborough next Wednesday," said an expectant Blues keeper Dave Beasant on two legs that would be played within four days. "We all know this is our last chance to salvage the season. We owe it to our fans, after all the disappointments we've put them through, to take them to Wembley. They will forgive us everything if we can do that. I don't mind if it's Leeds or Manchester United in the final. It will be a glamour game against either club. All I'm bothered about is getting there."

It was a sentiment echoed by his teammate Dennis Wise, who had joined Chelsea that summer from Wimbledon for a then-club record fee of £1.6million. "We are as good as any team in the country – including Liverpool and Arsenal," he said, even though they were sitting mid-table. "But we've got to start proving it. We have disappointed a lot of people this season, including ourselves. I came to Chelsea because they are a big club – a club where I can win major honours."

Alongside Wise, Republic of Ireland World Cup star Andy Townsend had arrived from Norwich for £1.2m. The considerable fees paid for Beasant, Graham Roberts, David Mitchell and Ken Monkou were still sharp in the memory and Chelsea also had international-quality talent such as Kerry Dixon, Gordon Durie, Tony Dorigo, Steve Clarke and 20-goal striker Kevin Wilson.

Had sliding doors been pushed the other way, Wednesday might well have been lining up against Carlton Palmer alongside Wise in midfield. As part of a fire sale of players at West Brom in 1989, Palmer had been told the club had accepted two offers; one from an ambitious Chelsea side challenging in the upper regions of the division and the other from a Wednesday side locked in a relegation scrap that would be fought off only on the last day of the 1988/89 season. The decision to re-join former Baggies boss Atkinson in the end was made on the advice of England World Cup winner Nobby Stiles, a coach at the Hawthorns.

"I had a long chat with Ken Bates, but I've never been a fan of London," Palmer later said. "I like going down for a weekend, don't get me wrong; a few drinks, nice meal and a show, but living there never appealed to me. We spoke on the phone, he told me what he was going to do, that he wanted to build things around me in midfield, but then Nobby came in and asked me what I was going to do.

"I said I didn't really know and that London wasn't really for me. He told me not to even think about it, to get up to Sheffield Wednesday with Ron Atkinson. There was a threat of being relegated, but he told me the big man would sort that out. And so that's what I did. I had fantastic years there, not just in football, in my personal life. It was a fantastic time."

Palmer describes Atkinson as the single biggest influence on a stellar career and the pair remain firm friends. When Palmer returned from his new home in Shanghai 27 years on from the 1991 season, Atkinson received a phone call from his former talisman revealing that he had driven to his village as a surprise. He walked into Atkinson's house at 3pm, a bottle or two were opened and Palmer left to book himself into a local hotel well after midnight.

Palmer was one of few of Ron's former players to come forward in defence of the manager when a derogatory comment towards Chelsea's Marcel Desailly caused national outrage in 2004. Like Paul Williams, Palmer laughs off the idea that the man to have played such a trailblazing role in furthering the role of black players in British football might be considered a racist.

"Ron and I hit it off from day one," Palmer said. "I'm a cheeky chappie and I'm a very positive person. Ron likes to have positive people around him. If we're 4-0 down with five minutes to go, I think we're going to win 5-4 and Ron is the same. I very rarely get down and I can't have people around me looking at things in a negative way. Ron is similar to that. He was brilliant.

"He loved football and he understood that supporters paid money to come and watch us play, so he wanted teams to entertain. We never got a bollocking for getting beaten; we got a bollocking for not trying to entertain people. He's larger than life and a great bloke. Since I knew him as a kid, I've never known him to be any different.

"It was very difficult for me when all the racist stuff came about. He hasn't got a racist bone in his body. He's just old school, Ron. Yes, he made a racist comment, but he didn't mean it like that. My mum and dad came over from Jamaica in the late '50s. They've known Ron all my adult life and they'll tell you he's no racist. You know when someone is a racist and he's not. It really affected him. I was disappointed afterwards to see that people he'd looked after all looked after themselves. That's what people do, but it's sad. At the end of the day if you know somebody not to be that way, you should stand up – even if it means you get some criticism. You should speak as you find."

The game had been moved to a midday kick-off, irking Wednesday fans making the trip to London and, if the first leg of a Rumbelows Cup semi-final wasn't enough motivation for the Wednesday players, race relations were. Chelsea have come a long way in the intervening years and have been praised for their handling of issues they have had, but in the early 1990s they were on a mission to modernise the club and stamp out a racist faction of their support who had abused both Palmer and striker Paul Williams – down to start on the bench –on previous visits.

"It was an added motivation for me," said Williams, unprompted. "At their ground there was always a sense of hostility there towards people of colour. When you're playing, you don't always take much notice of it and I think ultimately a lot of professionals tend to use it positively. Any time I felt any hostility towards me for any reason – whether that was for being of colour or like when I went back to Charlton and fans were booing – I used to turn that around and use it as a form of inspiration. Chelsea was one of the grounds you went to and you knew there was a risk of abuse.

"It was something we as players maybe didn't experience a great deal by then, but as spectators my family would often comment that some grounds were worse than others and Chelsea was certainly one of the worst ones. I had a habit of scoring consistently against them. I guess they knew I had a good record against them and I would have comments and chanting, but my family heard a lot more than I did.

"When you're playing, you tend to concentrate on what you're doing; it's only the very odd occasion when maybe the ball goes out of play that you switch off and you tune in to what people are saying or what is being chanted. I didn't take much notice of anything of that nature, but sadly it was a part of the game at some grounds that you went to at that time.

"A few years ago my daughter told me she wanted to go and watch

Chelsea with some friends. I wasn't all that comfortable with it. I told her that her grandmother used to go and watch me play at Chelsea and they were quite derogatory towards people of colour."

Cheered on by an incredibly vocal following, Wednesday players limbering up for the match were supremely confident, a feeling that had followed them from Harkes' goal at Derby and that overpowered any hangover from back-to-back defeats at Cambridge and then in the league at Swindon.

Even though they had a game in hand on all those around them, Wednesday's lead over the chasing pack had been cut to one point – fourth-placed Notts County were closest to the Owls' tally of 51 – while Oldham were second on 59 points and West Ham out in front on 63. A nervy trip to County was the next league match on the calendar and, although Atkinson's pre-match words reminded the world that promotion was priority number one for the club, any lingering worries would be put aside for four days.

Featuring on *Saint and Greavsie* ahead of the Stamford Bridge clash, Big Ron had a simple, thinly-veiled message to his players; they had every right to be confident and that their showing at Cambridge was one that would not be accepted. "We're at a crucial point now," he said. "What we do know is that there is no way in the world we can play as badly as we did in our last cup contest. You can bet money, whatever the score is against Chelsea, we will play a darn sight better than that. We were awful.

"We've been nice and relaxed in our cup matches. In fact we were half-asleep against Cambridge. But in the other games, against Coventry and Derby, we've been very relaxed and we've gone into those games with a good, open mind. What I do hope and will preach to the players is that they don't freeze in the semi-finals, that they treat it as something to be enjoyed and to make them realise just how close they are to the real big one."

All-yellow Wednesday weathered an early Chelsea storm thanks in the main to Chris Turner, a man who had been to this stage of the competition before and indeed one stage further during his time with Sunderland. A double save, first to deflect the dangerous cross of Townsend and then to deny Wise from close range, set the tone for the Owls' afternoon as they quickly grew into things in a remarkable atmosphere. Beasant saved Palmer's effort and Francis shot wide as both sides traded blows in an entertaining first half.

The second half belonged to the travelling supporters, who watched on as their yellow wizards began to play with the sort of pizzazz that Atkinson so desired. On 52 minutes Wednesday were awarded a free-kick on the left-hand side, offering an opportunity for them to dust off a routine designed to set Nigel Worthington free on the overlap down the touchline with all the world expecting a floated Sheridan cross. "You won't do it this time," sneered Wise in a one-man wall. They did.

As the Northern Irishman's cross escaped two Chelsea defenders, Peter Shirtliff found himself in enough room to poke the ball awkwardly goalwards past Beasant, who was wrong-footed by the defender's swinging left boot. For all the quality Wednesday had shown in that tie and for all the entertainment they had provided throughout the season, it was a scrambling goal by their big centre-half that set them on their way.

"It was a bit of a miskick," Shirtliff laughs now, "but it went in. I think you could probably tell I didn't score too many with my feet, to be fair. It was a move we'd worked on. Nigel Worthington went round the outside, Shez did a reverse pass and he got round the back of them, squared it and I managed to get it in the net. It wasn't a shock to us. Chelsea were favourites because they were in the league above, but we didn't feel like we were underdogs. We all fancied ourselves to beat them and I think that showed in the way we played."

"It was something we'd done a few times," Worthington said. "I didn't hit it exactly as I'd have liked, but I wanted to hit it low. Nigel Pearson was usually the target with all the goals he'd scored with his head; with so many important goals for us in that run in particular. We deserved it, we'd played well and gone down there looking to score goals. We were rewarded for our bravery, I think. And we enjoyed it."

Atkinson had gone for the experience and X-factor of Francis ahead of Williams, who was chomping at the bit to get on the field alongside unused sub McCall. Chelsea had their moments as Townsend and Graham Stuart caused particular strife for the Owls from the middle of midfield, but the Owls remained on top in search for an all-important second goal. Shirtliff again acted as hero, this time at his more familiar end of the pitch, when he headed a Durie-bound cross upwards for

Pearson to clear. The introduction of Williams, sent on in place of Francis to stretch Chelsea's defence, proved to be vital as his header put Hirst through to finish confidently with eight minutes remaining. Minutes later a save from the Chelsea stopper to deny Hirst a second was a minor distraction on an incredible afternoon. Kept in the ground for more than an hour after the final whistle, for fear of a backlash from Chelsea fans, nothing could dull the atmosphere in the away end. A two-goal lead away from home was the stuff of dreams, if not – just yet – celebrations.

After all, Chelsea had done this before, if not quite to the same extent. They had come from two goals down at Second Division Portsmouth to win 3-2 in the competition's third round and their disappointing 0-0 draw at home to Tottenham Hotspur in the quarter-finals was a blow they overcame by winning 2-0 at White Hart Lane. Those players who gathered for Atkinson's team talk before a packed second leg under the lights at Hillsborough knew what to expect; to be told to play attacking football, to entertain a crowd who had worked long hours in order to pay to watch them play.

The first goal, he told them, would be vital. It would be "criminal" for them to let this opportunity pass. Chelsea boss Bobby Campbell sought to pile on the pressure in the build-up. "In this tournament we've won all our games away," he said. "That's what the boys are talking about."

Manchester United were already confirmed as the opponents for whoever progressed, having breezed past Leeds United by virtue of a 2-1 win at Old Trafford and a late 1-0 victory at Elland Road. The prospect of facing the behemoth that is Manchester United, Ron's old club from whom many felt he was unfairly sacked, merely added to the majesty of a potential first major final for Wednesday fans in a quarter of a century.

At Hillsborough for the second leg the atmosphere was tingling and an early free-kick by Worthington that was curled in to the back post gave the 34,669 fans present a livener, as if they needed it, when Shirtliff again had the ball in the back of the net but for an offside flag to kill the celebrations. But Wednesday were rampant and Chelsea defender Jason Cundy later admitted that he and his teammates were taken by surprise by the noise generated inside the stadium. Owls fans were responding to Atkinson's brave call for a more vocal support with

VAT. Wave after wave of attack came and went before a lovingly familiar story; a well-worked corner, a pinpoint Sheridan cross and a fifth Rumbelows Cup goal of the season for their leader, Nigel Pearson. "This man gets more goals than most midfield players," shouted commentator Alan Parry over the pandemonic home crowd. He was not kidding. In all competitions, in the depths of February, it was his 10th of the season.

"Wembley, Wembley...We're the famous Sheffield Wednesday and we're off to Wembley," the crowd dared to sing, the prospect of throwing away their three-goal cushion diminishing with every confident tackle, pass and attack. When other sides may have been tempted to sit in on the counter-attack and accommodate the efforts of the away side, that was not the Owls' way under this manager, an evening 25 years in the making and in which their fearless side thrived. Wednesday went on looking for another goal, the one that would put the tie beyond all reasonable doubt and confirm the Wembley dreams of their boisterous support.

It came on the stroke of half-time and was a goal well worthy of such a moment. Shirtliff's long ball forward was won by the tireless Hirst, whose header into the box seemed to take an age to reach Palmer. Holding off both Monkou and Dorigo like a dad breaking apart fighting siblings, he nodded the ball to the oncoming Danny Wilson, who unleashed a sweetly-struck volley with the outside of his foot into the top corner of Beasant's net. Right in front of a packed Kop end, several fans remember it to be the greatest – and loudest – moment at the famous old stadium. At home Parry's television commentary of the goal gave Wilson a curious nickname "Didwell" – courtesy of the immortal line: "Palmer did well, Wilson..."

"The atmosphere was electric, absolutely amazing," remembered the goalscorer. "I was in the team to be energetic. I wanted to get forward all the time and, while we appreciated that I didn't always get there, I was always a threat to defenders, finding those little spaces, running box to box. When we went on those forward surges, I had the licence to get up with the front men. It fell perfectly for me. I just lashed at it and fortunately it went where I wanted it to go. I'd seen plenty of those go over the stand before, but it was destiny really, the way we were all going and the way we were playing. It is special to me that that was the goal that finished it.

"We were a good side and we knew that. We weren't scared of any-one, whether that be home or away and we knew we weren't really underdogs. I remember hearing on the radio on the way down to London that week; people tipping us not only to get to the final, but that we would go on and win it. We were a team in the Second Division! You look at the likes of Sheridan and Hirst, who were as good as anything in the First Division, so we were expected to turn up and give the top division teams a run for their money."

With what was Chelsea's only real chance of the second half, Stuart – their best player across the two legs by a distance – nodded home Dixon's cutback to earn a consolation, but the muted celebrations, with less than half-an-hour remaining, said it all. With the match in danger of fizzling out on the pitch if not on the jubilant terraces, Atkinson again brought on Williams for Francis and gave the perhaps under-appreciated Steve McCall another run-out.

And the two combined to lather icing on the cake for Wednesday one minute from time when the winger's pass over the top allowed Williams to lift the ball triumphantly over the onrushing Beasant. Beyond all doubt, with a 5-1 aggregate scoreline, Sheffield Wednesday were going to Wembley.

Across the previous decade under Wilkinson Wednesday had threatened to make a major final, but never had, falling short in six quarter-finals and two semi-finals across the two domestic cups. Hillsborough, for so long a neutral FA Cup semi-final host, so often witnessed the glory of other teams booking their place in the final. But that night, under the floodlights, under the adoring gaze of their own packed house, the night belonged to the Owls. Few could take a dim view of supporters who rushed from the Kop to congratulate their heroes. Special nights call for special dispensations.

"That occasion is probably the second-most memorable thing that I achieved in football," remembered Williams. "It was absolutely phenomenal and the spectators were out of this world; they just never stopped chanting. At the end, when we finally got through, I could have stared into those stands for a week. I have got to give credit to Sheffield Wednesday; their supporters are second to none. You've got to be there really to appreciate and experience it. That night for me was so special and was one that I couldn't forget. I went home and couldn't sleep that night, such was the adrenaline of playing in front of that crowd."

The changing-room was a scene of pure elation. With the players in high spirits, laughing and joking as they so often would, the club's directors and chairman Dave Richards were allowed to join the celebrations, as were members of the club's youth team. His mind drifting back to that Middlewood Road meeting all those months ago, Atkinson was keen to ensure the famous night belonged to the whole club, not just the 15 or so members of the first team. Interviews were interrupted as players threw towels at those answering questions and indeed the interviewers. In the background of camera shots youngsters grinned, wide-eyed and inspired.

"I think tonight we showed really just how good we can be," Francis said after the game, towel rested over his shoulders. "Tonight was a good, determined performance and across the two games we thoroughly deserved to win." Hirst was less circumspect: "We hammered them, didn't we? Nobody expected that from us and we hammered them." Images of the talismanic striker spraying champagne with Sheridan in the changing-room are among the most iconic in the club's history. With the camera pointed at his manager, Hirst feigned to pour the bottle over him mid-interview. "Oh, go on, it's cheap," the flailing reporter quipped.

Atkinson, chuckling through a throat sore from the exertion of two semi-finals in four days, did not miss a beat. "No, it's not, it's vintage," he said. "It's from the last time we were at Wembley."

After 25 years Wednesday were back at that famous old stadium. And they were determined to celebrate accordingly.

12

JOSIE'S

"As far as I'm aware, there are only two clubs in Sheffield," Ron Atkinson often regales to after-dinner audiences with a cheeky glint in his eye. "There's Sheffield Wednesday and then there's Josephine's!" The legendary nightclub, a regular haunt of Wednesday's legendary drinking school, was the venue of choice on the evening of their second-leg triumph against Chelsea, the bubbly still dripping down the walls of the Hillsborough changing-room as the first-team players made their way through the doors to the cheers of waiting supporters.

There had been a whisper that the players would be out en masse in the event of such a historic win, despite the fact that they had a hugely-important league match at Notts County just three days later and the club was packed with waiting punters ready to revel in their success. Owned by Dave Allen, the casino and club magnate who would later become Wednesday's chairman, it was as swanky a nightclub as the north could offer; all gold and silver and mirrors and glitter-balls. Alongside Hanrahan's, it was the players' most popular drinking hole, nicknamed "Posephine's" by those who could not get in; frequented by the famous and the wannabe famous, the high-ranking policemen and the successful.

Open seven nights a week, unlike most clubs at that time, Wednesday night was karaoke night at Josephine's, set up in the wine bar. As the first pints were pulled for the Owls players, Phil King jumped straight on to the microphone to the delight of the punters present. Wednesday players barely put their hands in their pockets all night as Allen threw on round upon round of free drinks. Danny Wilson paraded around with a thick Cuban cigar between his teeth and David Hirst glugged champagne from the bottle. They were having the time of their lives and were behaving like champions.

"All the football players, the Steelers hockey guys, 'Bomber' Graham, they were all given a sportsman's pass to get into the club," remembered Steve Bailey, the doorman at Josephine's at the time. "It was a clever move that. Josephine's became the place to be. The footballers tended to enjoy the wine bar to one side because it was a little quieter, a little more exclusive and the music wasn't so loud so you could have a conversation with one another and hold court a bit. And they never seemed to get any bother from people in there. They left them to it.

"Dave just wanted to keep it a nice place for nice people and it was. There was very rarely any trouble. It was a nice club, a great feel-good factor to it. Dave wanted to get the footballers, the boxers and the singers in because it gave it something the other places didn't really have. People liked rubbing shoulders with these guys. Both sets of footballers at that time didn't mind a night out, but it's fair to say the Wednesday lads liked a drink. They didn't mind letting their hair down and, like a few of the doormen around at that time, I got to know them quite well."

In late February 1991 South Yorkshire – and Sheffield in particular – was a region in the early stages of enforced modernisation from its proud history as a steelworks and mining community. Its nightlife was one thing, but from a dour 1980s best channelled in two dystopian films by locally-born filmmaker Barry Hines, 1981's *Looks and Smiles* and 1984's *Threads*, an ambitious city council set about building a brighter future. Meadowhall, an enormous shopping centre built on the site of a former steelworks on the outskirts of the city in September 1990 and advertised in Wednesday's matchday programme, was perhaps the most brazen example.

Wednesday players were involved in the promotion of the 1991 World Student Games, for which the Don Valley Stadium had been built at a cost of £29m along with Ponds Forge International Sports Centre and Sheffield Arena. The Don Valley was demolished in 2014 and a recent estimate suggests that the Games ran up an overall debt of £658m. The city's pubs were a success at least. Wednesday players made sure of that.

There was not much of a conversation about whether players would be sanctioned a night out or not after the Chelsea game. Ron's attitude to the club's drinking culture had always been that he trusted his players to make good decisions. It was a brave mantra, especially given the fact he had the likes of Carlton Palmer, David Hirst and so on in his side, but it was one that very rarely backfired, if at all. The days before camera-phones, he laughed three decades on, allowed players to get into drunken scrapes the Press, supporters and most importantly managers would rarely hear about. This was a night that was a little better behaved than usual anyway, given wives and girlfriends were invited along to enjoy the glory.

Back at S6 the youth-team players invited into the changing-room an hour or so earlier were left a whip-round organised by Nigel Pearson to wipe the surfaces down and tidy up. It was a job they would ordinarily have had to complete anyway, but spirits were high and the players were happy to hand over a little cash given the extra work. The youngsters, some as young as 16, smiled their way through it, not knowing that, after their jobs were done, they were to be invited to join the first teamers at the nightclub.

The senior men bought the wide-eyed youths pints all night and introduced them to some of Sheffield's fairer sex. That Wednesday received an angry phone call from one of the boy's parents the day after was a minor footnote to the evening. Atkinson was keen to ensure this was a win for the whole club and indeed the whole city. Well, half of it perhaps.

"I was standing in that changing-room, the lads were having a drink and we were all having a laugh and enjoying ourselves, as you do on a night like that," Atkinson remembered fondly. "I'd had a think about this earlier and I'd decided that, if they won, it was a good time for the boys to go bonding at Josephine's. We'd mapped it all out just quietly. This was the Wednesday night and we were travelling down to play Notts County on the Saturday, so it was a big call, but we trusted them to get the job done. And there was a second motive under it. Neil Warnock's a Sheffield lad, isn't he? I knew he'd get wind of this. Some of his mates were in the bloody bar with us. We wanted them to think we were distracted."

Pints followed pints and players were invited to stay on long after closing hours. King had taken a knock in the semi-final clash and had been asked to report to the training ground for a precautionary once-over. Stumbling out of Josephine's in daylight, he said that he jumped into a taxi home, took a shower and reported straight to Middlewood Road. If his ankle was fine, his head wasn't quite so rosy. But it was all worth it. Training before the Notts County trip was limited to a Friday kickabout. Atkinson took part in a thick sweater and woolly hat as usual, but for once was one of the more energetic participants.

"All the punters were buying us drinks and singing with us," Chris Turner remembered on a famous session. "I didn't get home until seven o'clock the next morning. That was one of the great nights I had with the lads. Across the course of a career you don't get many moments like that, getting to Wembley, and we knew how to celebrate, let me tell you.

"It's the way football was in those days, socialising. Carlton and Hirsty were great personalities when we went out and we had some great laughs. Pears was our leader and he was in charge on the nights out. This is stuff that, if it was done today, it would be rocket fuel for the media, but these were things you did. We trained hard and played hard. It was a proper set of lads."

"Oh, we had a night at Josephine's," remembered Peter Shirtliff. "A few of the lads came straight in the next day, I think; it wasn't just Kingy! A few of us liked a drink, there's no doubt about it, but we did it at the right time. We had a policy that meant that, when we achieved something, we went out to enjoy it and we'd certainly achieved something that night. I wasn't as bad as a lot of the other lads, I don't think; I left at closing!

"There were fans there, all the local lads had friends there. It was great. We had a sing-song and had some laughs. There's a point from which I must admit it becomes a bit of a blur. Superb. Hirsty would have been holding court, that's for sure. Shez was one after a couple of drinks as well. But there were loads, some great characters, some funny, funny lads. There were some big, big nights and that was certainly one of them."

Notts County had enjoyed something of a renaissance in the mid-point of the season to fall in a point behind Wednesday. Six wins and a draw between December 15 and January 19 meant that their tag as surprise packages inflated to the point they were widely recognised as genuine promotion contenders, especially given the four-up change in the rules. In Tommy Johnson they had a bright young thing on his way to 19 league goals that season. Warnock had already transformed the history of Scarborough and, in taking unfancied County from Division Three to the brink of promotion to the top tier, had by now developed quite a reputation – and one that he was relishing. In the coming months he would be approached to take on big ticket jobs at Sunderland and Chelsea.

Ron arrived at Meadow Lane entirely unable to speak – not the only ailment taken over from the week that was, as the Owls lined up for one of their biggest matches of the season without King, Wilson and Hirst. The Owls boss made it clear that the former pair were rested, moves he had become more comfortable in making after the reinforcement of his squad in earlier weeks, while Hirst would sit out the next two matches with a knee injury. With Nigel Worthington shuffled back into defence, the dependable Steve McCall stepped back on to the left of midfield and Anderson jumped in at right-back with Harkes shunted further forward. Paul Williams replaced Hirst up top and after three minutes of blood and thunder football, it was the former Charlton man who put Wednesday into the lead.

"I knew they thought they'd get us," Atkinson remembered. "They knew that we'd been celebrating, that the boys had had a drink and they'd think we'd relaxed too much. In all the excitement of the semi I'd lost my voice, so I took Frank Barlow along as the official shouter. Neil had got them pumped up for the game – this was their big chance and you could see they were so confident. They thought we'd been having a laugh all week, especially when I rocked up with a frog in my throat. Within a few minutes we were one up. We were playing on pure adrenaline. The boys are flying. I'll be honest, we couldn't believe it on the bench."

The game was deeply unpleasant and County's supporters played their part, baying the thousands of Wednesdayites who had travelled, cuddly toys and all, and barracking the Owls players, too. County had trained on the pitch the day before in their attempt to disrupt Wednesday's passing game and a firm tackle was never far away, particularly on Sheridan. Shirtliff hit the crossbar, Harkes received lengthy treatment from Smith after a monstrous tackle by Dean Yates and County threatened to steal a point but for Turner's efforts between the sticks. With Watson and MacKenzie thrown on for their Owls debuts, it was only when Dean Thomas nodded a Sheridan free-kick past his own goalkeeper that the points were sealed, continuing Wednesday's fine run against the division's stronger sides. In a battling performance against the odds of human condition, the four-point gap on Warnock's side had been restored.

"After the second goal Neil came climbing out of his dugout to have a go at something and started screaming," Atkinson remembered. "Little Danny Wilson wasn't playing, but had travelled with us that day. He turned to him and said: 'If you don't get back in that box, I'll put you in there.' Neil looked at me and I just said: 'Good lad, Danny, saves me getting involved in my condition.' That whole afternoon was fuelled by pure adrenaline. They had a good side, players like Tommy Johnson, Mark Draper. They were typical of Neil, very well-drilled and a tough side. A real threat. But that game gave us a big momentum swing over them. That was their big chance without any doubt."

A soft penalty tucked away by Sheridan at Hillsborough seven days later saw off old adversaries West Brom on an afternoon when Atkinson was awarded the Second Division manager-of-the-month award for February. Considering the month had yielded a draw with Watford, a defeat at Swindon and that 4-0 FA Cup thrashing by Cambridge, it is fair to say it was a gong handed over for Wednesday's League Cup heroics. Atkinson was presented with a magnum of champagne before the match and Wednesday fans sang his name. The bond was real.

Both postponements and cup involvement meant that games would come thick and fast. Addressing the fans in his programme notes ahead of the Baggies win, Atkinson spoke of a gruelling fixture list and the need to treat the 11 league matches scheduled ahead of their April 21 Rumbelows Cup date as cup finals in their own right. In the first, on a midweek night at Hillsborough, Wednesday dominated fifth-placed Brighton and went ahead through Anderson after just five minutes.

The euphoria of the semi-finals had yet to wear off, but nervous moans and groans began to emanate from the home crowd as the game became increasingly frustrating, especially when the Seagulls' striker John Byrne equalised with 12 minutes to go. Atkinson had attempted to lure Byrne from French side Le Havre the season before and his

"11 cup finals" talk could not bring about the desired result when the equaliser prevented Chris Turner from celebrating his 500th senior appearance with three points.

The sight of Hirst emerging from the bench, some weeks before Wednesday fans had been advised to expect him back in action, was a welcome boost, but the Owls had been dealt a blow earlier that week when Nigel Worthington, an ever-present up to that point, had landed awkwardly from a jump in training and injured his cartilage. Alan Smith considered it touch and go as to whether he would be able to make the cup final six weeks later. With Nilsson recovering well, but carrying no guarantees for Wembley, Wednesday were facing the prospect of being without two of their most dependable characters on either flank.

Including cup matches, the Brighton draw was Wednesday's 11th at Hillsborough that season and with no time to breathe, attention quickly turned to another monster match-up three days later at West Ham's Upton Park. It was a ground at which Ron Atkinson had never won and, in fact, it was a ground at which no opposition manager had won in a very long time. Under Billy Bonds, the FA Cup semi-finalists had peeled away from third-placed Wednesday and, although they were stalling a touch with one win in five games, they were unbeaten at their traditional old ground in 14 months. Their East Terrace stand, nicknamed the Chicken Run after the stand it replaced in 1968, was one of the most feared in British football.

"It worked for us; we all knew that," then West Ham midfielder Stuart Slater remembered three decades on. "When opposition players would come and play and take throw-ins, the Chicken Run was hardcore. Proper West Ham, East End boys, no messing about. They were funny and they gave banter, but they could literally touch a full-back or wide player as they came past.

"It would be absolutely packed in there and it would either make or break you as a West Ham player as well; you could hear everything. But for an opposition player there was no hiding place. They would either intimidate you and you would go hiding or it would inspire you. The characters Sheffield Wednesday had at that time – experienced players – we knew it could go the other way."

It was hardly ideal preparation for facing such a cauldron then that the Sheffield Wednesday coach was desperately late to the ground, having taken a wrong turn in the London traffic and hit every traffic jam in the capital. At five minutes to two the Wednesday cohort were still miles from their destination and a hurried Atkinson remembered that their teamsheet had to be in the hands of the referee. A panicked phone call to club secretary Graham Mackrell, the only official Owls' figure at the ground because he had travelled independently, led to the suited-and-booted businessman wandering the halls of the ground trying to find the officials to explain.

In the end Big Ron listed the team to Mackrell over the phone and he wrote it in pencil and handed it over, a little red-faced. With the West Ham side out warming up and time ticking down, Richie Barker was instructed to hop out into the smog of traffic to fetch the team kit from the boot of the coach as players began undressing. Atkinson delivered his team talk from the front of the bus, demanding that his players drew on their vast experience to get through another huge test.

Thankfully Wednesday arrived in time for kick-off. Hirst was pushed back into the line-up alongside lifelong West Ham supporter Williams, in a good run of form and desperate to nick a goal in front of hordes of friends and family all sitting in the home end. Setting off that afternoon, the polite and well-spoken forward leant back in his chair and thanked Atkinson for the opportunity to start at the ground that introduced him to football, explaining he had a good record against the club he supported.

Approaching the end of his Charlton contract two years earlier, Lennie Lawrence brought him into the side and told him in no uncertain terms that it was a do-or-die match in his career. As it happened, Williams scored two in a 3-2 win and did not look back.

"Without a doubt I kept a very close eye on West Ham's results," laughed Williams. "For me my ideal scenario was always going to be West Ham coming second and us winning the Championship. That would have been the ultimate season for me, a complete dream come true. That place was my football education, I loved standing watching West Ham while I was growing up and, although I wrote to them several times asking for a trial period when I was younger, they never replied. It is perhaps a slight regret that I never played for West Ham United, if I am completely honest."

Even though Wednesday might have been accused of dropping points in matches they should have won, particularly at home, results against those challenging for the three automatic promotion places had been good. Defeat to Millwall after injuries to Pearson and Nilsson was the only one on record against the division's top six. Alongside the famous cup nights, there seemed to be something in this collective, made up of individuals used to high-pressure games, that was lifted by the big occasion. So predictable then, so Wednesday, that they would smash three past their table-topping rivals in a display of quality, free-flowing football that by the end of the game had pockets of the Chicken Run applauding.

The goals, so often shared around the Wednesday changing-room, came from the two most predictable sources; David Hirst, turning smartly on the edge of the box to smash the ball past Ludo Miklosko on the half-hour mark, and a classy second-half brace for the bustling Hammer Paul Williams. His second, a beautifully-timed diving header, was particularly outstanding. West Ham one, Sheffield Wednesday three – the first home defeat for any of the top three sides that season and the first time Bonds' side had let in three in a game. In context West Ham went on to concede only 34 goals in total during their 46-game season.

Williams remembered the game with a wide smile: "I'd invited the world to watch me play for my new team, I scored two goals and I was ecstatic. For me I would have preferred to score those goals against West Ham more than any other team. They're my team and I remember those goals, all my goals against them, more vividly than any others I scored in my career. To be at that ground and score and win among all the friends I grew up with and spent time on those terraces with...it couldn't have been any better than that. And it was such a big result in our season, too. It was a special day."

As was traditional in the event of back-to-back games down south, Atkinson arranged for the side to enjoy a break away from Sheffield. Plymouth was the next destination on March 19, just three days on from the triumph of Upton Park, and, if the players had been spared the perils of a long journey, the same could not be said for Wednesday's supporters.

Three thousand of them traipsed down to see Steve MacKenzie

knock home a late, late equaliser on a terrible playing surface designed again to nullify the Owls' preference for passing play.

"Plymouth make it hard," said a frustrated Atkinson after the game. "They play in a way that is designed to spoil games and the pitch was not too clever. I knew it wasn't going to be pretty, but I didn't think it was going to be that bad."

With road closures affecting hundreds attempting to get back to South Yorkshire, several fans remembered getting less than an hour's sleep ahead of early-morning shifts in factories and steelworks across the region. After a cold midwinter of league uncertainty Sheffield Wednesday were six points clear of fourth-placed Middlesbrough, six shy of West Ham and seven behind league leaders Oldham. They had a game in hand on those in front and two on Boro behind. And Wembley was booked. Those hardy supporters on the road back north may have been half-asleep, but they were dreaming all the same.

13

ENTER SHERIDAN

R on Atkinson had learned to accept that from time to time he was not going to see John Sheridan's sparkling best during Monday training sessions at Sheffield Wednesday. The midfielder would often pull on a black bin-bag and wander his way through the session, eyes narrowed by an evening of Manchester lager the previous afternoon. The joke would be made by teammates that Sheridan's scent would make Oliver Reed recoil. "Shut up, you crisp packet," the reply would invariably come. As in his football, Sheridan's stock put down was different from most; one sprinkled with a little bit of mad genius.

Born into a Stretford council estate to two Irish parents, Sheridan had grown to be adored by the Wednesday faithful for his deft touch, an ability to pick a pass not seen at Hillsborough since and a penchant for the unthinkable. Above all else he just loved playing football, showcasing an attitude to playing in front of 30,000 people that he would have shared in front of a dozen on a Sunday morning. And therein lay the unspoken Monday-morning issue. Such was his obsession with the game that he had often made the trip home to play for his brother's pub team at the weekend before enjoying a skinful in the afternoon.

He thought Ron Atkinson did not know, but he did. Atkinson had eyes everywhere. But such was his delicate handling of his most talented player, he pretended he had no idea. He had rescued Sheridan's career, digging him out of the wasteland of Nottingham Forest's reserves after a bizarre fling with Brian Clough when Sheridan made only one League Cup appearance after a £650,000 move from Leeds United that seemed to make so much sense. Impressing on a fleeting pre-season tour to France, the midfielder started in a 1-1 draw with lowly Huddersfield before being told by Clough, by then staring into the abyss of alcohol addiction: "Young man, you've had a busy week – I'm going to give you a rest."

"It didn't matter how hard I worked; Brian Clough was never satisfied," Sheridan said after signing for Sheffield Wednesday in November 1989, just three months after his Forest arrival. "I couldn't get in the side or convince him I was fit to fill the gap left by Neil Webb. When he finally agreed to see me, he made it quite clear I didn't figure in his plans." Sheridan later claimed the coaches at Forest would almost beg Clough to put him in the team. "I could not show Brian what I could do playing in the reserves all the time," he added, "but he made it clear to me that I would not get into his side."

Sheridan's was one of the names most widely linked with a move away from Hillsborough when Wednesday were relegated from the First Division. Like Nigel Worthington, he had a release clause in his contract, but showed no intention of exploring the options available to him. "Ron gave me a chance by signing me from Nottingham Forest," he later said. "I owe him loyalty. Relegation apart, I've never been happier."

So happy, so effective, so loyal. And with hindsight crystal-clear, it is confusing that the man at the heart of Wednesday's success that season was subject to booing from a section of the Hillsborough support during their first home defeat of the season, to lowly Oxford United. The afternoon is a source of embarrassment for Wednesday supporters in retrospect. At a club and in a community so indelibly soaked in honest, working-class values, Sheridan for a little time fell down the pecking-order in the affections of some Wednesday fans. Some preferred the slugged-out stylings of his midfield partner Carlton Palmer or David Hirst. And when Sheridan missed two penalties in the April Fool's Day defeat to Oxford, tension boiled over.

It was a tension caused by a 3-2 defeat at Wolves and the feeling that, after it took a last-gasp Steve MacKenzie winner to beat Bristol Rovers at home the week before, Wednesday were just performing a little beneath the level they were capable of. That, with the glory of Wembley Way just three weeks away, the title was sliding from their grasp. Although the Owls had a game in hand, the Oxford loss put them 11 points behind an impressive West Ham side who were unbeaten since

Wednesday's 3-1 win at Upton Park and showing no sign of a further slip-up. Oldham sat between them, two points behind the Hammers.

Sheridan faced his critics head-on with typical honesty. In conversation with Alan Biggs in the following matchday programme, he admitted a drop in otherwise sparkling form. "My passing, which is my strongest point, has been letting me down a bit," he said. "Maybe it's because I've been trying for the miracle ball all the time. Instead of going for the hard ones and giving the ball away, I'm looking to play more simple passes. I was pleased with the way I started the season, but after that I wasn't happy with my game at all, particularly in home matches – and I don't know why that should be."

Most fans knew his class would shine through, as did his teammates. "What a player," said Hirst. "He had quality running all through him. He was a centre-forward's dream because he could put it on a plate for you. He was hard to play with, but that was because he was so vocal. I used to get absolutely hammered by him if I gave the ball away; he'd have a go at me, my family, everything. Some of the things he said were totally unrepeatable. But straight after the game he'd come over and say: 'I'm sorry about that, it just comes in and comes out.' It was just his way of releasing the tension and anger of what had happened. And to be fair, when I did lose the ball, he was the one who had to run around and get it back. Great bloke."

A second 2-0 defeat in five days, this time away at Portsmouth, saw Atkinson admit that Wednesday's title chances were sliding further from view. But there was some good news in the long-awaited return to action of Roland Nilsson, well ahead to schedule. The Swede added class and calm to the Wednesday side and would make an incredible impact on the final later that month. "He made a fantastic recovery," Smith remembered. "It was a record time back for an injury of that nature; it may still be a record. Incredible. We worked closely with a man in Stockholm called Professor Jan Ekstrom who was the world authority on the knee joint and performed the surgery on him. The Swedish FA were with us every step of the way with him.

"Roland was a great athlete with a great attitude, a smashing lad, and it was his attitude and commitment to the programme we put in place that got him back. He'd do anything we wanted him to because from his point of view it was his responsibility to be match-fit for when he

returned, nobody else's. He took it very seriously. We were the exper-
tise, if you like, but, if we said it was best for him to have a day's rest or
that it was time to go, he'd do that. He was the best professional I ever
worked with."

A left-field technique at that time, Smith had Nilsson performing
training drills in the swimming pool at the Hallam Towers Hotel to
ensure that his muscles were strong enough to re-join the Wednesday
effort as soon as possible without having to put weight on his knee
joint. Nilsson credits the Smith-Ekstrom combination with saving his
career: "It was really good to work with him [Smith]. He pushed me as
hard as he could without making things go wrong. I had no setbacks
and we had such a good understanding whether I was in England or
back in Sweden for a week or two to do something a bit different. It
was a really good partnership with respect to getting me fit.

"When you have the operation early and the doctor tells you they're
not sure if everything will be all right, it's a case of wait and see. That's
a big thing for a footballer to hear. But at the same time it was broken
down for me very clearly – that the operation would be one part, then
recovery from that and then building it up. Alan told me very early that
it was a case of working really hard and doing all the right stuff to get
myself back.

"After the operation they knew it would be okay. A new cruciate,
you hope, will hold for a very long time, but sometimes it doesn't sus-
tain everything and you have to do the operation again. There was a
lot of doubt regarding the knee at that time and it frightened me. It was
a very real possibility that, if things had gone wrong, I wouldn't play
again. It was emotional to play at Portsmouth."

With thousands of supporters having made the trip south yet again,
a similar number set themselves in for a long, cold weekend in the rain
on Penistone Road in search of a golden ticket to Wembley, which
were set to go on sale at 10am on the Sunday. The first to set up camp
at the ticket office did so at 6am on Saturday and watched as the queue
grew and grew. By 3pm camaraderie had grown and groups of strangers were huddled around radios to celebrate the return of the fan favourite Swede and curl in frustration as goals from future Owls Guy
Whittingham and Martin Kuhl, via a controversial late penalty, earned
the relegation-threatened side a deserved three points.

It was what happened after the penalty that cut deeper still. Carlton Palmer, who had given away the spot-kick when he launched into Steve Wrigley in a challenge that nearby Nigel Pearson later described as an excellent tackle, could not contain himself in protesting his innocence to the referee long after the fact. Several players remember trying to calm the fiercely-competitive midfield man down as he continued an extended tirade, all sense of reason lost in the disappointment of another match lost. A red card shown to the energetic 25-year-old registered little with the Wednesday players, least of all Palmer. Until he made his way to the touchline.

"You fucking idiot," snarled Atkinson, Carlton's long-time mentor. "Do you have any fucking idea what you've just fucking done?" The two of them would travel to London the following week in an unsuccessful effort to see the red card rescinded and the subsequent ban meant that Palmer missed two matches, effective a fortnight after the offence. Palmer, the engine to a Sheffield Wednesday side who allowed those around him to flourish, would miss the Rumbelows Cup final.

Classically philosophical, Palmer looked back on the incident with sadness, but no regret. Had he had the mindset to pull out of that tackle, he would have pulled out of hundreds more in his career and not achieved what he achieved. "I was just concentrating on the game," he said. "Our priority that season was promotion and I wasn't even thinking of the cup final; I was thinking of winning the football match and that was it. It was a reckless challenge; one I didn't need to make. It was frustration, I don't like losing and that was it."

"We were gutted for him," remembered Danny Wilson. "None of us clicked that it would be the case that he'd miss the final until we got back into the changing-room and Ron was tearing a strip off him. He was such an important part of that side and once the disappointment for your mate goes, selfishly you start to think: 'Well, that's a blow for us,' because he and Shez were so brilliant together in midfield. You're going into a game with Manchester United and all the midfielders they had and you're without one of your main men. I can't speak for the other lads, but it shook me."

Back at Hillsborough word had travelled through the radio. A spontaneous chanting of Palmer's name briefly filled the air, but the disappointment, both at the news of the suspension and of the result, dampened a previously jovial communal atmosphere. Groups of strangers had taken it in turns to nip to shops to buy food and drink and two workmen wandered back from a nearby B&Q with sheets of tarpaulin for people to hold over their heads and keep out the rain. As the afternoon stretched into evening, the queues wound way down Penistone Road.

Supporters who had made the long trip back from Fratton Park joined the masses and it was only when the pubs closed at 10pm and refreshed punters arrived looking for their place in the line that atmospheres were dented slightly. Such was the demand and to minimise the risk of any further trouble, Wednesday eventually opened up the gates and allowed fans to wait in the stands at midnight – still 10 hours before the tickets went on sale.

With only two weeks to go until the cup final, *The Star* and *Green 'Un* began running daily "Wembley Watch" snippets, offering insight into the Owls' preparations for the big day. And it was there, 13 days out from the final and two days before a now-vital league clash with Blackburn Rovers, that news of a knock to skipper Nigel Pearson became public knowledge. The nerves of Wednesday fans were being severely tested.

Led by experienced manager Don Mackay, Blackburn were at the start of a journey that would enable them to break the monopoly of the so-called bigger clubs and win a Premier League title just four years later. Industrialist Jack Walker, whose spending power sharpened that charge, had taken full control of the club in January and had set about making his presence felt, breaking the club-record transfer fee three times in less than three months; for goalkeeper Bobby Mimms, from Tottenham, and Coventry pair Steve Livingstone, a striker, and defender Tony Dobson. Rovers had recently beaten Oldham and it was through these three signings that they were pulling away from any notion of a relegation scrap. They would be promoted two seasons later.

Without Pearson, Peter Shirtliff took the captain's armband, Viv Anderson came in to cover at centre-half and Rovers went ahead when Alan Irvine, a future Owls manager, broke through to finish a bouncing ball across the box from Chris Sulley. Bloodstained from an early knock to the face, a bandaged Shirtliff spoke at half-time alongside Atkinson to inspire a much-needed second half comeback. Wednesday had not been poor, far from it, but therein lay the story of their season at Hillsborough. They had to win the football match.

Enter Sheridan.

Ducking, weaving and producing balls only he could see, the Mancunian midfielder burst into life as only he could, controlling the game from the middle of the park in defiance of the doubters who had dissented against him in their previous Hillsborough outing. Mimms, a former Rotherham stopper, was proving a nuisance, twice saving from Hirst and once from Francis, before the dam broke through Anderson's determined header on 54 minutes. Just 60 seconds later came a moment of pure sporting redemption under the lights that the fixture will forever be remembered for; a ball across from David Hirst, one touch, two, and a sweetly picked-out finish from 20 yards.

Veins bursting from his neck, Sheridan ran towards the Kop, swinging arms and gesturing to the crowd. Within seconds he was flooded by teammates. Hirst pointed to his great friend and made no secret of his anger about his Oxford treatment; Palmer lifted the goalscorer in the air before shouting into the Wednesday crowd in defence of his partner in crime. It was a moment, if one were needed, that proved the togetherness of the squad and their unabated desire to look after one another. For those who had doubted Sheridan just nine days earlier, it was a point well-made and taken on board; and one that would be hammered home when he netted a game-settling penalty in front of the same stand 15 minutes later.

"It was always going to be a matter of time for him," said Palmer 30 years on. "The fans don't know that he could hardly walk sometimes that season with his knee. He played with injections; his knee was fucked and there were times when he played in unbelievable pain. So of course there were matches where he wasn't the John Sheridan everybody knew. We were all disappointed by the way the fans were with him. We'd spoken about it between us and we said it was up to all of us to prove them wrong.

"But Ron told us what we already knew, that he'd turn the corner with them, which he did. He was always going to; he's one of the best footballers to play for that club. That's the way supporters can be at times. It's funny with some players. If Hirsty had been shit for a whole season, they'd never boo; that's just the way it is. It did affect him. It was always going to. But all the lads were fuming about it and we made sure we had his back. He knew that."

Phil King, who later became the godfather to Sheridan's footballer son, Jay, looked back on a generational talent. "What he couldn't do with a football wasn't worth doing," he said. "He used to come into training in all sorts of states, I'll be honest. There were a few of us like that, but he was always the best player on the park.

"He had ups and downs with the fans, but in the end he became a Wednesday legend. You're never going to keep a player like that down. And someone with his determination? No chance. We had a great relationship with the supporters in and away from the ground, but that was a moment for us to get behind our boy, if you like. I still get goosebumps thinking about it now."

Days earlier Sheridan was one of four players with Nigel Pearson, David Hirst and Carlton Palmer, to be named in the Division Two team of the season, a list that surely would have also included Nilsson had he not suffered his injury. The gongs kept coming, too, vindicating the "one-club" mentality Atkinson had spoken about all those months before; Dave Barber and his team of six ground staff winning the second-tier groundsman-of-the-year award for producing the best pitches in the division. Handing over the award, Ron Atkinson commented that it had been sponsored by Rumbelows. A good omen, he suggested.

Across the Pennines Manchester United were busy planning for the final of the European Cup Winners' Cup, having beaten Legia Warsaw 3-1 away from home. Their powerful frontman Mark Hughes was voted PFA player of the year with promising winger Lee Sharpe winning the young-player gong. But the Owls had no reason to care.

Those who had secured tickets for Wembley clung to them dearly and made travel plans while, within the halls of Hillsborough, focus on the job at hand remained steadfast. Middlesbrough, all season one of the sides clawing at the coat-tails of the front three, were next to visit and after a horror start to the new year had won two in two, a 4-0 win over Port Vale last time out building confidence that a late charge was still not out of the question.

Atkinson's side had spent just one week outside the automatic promotion places and saw no reason to dip out again, a late 2-0 win thanks to two Paul Williams goals effectively all but knocking the Teesside club from contention. The Owls were now five points clear of Millwall in fourth.

With prizes for the ground staff and prizes for individuals secured, and the prize of an immediate return to the First Division growing more and more real, Sheffield Wednesday were just a week from their big day out in the Rumbelows Cup final. But away from the first team, Ron Atkinson had demanded success at every level of the club. And that is exactly what he got.

14

A TALE OF TWO RYANS

The red-hot Sheffield sunshine was burning bright and, as Ron Atkinson continued in his mission to pick up the pieces of Sheffield Wednesday's first team's relegation from the First Division, he called a meeting in his office with staff and some senior players and outlined his blueprint for the season ahead; that success breeds success. "This is not just a season for the first team," he said. "It is for the juniors and the reserves. I want every team that pulls on a Sheffield Wednesday jersey this season to achieve success in whatever form it comes."

It was his attempt to cultivate a spirit that would run through the entire club, one that would bounce through the corridors of Hillsborough and through every blade of grass at Middlewood Road. In that meeting before the start of the season he told those present that the first team should act as a marker for those beneath them. Established players should be on hand to assist with the youngsters; reserve-team football should be taken incredibly seriously. It was the original big society.

By the time that spring had sprung in April 1991, his vision had long since been realised. Both sides, bubbling along under the radar of the first team's road to Wembley, had done exactly what they were told. When David Hirst and Phil King left Hillsborough in the hours after relegation from the First Division, the ladies on reception were crying. A few months on the stadium was filled with smiles, from those ladies on reception to the big man in the dugout. The transformation had been incredible and beneath the first string had been led by two men in the main – Frank Barlow and Albert Phelan.

Barlow was in many ways the most popular figure at the club. Experienced, unflashy, mild-mannered and an excellent man-manager, he went about his job as reserve-team boss with a quiet assurance. His side were challenging for the title of Pontins League Division One champions and in a division including many of the country's footballing behemoths, such as Manchester United, Liverpool, Everton and Nottingham Forest, Wednesday had stayed the course.

Their young central defenders Jon Newsome and David Wetherall went on to have hugely successful Premier League careers elsewhere and the experience of Lawrie Madden, Steve MacKenzie, Steve McCall and others proved to be an irresistible mix. But the man at the steering wheel was Barlow; motivating players who often thought they should be playing elsewhere and often glancing longingly at those in their positions limbering up for Wembley.

His, many said, was the hardest job at Wednesday; ensuring players featuring in the second string were fully motivated and hungry despite the relatively-settled nature of Big Ron's top dogs. He would hold regular conversations with players, taking them into the dugout of Hillsborough for pep talks and using the scenery to remind them that they were playing for one of British football's great clubs. When players required days off from the rough and tumble of the reserve league, they would get them. But in the main players wanted to play. Looking back, Atkinson himself said that the spirit of the reserves and youth team was a key factor in the success of his side and credits Barlow with much of that.

"Frank Barlow was a godsend to me," remembered Kevin Pressman, who at 23 was struggling with what he felt was an unjust exit from first-team involvement at the season's halfway mark. "He was the one who kept me on the straight and narrow. I spent many an hour sitting in the dugout at Hillsborough asking him what he thought I should do. His guidance was second to none and he helped me through some dark times that season. It might sound a bit extreme, but he was my rock.

"I spent a lot of time with him and he was always there for me and the other lads when they were struggling. I spent so much time with him and I owe him so much; he was a big part of the reason my career went as it did. It was all part of the success of the football club. When the reserves are doing well, the club is usually doing well. It was a very well-balanced squad of players, but Frank held the whole thing together."

Barlow himself was more modest on reflection. Although he accepted that he played an important role in the club's success that season, he said that there was no secret to good man-management; he was simply a good person to frustrated footballers and made time to listen to their grievances. "Disappointment is a natural feeling," he said. "You do not have to feel guilty about feeling disappointed. With the 'keepers, on both occasions they turned in, trained properly and played properly.

"That's why they did so well, the pair of them. When you're the reserve-team manager, you've got to accept that the people you are going to have playing for you are not happy for one reason or another. If you get an international player with you in the reserve team away at Preston, their motivation is not the same as if they're playing at Wembley in a cup final. You have to accept that their mental approach is different. Sometimes those coming down would do their best to straddle a line of acceptability.

"The biggest thing is getting them to enjoy themselves, just to go out and play. Sometimes it would be about making sure it was an environment for them to go out and enjoy it, asking them to show the younger lads what it was about. We had some good players there. Jon Newsome and David Wetherall were the two centre-halves, great development players who had excellent careers at the top of the game. They barely played a game for Wednesday, of course, but that's another story. That team won the league because of their attitude, basically. It was better than all of the other teams we played against. They had huge ability and there were some very talented players in there, but they had their heads screwed on when other teams flounced around a bit."

Barlow's reserves romped to nine wins and a draw in their opening 10 matches, which included an October run of four clean sheets in 19 days against Leeds United (3-0), Manchester United (1-0), Derby County (3-0) and Coventry City (1-0). But they suffered a mid-season wobble when defeat at home to Newcastle was preceded by back-to-back defeats at the two Merseyside clubs stacked with first teamers; Wednesday were torn apart by a young Steve McManaman in a 2-0 defeat at Liverpool before Peter Reid and Kevin Sheedy, earlier offered to Wednesday, inspired a 5-0 hammering by Everton.

"We didn't have it all our own way," remembered Newsome, who was 20 at the time. "There were some very tough games and we lost a few. But we had a good team and we knew that; there was a spirit to us that I'm not sure many of the other teams had and we were hungry. Frank and the experienced lads helped that along. It was brilliant. Frank and Albert were great, really good coaches, but at the same time great man-managers."

Even though Atkinson would keep a constant and keen eye on the reserves, having regular talks with the coaching team and watching matches midweek, the set-up at Middlewood Road meant there was a natural separation between the firsts and the rest. The training ground's controversial four-changing-room system, blamed in part for the split between the British and foreign players ahead of Wednesday's relegation from the Premier League nine years later, provided a physical barrier between those in favour and those in the second string. It was one, though, that helped to cultivate a "team-within-a-team" mentality.

Although most remember a jovial and joined-up atmosphere throughout the club, one reserve player, who preferred to remain anonymous, said he felt the reserves were at times treated "like lepers" at the training ground, adding: "We might as well have trained with a bell round our necks." In busy periods, he recalled, they would be called to train with the first team as "dummy-runners and mannequins," bodies for the first-team players to awkwardly play around.

Newsome remembered being called in early the morning after an evening reserve game and being asked to train at odd times, most often on the whim of Atkinson. "We'd do extra running after training, which is fine," he said. "But we'd be dead on our feet, getting changed to go home and Frank would come in and say: 'The gaffer wants a five-a-side this afternoon at four o'clock; you've all got to meet at the gym.' It'd just be all the reserves and Ron.

"He'd be staying over Friday night so, to give him something to do, he'd call us in for a kickabout. He'd join in and play and he used to think he was a bit of a player, but whoever had him in their side was always a man down and would usually lose. He didn't like losing and so, when you lost, he'd make you run your bollocks off afterwards."

With the reserves packed full of experience, opportunities for players in the club's exciting youth side were a little scarcer than in an ordinary season. But they were having an extraordinary season themselves, bouncing back from a run of four consecutive defeats at the start of the season to go 17 unbeaten and tick along nicely in the Northern Intermediate League. But the headlines centred on the fact that Phelan and his hard-working young side were building a historic cup run that by the middle of April in which they had gone further than ever before in the club's history.

In the 1991 FA Youth Cup semi-final between Sheffield Wednesday and Manchester United, one side had a star midfielder called Ryan, who had won Wales youth caps and was tipped for very big things. Blessed with energy and a stand-out ability to threaten the opposition goal, he had scored a sensational hat-trick in the competition's earlier rounds and was the latest in a long line of talented youngsters at the club who would go on to star for the first team. The other side had Ryan Giggs.

Wednesday's Ryan Jones was just 17 when his boyhood club lined up in the second leg of the semi-final at Old Trafford in front of 4,000 spectators, in a game they were expected to lose handsomely. Such was their confidence that Big Ron's old mate Nobby Stiles, one of a handful of support staff whom United's youth side had at the time, had not bothered with the first leg, a close affair which had been drawn 1-1 under the lights at Hillsborough, instead preferring to travel to West Ham to file a dossier on Millwall, their likely opponents in the final.

United, with Giggs as their star man, had internationals across the home nations. It was a well-known breeding ground for future internationals. Although it had produced the likes of Pressman and Shirtliff in relatively recent years, Wednesday's youth set-up was a little more grounded.

"We had a really good, close set of lads," remembered Jones 30 years on. "A lot came down from the North-East, a couple from West Yorkshire and a couple from Mansfield way, but the majority of us were from South Yorkshire, most from Sheffield. We all knocked about together when we could. We were like the first team; we lived in each other's pockets a lot of the time, very close-knit.

"We spent a lot of time together because there were days it wasn't worth going home; we'd be at the ground doing a reserve game, cleaning up. We'd get to the ground at eight o'clock some mornings and not get home until half 10 at night. They worked us hard, but it was good fun. It didn't feel like work a lot of the time. You were bouncing around a football stadium with your mates. We were living the dream."

Although the midweek drinking culture of those above them did not quite trickle down to the youngsters, Dave Allen's wish to get the stars of the future through the doors at Josephine's meant there was a fairly relaxed attitude towards the Wednesday players who were under 18. They too were given passes to fly past the queues and, as 17-year-old lads with a golden ticket in their pocket would be expected to do, they took full advantage of them.

Wednesday's youngsters had reached the last four of the Youth Cup via a long and winding route through what had been recognised as the "gentler" side of the draw. Back in December in sideways rain under the Hillsborough floodlights, they had pressed on past a hapless Bury side, striker Nicky Robinson scoring within a minute of their campaign and Chambers bagging a brace in a 4-1 win.

With their league season by now well in check, two weeks later they made the trip to Aston Villa's Bodymoor Heath training ground, just a few minutes up the road from Ron Atkinson's house. Shortly before kick-off the big man emerged from nowhere, trademark aviator sun-glasses and all, wandering through to the side of the pitch to check in on the action.

He was not let down. A stunning Jones volley from 20 yards beat future Premier League keeper Michael Oakes to put the Owls ahead before Villa rallied to take a 2-1 lead into the break. It was here that some Phelan words of hard work and determination, drawing on their long, unbeaten run, came to fruition and Villa were left shell-shocked by a stunning effort by Chambers, who beat three men to hammer the ball home from distance. Robinson claimed a late winner to cap a classy second-half fightback and win it 3-2; Atkinson waved his fist in tri-umph before departing without a word, leaving Phelan and his players to take the glory.

Among the players to have travelled down from the North-East to stay in the club's modest Oughtibridge digs were the Linighan twins, Brian and John. Brian, a gangly right-back who was an ever-present in Phelan's back-four, was seen as a future first-teamer with John waiting in the wings at left-back behind Gareth Dunn. The pair were the latest additions to something of a footballing dynasty, older brother David having forged a successful career with Ipswich.

Another brother, Andy, had been signed by George Graham at Arsenal for £1.2m the previous July and would go on to hurt Wednesday in the most conceivable way, scoring the extra-time winner against them in the FA Cup final two years later.

Brian was one of the heroes of the third round, clearing a Roy Hunter header from the line late on with his side 2-1 up, and goalkeeper Paul Robinson had made a handful of outstanding saves. The stand-out performer, however, was Jones, who scored what proved to be the winner after Chambers' early effort.

By now proving himself to be the star of the show and earning himself the first of seven appearances for the reserves that season, he was pulled aside by the watching Ron Atkinson as he trudged off the field. One of the country's great prospects, who would go on to represent England, had been marked out of the game by a rough-and-tumble young fella from Sheffield.

"Ugo Ehiogu was at West Brom," smiled Jones at the memory of his early encounter with a classy Premier League centre-half, who sadly passed away in 2017 aged just 44. "He was a brilliant player. A lot of the time players at that level all played at a similar standard, but he stood out a mile for West Brom. He played in midfield and I marked him. I remember Ron pulling me for a chat after the game – he'd had his eye on Ugo from way back – and he told me I'd done really well marking him, so I must've done all right.

"He wasn't always that forthcoming with praise, Big Ron. Ugo was a big lad and he had an engine; he was all over the place, which suited me because I loved getting round the pitch as well. It was a good game and a good battle. We shook hands afterwards and had a chat. I was gutted to hear that he had passed away. Such a good player and a nice kid as well."

With Manchester United lying in wait in the semi-final, it fell to either Wednesday or equally unfancied Hull City to take their chance. United, with legendary youth coach Eric Harrison at the helm, had seen off three of the country's most renowned academy clubs – Liverpool, Everton and Southampton – and had a number of exciting prospects, including the boy national newspapers were calling "the next Georgie Best," a 17-year-old Giggs.

It all sounded glamorous, but there was little of it in Wednesday's back-to-back quarter-final draws with Hull, played in shocking, turn-of-the-year weather at Hillsborough and then Boothferry Park. Both 1-1 draws were low on quality, the first played at S6 with a few hundred spectators squinting through the thick Sheffield fog. The third clash couldn't have been more different. Wednesday won 5-1.

"Those Hull games were hard work," Jones recalled. "They'd been properly horrible tight cup ties and that fortnight took a hell of a lot out of us. They felt like a slog, those first two cup games, and we went into the third game prepared for another one. Well, they rocked up at Hillsborough and they must have just wanted to get out of it. We beat them easily. To play two draws that were so tight when they were the same teams and everything…it was weird, to be honest. But we hammered them from start to finish, one of those nights when they were a bit off it and everything went our way."

Jones scored a classy hat-trick to take his Youth Cup tally to five in as many matches with Brian Linighan and Richard Curzon bagging the others. Fearing fluttering eyelids from elsewhere, Wednesday stepped in fast to sign Jones to a professional contract. "It was an unbelievable experience," he said. "We just kept going and going. We got told after the Bury game we were going to get a bonus after every round we got through. Well, you can imagine the excitement in all us young lads who didn't have two quid for a chip butty.

"It turned out we were getting all the cast-offs as bonuses, stuff that nobody else wanted. But we were ecstatic! First round we got these old jackets, second round a pair of boots and so on. That made us all hungry and up for it. We loved all that stuff and that's how it was back then. We were playing for scraps and hand-downs basically."

By now Barlow was working more closely with the youngsters alongside Phelan, sent by Atkinson to assist with shape and on technical aspects that he felt could take them on to a famous Youth Cup title. The pair and chief scout Clive Baker were seldom seen on the training field, but were constant mentors to the youngsters around the club and a hugely popular coaching team who were getting the best out of their side with hard work and togetherness.

On Wednesdays youth 'keeper Paul Robinson worked with Alan Hodgkinson, Kevin Pressman, Chris Turner, Lance Key and talented youngster Marlon Beresford in what Robinson described as "eye-opening" training sessions. The outfield players joined him in the days before matches and line up in the defensive system of their Saturday opponents for the seniors, who would take no prisoners. "I remember a cross coming in from Nigel Worthington and racing off my line to come and grab it," remembered Robinson, who played for Scarborough before enjoying a successful non-league career with Whitby and Bridlington Town.

"I claimed it really nicely and stood there with the ball in my hands, looking really pleased with myself. A second or two later Nigel Pearson came in and absolutely cleaned me out, smashing me into the back of the net. Albert shouted on: 'Come on, Nigel, that was a bit much.' He said: 'He has to learn.' And he was right – I was holding on to it too long. It was ruthless."

Another time Pearson covered an apprentice in boot polish for failing to clean his boots correctly. And other youngsters would be thrown into large sacks by senior players should they have not carried out their jobs properly, from sweeping changing-rooms to cleaning boots and washing kit. Ruthless they may have been, but there was a duty of care that the senior players took very seriously.

Training on separate pitches at Middlewood Road, Ron's lot would sometimes stay on to watch the end of junior training, which would often finish in a round of shooting practice against Robinson. On occasions they would step out on to the field to join in, the likes of David Hirst and Trevor Francis passing on shooting tips to the strikers. The rough came with the smooth.

Barlow now looks back on the achievements of the youth side that season as a career highlight and spoke fondly of Phelan, a gentleman with a gentle approach to coaching the talented youngsters: "Albert was dedicated to it, totally obsessed with getting the best out of those boys and the bottom line was that he was an excellent coach. We had the odd player coming up and down so we spoke a lot. He and Clive Baker took them and, once they'd won a game or two, we all thought we had a really good chance."

"He was brilliant," said Robinson on Phelan. "He took time with you; he got to know you. He made you feel a million dollars and knew when to build you up and knock you down a peg or two. If you made a mistake, he'd let you know, but he was everything you'd want in a youth coach really. He was brilliant with us."

The semi-final came around quickly, to be played over two legs on April 8 and April 18. With Giggs away on international duty, Wednesday had the best of the opening stages of the first leg at Hillsborough, shocking the United staff. With several first-team players and the entire staff watching on with nearly 2,000 supporters, Leroy Chambers showed the sort of form that earned him a professional deal by setting up Curzon's opener, although it was short-lived when United equalised soon afterwards. Wednesday's players walked off the field to the applause of the watching Wednesday fans knowing they had a lot to do 10 days later.

In the Manchester United side that day had been forward Marcus Brameld, a friend of Jones during childhood and a boyhood Wednesdayite who later became head of community at S6. Brameld and Jones had been invited for a trial at Old Trafford three years earlier and only the forward opted to stay on. Looking ahead to the semi-final that year, he was as excited as anyone. "I was desperate to play at Hillsborough," Brameld remembered.

"But there was a lad called Ryan Giggs they kept playing in my position. He was only a year younger than I was and he wasn't bad, to be fair. Then a few days before the first leg the club got a call and Giggs went away with Wales. I was well chuffed, as you can imagine. It was great for me to be able to play there."

The second leg came just days before the Rumbelows Cup final and much to the disappointment of the Owls youngsters hoping to impress Atkinson on the big stage of his old stomping ground he was called away on an engagement with the competition sponsors. At a meeting before the trip to Manchester, Atkinson had called the youngsters together to give them a word or two of advice about playing at Old Trafford. "Don't worry about them, lads," he smiled. "They've got a lad called Ryan Biggs playing apparently, but I wouldn't worry about him."

Calling through to Old Trafford with a minute or two remaining of normal time, Atkinson was told that, despite a 90-minute onslaught from the Giggs-inspired United, the tie would be going to extra time. He hung up, believing Wednesday's youngsters would run out of legs. But extra time never came. Instead he received an excited call from Albert Phelan, who reported a plucky, hard-working performance and a last-gasp 1-0 win.

The young Owls had been inspired by a number of saves by Robinson, who was born into a family of Manchester United supporters. "They're the worst bloody side we've played," mumbled Alex Ferguson to a stranger at the bar in the players' lounge afterwards. "If it wasn't for their goalkeeper, we'd have battered them." That stranger was Paul Robinson's dad.

"It was one of the most one-sided games that I ever played," Jones admitted with a knowing chuckle. "They absolutely battered us and with what was pretty much the last kick of the game Nicky Robinson had this shot that was going out for a throw-in. It hit this lad on the back of his leg, wrong-footed the 'keeper and went in. Unbelievable. I remember lining up again and Giggs asking the referee how long was left. He said that the next time the ball went up in the air that was it. So some lad tapped it to him, he beat three or four of our lot, hit one from 35 yards and it missed the top corner by about two inches. That was the end of the game. It was an incredible feeling.

"We'd played against some good players, like Ugo, but Giggs was in a different class altogether. Brian Linighan was marking him and he did as well as anybody could have done. But we knew after the first five minutes that, as soon as the ball went out on that side, we had to drift across just to help Brian out. He'd end up with two or three behind him, just defending this one bloke. That was an attitude thing as well. We wanted to win, but we didn't want to leave Brian out there on his own. We were helping out our mate."

The first leg of the final on May 1 was something of a damp squib as Millwall, inspired by future Wimbledon and Crystal Palace midfielder Andy Roberts, won 3-0 in front of a disappointed Hillsborough crowd on a painful, bittersweet evening for the Owls. Again Wednesday started the better of the sides, but ultimately ran out of steam with goals from Brian Lee, Sean Devine and Lee Walker all coming from lapses in concentration that simply had not existed to that point in the season. A goalless return leg in front of a ruthlessly abusive crowd of 6,000 at The Den followed a few days later and Wednesday's Youth Cup dream was over.

Of the youth side who made history in 1991, only Jones went on to make any sort of impact in the Owls first team. He made 41 appearances in a golden period between 1991 and 1994 before injuries forced him to retire at the age of just 23. He'd become a fans' favourite in that time for his energetic performances and earned a full Wales cap, lining up alongside Neville Southall and Ian Rush in a 2-1 win in Estonia in 1994. Leroy Chambers played for Wednesday on two occasions, scoring once; midfield man Simon Stewart featured a handful of times and Brian Linighan made just a single appearance before moving on to Bury.

"You have people swear blind they saw these players when they were 15, that they warned everyone he was going to be the next big thing," said Barlow. "That's not how it works. You see somebody and you think they can play, but you have no idea that they're going to develop into a top-class player, a first-team player, an international player. There are so many other factors involved. You can spot promise and you can spot potential, but you cannot tell whether he will or he won't. And that's the fascination of it. It's sometimes sad, but that's the fascination."

The reserves' quest for silverware ended rather more happily on May 9 when they earned a point at home to Derby County to secure a first Pontin's League Division One title since way back in the 1960/61 season; the year their first team finished second only to Bill Nicholson's historic, double-winning Tottenham Hotspur side. The celebrations were low-key, the feeling one of satisfaction rather than euphoria coming the day after the first team had done a little celebrating themselves. The reserves had been dragged over the line not only by the continued form of Pressman and central defensive doormen Wetherall and Newsome – both stolen away on free transfers by Howard Wilkinson at Leeds a few weeks earlier – but by the goals of hot prospect Gordon Watson, by now a reserve-team regular.

Watson had been signed from Charlton by Big Ron with the future in mind, but hit an incredible 11 goals in 13 reserve games to announce himself to an expectant club and Wednesday support. "I was in-between both and that wasn't easy," Watson remembered. "But let me tell you, Frank Barlow was brilliant. We drew 2-2 against Huddersfield and I scored two, then I got a hat-trick a few weeks later and I thought that was me away. I thought that was me made at Sheffield Wednesday.

"But I had to wait. Frank had one of the hardest jobs in the club, dealing with us lot moping around. It's the hardest job in football. You've either got the cast-offs or players who are half-injured or they're too old for the first team.

"What made it easier was that they had a really strong group of players who had come out of the youth team; then we had Kevin Pressman in goal, Steve MacKenzie, Darren Wood, Steve McCall, David Johnson, Wethers, Newse. It was like another squad beneath the squad. It was built out of the two centre-halves really, they were really strong and had a good understanding; then I came in halfway through the season and scored the goals that got us over the line. That little injection that I brought, that bit of something different."

To celebrate their title win, the FA and the competition's sponsors had thrown a post-match dinner for Wednesday's players to enjoy with little fanfare in the directors' lounge at Hillsborough. They were presented with tankards, some of which were engraved with the wrong season. During the previous months the players had been reliably informed that winning the title would result in a week's holiday at a Pontins resort for all who had played a certain number of matches. Making plans for a few beer-soaked days in the Skegness sunshine and inquiring about dates at the dinner, the company's embarrassed representative quietly told them it was an offer that had been quietly discontinued the season before.

Still a trophy is a trophy, or in this case, a tankard with "1989/90 Championship" inscribed on the side. And besides it was hardly the only bit of success the club had had that season. Something a little bit special had happened down at Wembley Way two weeks earlier.

15

A WEEKEND AT WEMBLEY

W hile his players threw back pints at Josephine's in the hours after that famous Hillsborough victory over Chelsea, Ron Atkinson's preparations for the Rumbelows Cup final had already begun. The mind's eye of some would transfix on opposition players, opposition tactics and their manager, but the big man jumped to a different place; how best to ensure his squad saw themselves not as underdogs, but as favourites.

Sheffield Wednesday Football Club, a proud club, one of great history and standing in the game, were not especially accustomed to all this; the towers, the walk up Wembley Way, the pageantry of the most famous stadium in world football.

Their last visit – save for an appearance in the final of the ad-hoc Mercantile Credit Football Festival, hastily arranged to mark the 100th year of the Football League three years earlier – had been in the 1966 FA Cup final when they surrendered a two-goal lead to lose to Everton and embarked on the first losers' lap of honour around the pitch. Their last major trophy win had been in 1935, when an Ellis Rimmer double helped to secure them a 4-2 FA Cup win over West Bromwich Albion. They had a squad of highly-experienced players of course. But as a collective, as Sheffield Wednesday, this was foreign to them.

That was not the case for their illustrious opponents, who had all-but secured their place in the Cup Winners' Cup final a week earlier. Manchester United had won the FA Cup at Wembley the previous season as well as in 1983 and 1985 under Big Ron. They had won the League Cup in 1986 and in recent seasons had played in a further round of Cup Winners' Cup semi-finals and a UEFA Cup quarter-final. United had been to Wembley eight times in the past decade. Green to the occasion they were not.

Ron wanted his players to wander on to the Wembley pitch as if they owned it, as if they had been there a million times before. Or at least more than eight times in the last 10 years. Cup finals are so often played between the ears, he would later surmise, and it was his job to ensure his unique and immensely-talented blend of experienced professionals, streetwise scallywags, international stars and bin-bag-wearing trainers came out to fight, not freeze. Against Alex Ferguson and his team of Wembley veterans, he would have to think outside the box. And he was meticulous.

A vital date in those plans, though, had been scrapped some three weeks earlier at short notice. With his feet up in his Hillsborough office, not long after the semi-final win, Atkinson sat talking with Richie Barker. "Get Richards on the phone," he said all of a sudden, almost spilling his tea. Francis, Turner and Wilson had felt the tingle of Wembley grass beneath their studs on previous occasions, but the rest of his squad had not and he planned to remedy that. Dave Richards, who would in 1999 become chairman of the Premier League, had already begun rubbing shoulders with the who's who of football governance down south. His was a ladder set up for climbing early doors.

Ron's plan was to set up a date with the FA for his Wednesday side to hold a training session at Wembley, on the pitch itself. Richards' contacts, he hoped, would allow that. A few calls back and forth, a comb through some prospective dates and an afternoon was found; Thursday April 4, fitting in a London stop-off on their way to their league match at Portsmouth.

He told the players of his plan 10 days previously, to great excitement from the likes of John Harkes, Carlton Palmer, David Hirst and Paul Williams – bustling 20-something players who had dreamt of playing beneath the two towers throughout their young careers. Plans were made, the hotel booked, a restaurant sounded out for the evening entertainment. The plan was to mirror the events of Wembley weekend and walk the players through every step.

That was until their worst run of form of the season struck as March turned to April; that draw at Plymouth, the stodgy win against Bristol Rovers and back-to-back defeats, first at Wolves and then at home to

Oxford. That was their only home defeat of the season, but there was gross concern that, as the Wembley date grew closer, Wednesday's focus on promotion fell away, prompting the fan reaction afforded to Sheridan in the Oxford game. Atkinson agreed.

The Wembley dress rehearsal was torn up. "I cancelled the trip to concentrate all our thoughts on Saturday's game," he said. "It was the only day the authorities could offer us, but we've postponed the visit because we don't want any distractions. It would seem that we might struggle to get an alternative date to train at Wembley, but that's one of those things. We have a number of important games before the final." With renewed concentration, Wednesday went straight to Portsmouth. Palmer was sent off as they lost 2-0.

From there the Owls' form did pick up thanks to those vital back-to-back home wins over Blackburn and promotion-challenging Middlesbrough, but one fixture remained before the final – a league trip to mid-table Newcastle just four days before the big Wembley date. Wednesday laid on one of their worst performances of the season and lost 1-0 to a goal that perfectly summed up an evening of half-tackles and missed passes; Kevin Brock miskicked his cross goalwards and the ball careered off the post, off the face of Turner and into the back of the net.

"I shouldn't admit this, but I have to say I did have a little chuckle at that one," said Hirst later. "We used to have a thing in training when the goalkeeper would shout: 'Over me' whenever there was a shot or something that was going miles off target. Anyway the Newcastle lad miskicked it and out of nowhere Chris said: 'Over me!' It came back off the post, hit him in the nose and went in. We were awful that night, I must admit."

The manager was less amused. Arriving in the St. James' Park changing-room with his players caked in mud and on a run of five defeats in their last seven matches, Big Ron let fly. Several players had to dodge teacups and training equipment as Atkinson told them exactly what he thought of what he perceived as a lack of professionalism, a lack of focus on the job in hand. The media, huddled outside waiting to collect their post-match quotes, were made to wait while he had his say. He emerged the best part of an hour later, red in the face and with a stern expression – one they had not been particularly used to.

"He had a point I think, to be fair," said Phil King. "Whether it's sub-

conscious or not, you see it all the time; players putting in poor performances before a big game like that. At the end of the day there's
something in the back of your mind that doesn't want to get injured
and you find yourself pulling tackles and not going hell for leather. You
don't do it deliberately, but it's something there. He made his point and
we knew exactly where we stood."

The Newcastle game was played on the Wednesday evening before
Sunday's final and such was the tight schedule facing the Owls that the
same media pack arrived at Hillsborough on Thursday morning with
little sleep after a miserable, rain-soaked journey back from the North-
East. It was the club's pre-Wembley Press day and journalists were invited to interview players and staff while they went through their last-
minute preparations for the final – with suit-fitting the new priority.

Given the mood Atkinson had been in when they left him the night
before, those members of the media were a little on their guard. But
they needn't have worried. "Right then!" Atkinson boomed, pushing
the door open with huge gusto before striding forward and rubbing his
hands together. "Where are we, then? Lovely jubbly."

**

Big Ron's cunning web of Wembley plans kicked into action the following day. Waved off from Hillsborough by dozens of adoring supporters, Wednesday travelled south in immensely relaxed mood, playing
cards and sharing jokes as they always did, playing up to the cameras
that were allowed on board to capture what they hoped would be a
historic weekend.

David Hirst laid on one of his comedy routines with John Harkes
as his straight man, taking on the persona of an American beach bum;
Paul Williams interrupted an interview to comment on Phil King's
flowing ginger hair. With the cameras rolling, Danny Wilson joked
that he wanted to order a gin and tonic from the buffet car. Little did he
know that there would be plenty of opportunity for that later.

Arriving at the plush, but relaxed Royal Lancaster Hotel, the players were told that they would be training that afternoon after a quick
bite to eat. Wednesday had been offered use of Tottenham Hotspur's
Brookfield Lane training ground by Terry Venables; Spurs had been
granted the use of Middlewood Road ahead of a Rumbelows Cup tie

the previous November and the Owls would often use the facilities of Charlton Athletic on away trips to the capital.

But this time, two days from a date at Wembley, Atkinson stripped things back. Dressed in dashing shell-suits, his players and staff were told to wander across the busy Bayswater Road, dodging bicycles and red London buses. They spent the afternoon kicking a ball around Hyde Park.

"It did surprise me," recalled Roland Nilsson, who months earlier had been exposed to no-stone-unturned Scandinavian efficiency at the World Cup. "It is only afterwards you could see what he was doing, to relax everybody and enjoy. That was the theme all weekend and even when we got to Wembley itself. And we did." With Roger Spry, by now fully recovered, leading the effort, players laughed and joked their way through what must have felt in many ways like a Sunday League training session, dodging tree roots and dog mess.

In a skit set up by the media, Howard Feggins, an American football player stationed in the big smoke with the London Monarchs, staged a light-hearted, if slightly awkward interview with Harkes. Remarkably, even with television cameras documenting their afternoon, the only flicker of attention they received from passing park-goers came when an elderly lady tapped Atkinson on the shoulder. "Who are you lot then?" she asked.

Atkinson revealed the method in his madness when speaking to the media with a typical glint in his eye. "We're doing our utmost to ensure that our players go in with no fear," he said. "Basically we go there, in everybody else's eyes but the people in South Yorkshire, as underdogs. If we play as we can play, that will be good enough for me. Not many of the boys have been in this situation before and the last thing we want to do is get too many hang-ups about the thing and start worrying. We've come down to enjoy the occasion and savour it. Our main priority of course is to come down and win, but I don't want everybody biting their nails for the next 48 hours."

It had been a session both leisurely and bizarre in equal measure, the first lines on a truly unique blueprint for success that Atkinson had drawn up weeks earlier. The players' wives and girlfriends had also been invited to London, travelling on a separate coach, and the players were allowed some free time for the rest of the afternoon to enjoy themselves. Some wandered for a coffee, some played with their children in the lobby and some got some sleep ahead of what they had been told would be a night of celebration; it was Trevor Francis' 37th birthday.

They were told there would be a party with partners invited before the group moved on to Ron's favourite Italian restaurant; a nod to Francis' five-year career in Italy. Aside from that they did not quite know what to expect. Suited and booted, Hirst and Sheridan sneaked down to the hotel bar for what they thought would have to be a secret pint away from prying eyes, but they soon realised that they need not have worried.

At a reception laid on by the club in one of the hotel's vast conference spaces, champagne was made readily available to players who might fancy a glass or two. Or three. Of course the majority duly obliged. It was an evening of relaxation and enjoyment, more akin to an event held for the winners of a cup competition; not one for players who would be playing in a major final two days later.

All of a sudden the doors flew open to what appeared to be a telegram delivery with a birthday cake. Club captain Nigel Pearson held the room: "This is a very special occasion, the birthday of one of our oldest players, our oldest player. We couldn't get enough candles, but happy birthday, Trev." Having blown out all the candles they could fit on the cake, Pearson read out the telegram and announced with great ceremony that it had been sent by Giorgio Armani. Francis had mentioned in a changing-room conversation earlier in the season that the superstar Italian fashion designer was an acquaintance. The birthday boy took hold of it with a smile.

Asked about the surprise telegram three decades on, Atkinson broke into roars of laughter. "From Giorgio Armani? Of course it wasn't! I'm not sure Trevor even knows to this day. The boys had set it all up! That was typical of the sort of thing we got up to."

Among the guests enjoying themselves at the reception was one from outside the Wednesday clan, an old friend and indeed employer of Atkinson. Manchester United director Martin Edwards, down on business and putting the finishing touches to United's plans for the final, looked more than a little startled by the party atmosphere, not least the drink that was being taken by Wednesday's players. United were due to arrive at a hotel across London the next day.

"I'd got wind that he was staying there and I invited him to come and have a drink with us," Atkinson said. "He thought we were mad, that this was a couple of days before the final. In a way I was playing the same trick I'd played on Warnock, having them believe we were having it off, like. I knew it would get back to them."

"It was clever that, the Martin Edwards thing," grinned Carlton Palmer, looking back. "We were all pissed and, if I remember correctly, United changed their plans because of it. They thought we were on a stag do and they came down in the afternoon instead of the morning. They didn't have a fucking clue – half the team liked a beer and Ron knew that. We worked hard and played hard and nine times out of 10 we got the job done. Ron played the whole thing clever all the way through."

Taken out by bus to Mayfair for the evening, 20-year-old striker Gordon Watson, cup-tied for the occasion with Viv Anderson and Steve MacKenzie, couldn't believe his luck when they pulled up outside a restaurant he and a handful of then-fellow Charlton players had known as a second home just a few weeks before.

"It was a lovely little place called Siberius," he remembered. "Two months earlier my girlfriend and I were going in there for our Sunday lunch every weekend and all of a sudden we're down there with my new teammates. It was surreal. But because we knew them, they made a fuss of us and did I get some stick for that!

"You can imagine all these senior professionals dead excited that they're going to the top Italian restaurant in London, and we've swanned in and they're calling us by our names and giving us kisses. There was wine on the table and, before you knew it, some of the lads were battered. Some were having to get help to get back on the coach back to the hotel. Only Ron could do that. It was all designed to stop the lads thinking about the game on the Sunday."

The message to "be sensible, but enjoy yourselves" which had been extended by the Wednesday staff at the start of the night flew over the head of some. Watson remembered stumbling through his hotel door at about two in the morning, having spent a little time enjoying the facilities of the hotel bar. But then again he was not playing. Phil King, the likely starter at left-back, said he got to his hotel room nearer four. "Absolutely bloody legless, I was," King chuckled three decades on.

"A few of us were, to be fair, although I'm fairly sure I was the last to bed. At the end of the day you can't put a load of bottles of wine in front of that lot and expect to get away with it!"

There was a slight whiff of alcohol on the breath of some players the next morning, then, when they kissed their significant others goodbye for the weekend and truly prepared to get down to business. Dragging their training bags with them, they were on a coach at 9.30am to make the trip to check into the Oakley Court Hotel in Windsor, a stunning, grandeur building set a short walk between a racecourse and a marina, backing on to a babbling stretch of the River Thames. They moved there partly to separate themselves from the possible distraction of loved ones, but also out of superstition; Big Ron always brought his teams here the night before a day out at Wembley.

It is based a short drive from Bisham Abbey, the then state-of-the-art sports centre used from time to time by Graham Taylor's England and the English rugby team. There the players were put through an intense session and were barracked by Atkinson and Barker whenever they put a foot wrong. Early on Harkes, laughing after he had timed a run incorrectly, was lampooned for being "brain dead" by his manager. They were worked hard and the message was simple; they meant business.

"I wanted them to be tired," Atkinson said. "Not blown out, but tired. It was a really hard session, certainly harder than some of the sessions we'd run in Sheffield the day before matches, but the idea was to get some football in their legs. To work on a few very specific things and, above all else, to make sure that they had a good night's sleep that night. It was unusual, I suppose – you'd usually take it easy the day before a final like that – but it was another way of relaxing them that night. That said, we had serious things to focus on as well and we had taken it easy the day before."

The central focus from a tactical point of view was on stopping Manchester United's biggest attacking threat. Although Alex Ferguson's side had immense quality all over the pitch – every member of their matchday squad for the final barring highly-rated goalkeeper Les Sealey was a full international – it was on the left-wing that it was felt the main danger resided in hot-shot young player of the year Lee Sharpe.

A flash thing taken from a YTS scheme at Torquay at 18 for a record

£200,000 fee, Sharpe had made his England debut the month before the final and was hugely in-form, having burst into the national consciousness with a stunning hat-trick against Arsenal earlier in the competition. A dazzling dribbler with huge pace, he was the one Wednesday wanted to stop – believing a quiet afternoon for him would stop the game from stretching and dramatically reduce the service to the likes of Mark Hughes and Brian McClair up front.

With Atkinson and Richie Barker, Nilsson, Sharpe's direct opponent on the day, hatched a plan to double-mark him alongside John Harkes, who was set to play on the right of midfield with Danny Wilson pushed inside to cover the absent legs of Carlton Palmer. Nilsson would show Sharpe towards the touchline, but Harkes would hurry back to block off any potential route inside. With Steve McCall imitating Sharpe's movements at Bisham Abbey, the young American hung on every word the experienced Swede could offer.

"Sharpe was in great form," remembered Nilsson. "If we could stop him on the left, we had a good advantage and we could be part of something really good. John and I worked on a couple of things in the training sessions the weeks before that could help, both defensively and attacking-wise, because we knew we couldn't just defend. That was the thing; we had to go out and play football. We needed to do good things otherwise it would be a very tough game. It worked very well. John was a good listener and was very understanding of the role I wanted him to play and I supported him on the other hand when we were attacking."

The squad would be absolutely confirmed only at the end of the Bisham Abbey session, but Harkes and Nilsson had held meetings with Atkinson in the lead-up to the game in order to prepare them best for the starring roles they were expected to play. The pair met for lunch in the build-up to the final and it was a conversation never far from their lips, Harkes remembered. "The gaffer told me weeks before the final that I was going to be playing that role with Roland. He had his own ideas on how we were going to shut down Manchester United. Our double-teaming and making sure we had a good time, closing down that space and limiting his opportunities was so important. Lee was becoming a really, really quality player.

"Roly and I worked so hard on shifting our position, doubling in the space, running him where we wanted. It wasn't easy. That was intense work. Learning how to play with the ball was one thing; without the ball it was another. And that took a lot of work and dedication. You think about Ron Atkinson and where he goes with things. The obvious thing might have been to focus on shutting down Paul Ince's distribution in the midfield. Everybody had their jobs to do."

Instructions imparted and roles crystal clear, Atkinson took his players off the field satisfied by more than three hours of hard work. The players headed back to Oakley Court to relax and get some sleep. Stretching and yawning, they met for dinner – although this time not greeted by wine – laughed a lot and told each other stories.

Although individually it was such a varied group of men, this was a band of brothers brought together by the heartache of the previous May and who bonded on the journey they had taken together in the month leading to the most important weekend of most of their lives.

"It was a wonderful night, that – one of my highlights of the trip," Atkinson said. "And the training session worked a treat, too. The next day we were down at breakfast and usually for a game like that you'd have lads rattling round reading the papers or pacing the corridors at six o'clock in the bloody morning. Well, a couple of the lads I wasn't sure were going to get down for breakfast, you know! There were lads coming down saying they'd had a stunning night's sleep. It went like clockwork."

Paul Williams, mentioning that he often struggled to drift off the night before a big match, had been handed a couple of sleeping pills by Atkinson at dinner. He swallowed both immediately and they kicked in even faster. Williams cannot remember leaving the table as he was carried upstairs by teammates and panicked the next morning when he woke up surrounded by red-soaked sheets. On closer inspection he realised he had not cut himself, but had reached for a bedside glass of blackcurrant squash in the night and fallen asleep with it in his hand. Despite the drama it was the best night's sleep he can remember having and he woke up with a skip in his step.

That same night John Sheridan wandered into Carlton Palmer's room for a chat before bed. The two were thick as thieves and confided things in one another that other pairs of teammates perhaps wouldn't have. "I tell you what, Carlton," Sheridan said in a deadly serious tone. "I've got a feeling I'm going to score the winner tomorrow."

16

DINK

"I don't think you're gonna win," came a cheeky Scouse timbre from between the breakfast tables at the Oakley Court Hotel the morning of the 1991 Rumbelows Cup final. "Hey, that camera's not supposed to be here; I'm with a bird." That was the opening gambit offered to Sheffield Wednesday players by Stan Boardman, the legendary comic and close friend of Ron Atkinson, whose role in the Owls' weekend is the stuff of legend.

Such was the secrecy of his appearance that not even Alan Smith, Frank Barlow or Roger Spry knew Boardman was coming. Several players remembered not cottoning on to the fact that Boardman's appearance was one organised by Atkinson until long into the morning, believing he had been a guest at the hotel by coincidence and, in the classic trope of a true performer, that he had simply taken it upon himself to steal a bit of thunder. But of course it was an Atkinson plan, another masterstroke in his desire to keep the players calm, relaxed and focused on the big day. As players finished their food and went off to play snooker or read the newspapers, Boardman threaded himself in and out of conversations, keeping the mood light and thoughts away from Wembley.

Danny Wilson, who later became a successful manager in his own right, described the surprise as the best piece of man-management he ever saw. "Ron had seen a nervousness in us in the games prior to going to Wembley and in his mind, there was the desire to get us into a frame of mind that was very relaxed," he said. "We'd had a relaxed build-up during the two days and woke up thinking that'd be that. But the fact is that you're going to get the nerves on the day; you're going to wake up with butterflies in your tummy.

"Well, we went down for breakfast and we didn't have time to think about Wembley or Mark Hughes or anything. We were busting a gut laughing. Stan had done his homework and he knew one or two of the players, but he just never stopped. It was like a comedy show you might go to, but it lasted four or five hours. On the coach on Wembley Way, there were jokes everywhere and we couldn't concentrate on what was going on. By the time we were going out to warm up, we all had smiles on our faces. We were playing Man United at Wembley and we were so far removed from what we were doing, it was amazing."

But before Wednesday boarded the coach for Wembley – and despite Boardman's routines – Atkinson noticed that one face was not smiling. And he took great issue with it. Goalkeeper Kevin Pressman had not been himself since he had been dropped in favour of Chris Turner as Wednesday turned into the new year. He prepared himself for reserve-team games with professionalism, but around the training ground, by his own admission, he dragged his bottom lip through every corridor.

One of several players in the travelling party who were not in the matchday squad alongside Anderson, Watson, MacKenzie, McCall, youngster Graham Hyde and the suspended Palmer, 23-year-old Pressman could not have made it more obvious that he felt this should be his big day. Rising from breakfast, face glum, Atkinson said he wanted a word. He spoke in hushed, but firm tones.

"I knew I was in trouble but on some level I was pleased I was making a point," Pressman recalled. "I said: 'Gaffer, you wanted to see me?' Well, he tore a strip off me. He said: 'Yeah, I do. Your attitude stinks. I'm leaving you out because I want to teach you a lesson. People don't get into my teams with attitudes like yours. If you want to get back into my team, you change your attitude. And if you do get back in, it's up to you to make sure you stay in.'

"The cup final was the greatest thing for Sheffield Wednesday, but for me it was the worst. Obviously we didn't have sub goalkeepers back then; we only had space for two on the bench, so I wasn't even in the squad. I was sitting there full of self-pity and anger."

It was something Atkinson did not have to worry about when it came to the other non-playing party members. The two Steves, McCall and MacKenzie, were invited not only because of their hugely-important supporting roles in the league that season, but to impart their vast experience on to the group. Gordon Watson, full of energy and enthusiasm, was given the responsibility of documenting the weekend on video by Pearson, who was due to record a "captain's log," but got fairly tired of the thing early doors. Watson, a bundle of enthusiasm, took on the role with delight. But the star turn fell to Palmer. His legs and quality in midfield would be lost, but Atkinson was determined to make sure that the energy that he offered off the field was not.

"Ron had a chat with me before we went down," Palmer said. "He told me: 'I need you to be you. I can't have you down there not being yourself, the lads are already gutted you're not playing and they're feeling it, but you've got to play your part now and they'll do the rest for you.' It was tough because I was gutted I wasn't playing, but it also wasn't because I got on so well with all the boys and I just really, really wanted them to win. I got involved in everything.

"Ron had me by his side all day. I sat right next to him in the dugout and he would not leave me alone. He was like a football dad to me and you could see he was hurting that I wasn't playing because we both knew I fucking deserved to. I just wanted them to win, to play well and to show what a good side we were. You have your important players, but a team is a team; you have to have a good squad. Players have to come in and do a job and play well. We had players who would do that and you'd find these players would come in and go to another level."

The journey from Oakley Court to Wembley Stadium takes three quarters of an hour on a good day. On a Sunday you can add a few minutes on. On cup final day? Despite the police escort you are looking closer to an hour-and-a-half. It could have been a nervy journey, images of Bryan Robson and Hughes and Sharpe bouncing between the ears. But Atkinson had the ultimate distraction with Boardman on the microphone at the front of the coach.

Trevor Francis' young son, dressed in the same tracksuit as the Wednesday team, was another special guest on the bus and drew a laugh almost as big as anything Boardman could offer when he was asked who his favourite player was. "David Hirst," he replied. "He scores goals."

"There's a curfew in Poland," Boardman quipped in between the Irish gags for which Nigel Worthington copped most of the punchlines. "They said if you weren't in your house by six o'clock, they'd shoot you. Anyway, this Russian soldier saw this Pole about half past five and went: 'Bang', shot him dead. The sergeant said: 'What are you shooting him for? It's only half past five! We're not supposed to shoot them 'til six.' The soldier replied: 'I know where he lives; he'd never have made it.'"

Physio Alan Smith described the Boardman stunt as "an absolute stroke of genius" and Wednesday's players laughed all the way to Wembley, giving hardly a thought to the match itself. But as the coach made the turn into Wembley Way a good two hours before kick-off, the players' attention switched from the man at the front of the bus to the thousands and thousands outside it. Expecting to see a heady mix of blue and red, they were met with only blue. Thousands upon thousands of Sheffield Wednesday supporters, some on their knees praising their team bus and floating club flags in the April breeze, had taken over London.

A proud football man, Boardman had earlier been an apprentice at Liverpool before signing for Tranmere Rovers. "Now look at this, lads, look at this," Boardman said on the microphone, serious for just a moment as the players climbed over one another to take in the scenes. "It doesn't get any better than this, does it? You're not going to let these lads down today, guys, I'll tell you. You can't let this lot down. They want to see you win the cup."

Once they had filed into the stadium, Wednesday's players were greeted by resplendent blue and white shirts outstretched on the benches around the changing-room with a one-off Asda sponsorship on the front and the embroidery spelling out "League Cup final 1991" beneath the iconic black and yellow Owls badge. Phil King's parents had arranged for a cake to be delivered – for consumption only after a famous win of course – and Atkinson opened letters that had been sent to the stadium ahead of the match from well-wishers throughout football. If a relaxed mood was what he was seeking, a relaxed mood he got – at least from the majority of his players.

Smith remembered a very specific moment that led to one of the more famous pre-match moments in the club's history. "The mass of blue and white outside the ground had been enormous," he said. "And while some were very relaxed, it hit some of the players emotionally – in particular Johnny Harkes. He went white as a sheet and he was sitting there in the dressing-room with his head in his hands. I went to sit down next to him and said: 'Are you all right, John?'

"I didn't even have to say anything, but I looked up at Ron and he knew. Just a glance. Ron realised that one or two of the lads had been hit by what they'd just seen. Straightaway he said: 'Right, lads, out on the pitch. We're going to walk around the pitch slowly, enjoy the atmosphere and say: "Hello" to our fans.' It was an absolute masterstroke of man-management.

"When we got them back into the dressing-room, they were a different set of lads; laughing, joking, taking the mick out of one another. The whole situation was diffused for the time being; the nervous lads had been taken out of the little pressure cooker and had walked around like gods. They felt 10-foot tall. In terms of preparation, it was incredible."

That slow wander round the ground before the starting whistle, before the twists and turns of the match itself, is remembered by many as the best moment of the day. As it had been on Wembley Way, by quarter to two the stadium was utterly dominated by Sheffield Wednesday supporters. "Our end was totally full," skipper Pearson remembered. "It left a big impression on us. It meant more to us. Manchester United were so used to success that maybe they approached it with more of a blasé attitude. Our fans had not been to Wembley since 1966, which we were constantly reminded of throughout the build-up."

As they had done all season, the sea of blue rose in fine voice, spinning through the full repertoire; *Atkinson's Barmy Army, Singing the Blues* and the rest. Regardless of what was ahead of them, Sheffield Wednesday were at Wembley and they were determined to make it a day to remember. Alongside the shouts for Big Ron, one man took much of the fans' focus as the London air was filled with the assurance that there was, in fact, "only one Carlton Palmer."

Palmer, a man whose image and demeanour suggested nothing could touch him emotionally, welled up. "I'm not going to lie, I'm not going to say I wasn't down about it, I wanted to play. But the reception I got when we went for that walk helped and I will be forever grateful to the supporters for spotting that moment. Still to this day I put it on and watch it; it's one of my favourite moments. Having 30,000 fans singing your name on a day you weren't even playing is something that will never leave me. I don't think it could leave anyone. I'm not sure you can really see it on the video, but my eyes were streaming. It was such a special moment."

His left-field preparation complete and his players going through their final talks and stretches, Atkinson took a moment to compose himself, wandering out into the communal corridor holding a poly-styrene cup designed for coffee, but filled with a double measure of brandy. Like Palmer, the manager liked to calm the nerves before a big one. There he bumped into Alex Ferguson, the man who had replaced him as Manchester United manager five years earlier.

The Scot, who would become the most decorated British boss in his-tory by earning 13 league titles, five FA Cups, four League Cups and two Champions Leagues, was pacing the floor, chattering to himself. "This was before Fergie had won all those trophies and he was on pins," Atkinson remembered. "I told him not to worry about it, that his boys would sort it and to come and have a drink with me. I offered him a brandy. He looked at me like I was an alien."

***

"And the team for Sheffield Wednesday..." the tannoy bellowed to the adoration of those on the blue side of the ground. The noise could not only be heard, but felt in both changing-rooms in the bowels of Wemb-ley. Chris Turner was in goal with a left-to-right back four of Phil King, Nigel Pearson, Peter Shirtliff and Roland Nilsson. Nigel Worthington was on the left of midfield, John Harkes on the right, Danny Wilson shuffling in alongside John Sheridan in the centre. Paul Williams up top with David Hirst. That was the side Ron Atkinson had named to take on Alex Ferguson's Manchester United in the 1991 Rumbelows Cup final.

Wednesday's two-man bench was full of wisdom, too. Trevor Fran-cis, who later admitted he felt aggrieved at not starting, given his im-mense experience of big-day football, would provide cover for the side's attacking players. In the absence of Viv Anderson, Lawrie Mad-den covered the defenders. In part, it was a worthy nod to a man who had given the best years of his career to the club. Combined, the two substitutes were 72 years old.

In the red corner there was huge top-tier quality. Les Sealey between the sticks, Denis Irwin and Clayton Blackmore on either side of a stoic centre-half pairing of Steve Bruce, a future Owls manager, and Gary Pallister. In midfield United named powerhouse pair Paul Ince and Bryan Robson inside Neil Webb on the right and the dangerman Lee Sharpe on the left. Up top, PFA player of the year Mark Hughes and Brian McClair. Mal Donaghy and Mike Phelan, both outfield players, sat on the bench.

Wednesday's form had stuttered greatly heading into the clash, but United's was crystal-clear; nine without defeat. But, as Atkinson had told them in no uncertain terms, the final was a one-off, a chance to achieve something extraordinary. Several players remembered a feeling of huge confidence, absolutely no doubt that they would topple United and win the club's first major trophy since 1935. To the roar of 30,000 desperate Wednesdayites, the ball was rolled from Hirst to Williams and the biggest match in the modern history of Sheffield Wednesday Football Club was under way.

It was a nervous start. Nilsson miscontrolled, King almost allowed Hughes in with an undercooked back pass to Turner, Williams crossed high over the goal. United looked little better. The markings of an American football match were visible on the pitch; incredibly the London Monarchs had played against the Montreal Machine in the inaugural World League of American Football less than 24 hours before. Although the condition of the pitch was reasonable, all things considered, the centre of the pitch in particular raised a bobble or two. The Monarchs ran out 45-7 winners on their way to lifting the "World Bowl" trophy, as it happened. Go Monarchs, go.

In a frantic first few minutes both sides had shots on goal, but neither particularly tested either Turner or Sealey. Sharpe, the much-hyped main man for United, had been kept largely quiet after Wilson had left plenty on him in a tackle inside the first couple of minutes. But then came his first real moment of the final; a darting run to get the wrong side of Nilsson, burning him for pace and crossing from the byline. Pearson cleared, but it served as a wake-up call for the Swede. With Harkes, and increasingly Wilson, he ensured that Wednesday's hard work in the days leading to the final paid off, keeping the rambunctious youngster at bay from then on in.

"To this day Sheffield Wednesday fans give me stick and tell me I'm still in Roland Nilsson's pocket from that final," Sharpe said after three decades. "I just remember being double-marked by Nilsson and John Harkes. Speaking to Ron since, he's told me they'd seen me as a bit of a danger man and that they'd brought one of their young lads down to practise doubling-up on me in the game.

"Nilsson in particular was a very good player. He was aggressive and he was quick and it was always a tough battle against him. But at that time I was probably a little bit cocky and didn't really worry too much about who I was playing against. If I could get the best out of myself, I'd have given anybody a tough game; it was about dealing with my own head. I definitely remember not having a lot of joy with the ball."

As both pairs of centre-halves stood typically firm, the two teams danced around one another, jabbing, but not committing to any real attempt at a killer punch. What was developing was an enticing battle between Nigel Pearson and Mark Hughes, who, with Sharpe and Paul Gascoigne, was the competition's top scorer with six goals. Centre-half Pearson was only one behind them on five, but he had a defensive job to do at Wembley against the Welsh international's forte for backing in, all shoulders and elbows.

A clear pattern of play yet to be deciphered, the game changed on 37 minutes when referee Ray Lewis blew for a free-kick on the right-hand side of Wednesday's attack. Nilsson had attempted to flick the ball around the corner to Harkes, but it hit the hand of Sharpe. In a small twist of fate Lewis was the official who presided over the very worst day in Sheffield Wednesday's history, the Hillsborough Disaster, and now one of their very finest.

"Wednesday were a strong Second Division team at that time and they were probably the better of the two teams on the day from where I was standing," Lewis remembered. "They had big personalities. You'd get a little bit of talkback, but nothing over the top. From what I remember it was a fairly tight game and a good cup final, very competitive. And the noise from the crowd was immense." The weekend before he had refereed the famous semi-final between Tottenham Hotspur and Arsenal; he had awarded a free-kick which Paul Gascoigne smashed home in one of the more iconic moments in Spurs' history. Now, for Sheffield Wednesday, perhaps another.

"It's a free-kick now, to Sheffield Wednesday..."

Legendary ITV commentator Brian Moore's words provided the backdrop as Lewis marked out 10 yards for the two-man United wall in the 37th minute. Halfway into the United half the free-kick provided an opportunity to plummet the ball into the box. The Owls' goalscoring threat from the back, who would contribute 16 goals between them in that famous season, bundled up for a closer look.

"They've brought Shirtliff forward as well and Pearson. And Pearson has certainly scored some important goals this season; he's on 12. There's Shirtliff..."

Pearson, broad of chest, put both hands in the air to signal that he wanted the ball to come in his direction. Watched closely by Pallister and Bruce, United were all too aware that it could spell a trick ploy. Wednesday had enjoyed huge success with their reverse free-kick, most notably in the first leg of the semi-final at Chelsea with the full-back overlapping to cross from a by-line angle.

"What we may well find is Worthington ducking over it or rather playing it down the byline for Harkes who might well make a little run down that right-hand side..."

With the left-footed Worthington standing over it, Harkes made his move, stepping over the ball and darting towards the corner. It took Clayton Blackmore out of the wall to cover. But this time Harkes was not the target. Worthington floated a curling ball into United's box.

"There he goes, there goes Harkes. Will Worthington play it? No, he plays it long this time. It might come..."

Steve Bruce rose up against Pearson. It was meaty centre-half against meaty centre-half, number six against number six. For once the Wednesday skipper failed to get any connection on the ball, the United man stretching in his attempt to head to clear. But Pearson's efforts had thrown Bruce off-balance and the header was directed straight down the middle of the pitch. It took one bounce and fell into the path of the onrushing John Sheridan.

For that split second the stadium stopped. As the ball came back down towards the ground, as Sheridan reacted faster than Neil Webb on the edge of the box, half a career flashed by; of his undignified expulsion by Brian Clough at Forest, of Acqui Terme, of his knee troubles, of the gripes of supporters just 20 days earlier in the Oxford defeat. Catching the ball just before the half-volley, he connected sweetly, a strike good enough to win any cup final. The ball breezed through the crowd in front of him, burst through the hands of Sealey and clipped the post politely on its way into the goal.

"A terrific goal! By Sheridan! A terrific goal for Sheffield Wednesday! That really rattled off the post and into the back of the net beyond Les Sealey. And the Second Division side go into the lead here at Wembley. John Sheridan! What a rifling shot it was!"

Even without the video footage and with the iconic Moore commentary stripped away, the very sound of the passage remains instantly recognisable to any Wednesdayite. The thud of the ball from Sheridan's boot, the slap of the ball against Les Sealey's gloves and the unmistakable *dink* of the ball against the post on its way into the Wembley goal.

"I will never forget the sound of the ball hitting the post," Nigel Pearson later remarked. Say the word "dink" to a supporter in the blue half of the Steel City, young or old, nowadays and they will know exactly to which moment you are referring. It was the sound that signalled the single greatest moment in the modern history of Sheffield Wednesday Football Club.

Half-time came and went in a blur; the usually cool and calm Atkinson a bundle of nerves, talking largely gibberish. "We didn't think that at half-time we would be in that position," Williams later said. "We were in front. Reality started to hit us. Everyone was trying to get a grip on the situation, saying to each other: 'Come on, we can win.' I was surprised at how important it was to win. I had always thought that if you got to Wembley, then it didn't matter if you lost. But that's not true. At half-time I decided that, if we lost, I would not go up to get my medal."

Atkinson did manage one moment of clarity in a frantic 15 minutes, explaining the situation ahead for the substitutes by calling Francis and Madden to one side. He said that, if the score remained as it was, Madden would be sent on to respite for one of the tired defenders; if United equalised, Francis would be sent on to provide a touch of magic.

In the second half chances were as rare as they had been in the first, both sides largely cancelling one another out both in midfield and at the threat of any attack. Soon after the break Worthington hesitated on a shot, allowing Bruce to block, and Hughes had an effort from distance. Not long afterwards, bounding on to the towering cross of Mike Phelan, the Welshman bundled both the ball and Turner into the net. Thankfully for the 30,000 watching Wednesdayites it was quickly disallowed, although there was confusion in the commentary box.

"Years before that would have been deemed a fair challenge," Turner later said. "In life you need a bit of luck but we deserved it. You couldn't have picked a more assured performance from a team." Referee Lewis, who ruled the goal out with his assistant Mike Bullivant, took solace in the fact that Ferguson did not mention the incident after the game.

With the minutes dwindling, Turner was called upon to be the hero. Five United players made their way into the box and Irwin's cross from halfway inside the Wednesday half held in the air for an eternity, heading menacingly towards Brian McClair on what felt like the only occasion when a red shirt was left unmarked the whole afternoon. Timing his run perfectly, the Scot made a stunning connection – only to watch on from the floor as his former teammate stuck out his left hand to career the ball over the crossbar and claim a match-winning reaction save.

"It was one of the saves you train for, but to do it in a game like that, at Wembley against the biggest club in the world, was special," Turner reflected. "It was a very, very important save because we were winning 1-0 with 15 or 20 minutes to go. If that goes in, who knows what might have happened? You don't really think about the save as the game goes on, but nearly 30 years later people talk about it. As you get older, it's really nice to have memories like that. We defended very well as a team that day.

"Nigel Pearson was inspirational on and off the pitch. He was never afraid to put his head in where it hurt and got injured many times. He was a leader who galvanised players. He took nothing from anybody and dealt it out, a great character and a lovely lad. It was an unbelievable game for me in front of nearly 80,000 people, playing for the club I support with my schoolmates in the stands, winning a major trophy against Manchester United when a lot of people expected us to lose. It was one of the best days of my life, without doubt."

By that point Turner's opposite number, United's Les Sealey, was grimacing with every movement after a dramatic collision with Williams badly injured his left knee. Williams remembered feeling sick at the sight of the open wound and referee Lewis recalled being able to clearly see Sealey's knee bone. Despite the fact that they had no substitute on the bench, he was told to come off by United physio Jim McGregor and Ferguson himself.

But Sealey refused, screaming to the sidelines that he would finish the final. Whether brave or stupid, Sharpe remembered that the decision could have ended in tragedy. "Usually after every final we'd have a party in London even if we'd lost, but this time we didn't because we had the Cup Winners' Cup semi a few days later. So we went straight to the airport and Les just collapsed. It was terrifying. They reckon if we'd got on the plane, gangrene would have set in and he would have lost his leg."

The tension became unbearable as the minutes counted down. Several Wednesday players received treatment for cramp, hero Sheridan received a knock to the head and Worthington took one to the calf. Tick followed tock and United went more and more direct as an opportunity for silverware – what would have been only Ferguson's second trophy with the club – slipped slowly and shockingly from their grip. Blackmore crossed, Shirtliff cleared. McClair crossed, Blackmore shinned the ball across the face of the goal. Wednesday were clinging on.

There were seconds remaining, Brian Moore reminded the nerve-shredded television audience, when 35-year-old Lawrie Madden, on for John Harkes late on, picked up the ball in his own area. When less experienced men might have cleared aimlessly, he skipped past Bruce in his own right-hand corner and made a dart down the wing – possibly the first of his long and storied career. The ball cleared, Hirst controlled and booted the ball up towards his partner-in-crime Williams, who long into the last minute of injury time would have run until Christmas had it been required. It was not. As Sealey collected the errant ball, three toots on Ray Lewis' whistle were met by scenes of pure elation in the crowd.

Sheffield Wednesday were the winners of the 1991 Rumbelows Cup.

The effort had been incredible. Pearson was named man-of-the-match for his handling of Hughes, but credited his sidekick Shirtliff with half the job. Turner could have quite easily received the award for that incredible save to deny McClair or Sheridan for the dink that won the cup. Wilson and Worthington were as dependable as ever, offering untold legs against United's hard-working midfield.

King was a threat going forward and was strong in defence. Even though they saw less of the ball than they would have liked, Hirst and Williams battled and harried as if their lives depended on it. And on the right, with a series of Wilson cameos, Harkes and Nilsson completely dethroned the would-be prince Sharpe. It was a truly incredible team performance.

At the final whistle Wilson admits that he "lost it." "I went round hugging everyone," he said. "We were massive underdogs and to take Manchester United on and play as we did...incredible. To see the fans as they were; they came down in numbers and they were enormous for us. They outshouted Man United and all we could hear all game were our fans. It lifted the lid off when the final whistle went."

A six-foot South Yorkshireman from mining country, boyhood Wednesday fan Shirtliff embraced the matchwinner Sheridan and promptly burst into tears. "It is an amazing feeling; it really is," he fawned all these years later. "I can't really express it, just surreal. You don't take it in as much as you should; you can't quite compute the show of atmosphere and the feeling. On the way in Trevor had spoken to the players about stopping to savour the moment, about taking every chance we could to remember the experience. But it all went out of the window when we realised we'd won it. We ran around like loonies."

After a moment or two, after the initial burst of ecstasy, the pitch was invaded – not by fans, but by the well-known football figures who had had to watch from the sidelines. Ron Atkinson congratulated each of his players with a hug. Carlton Palmer raced on to throw his great pal Sheridan into the air. Roland laughed with Trevor Francis, Steve McCall high-fived his left-side rival Nigel Worthington and Gordon Watson danced around in a sombrero.

On the terraces grown men cried, fathers held sons and friends embraced. Striding on to the field with a stern face, the losing manager Ferguson went straight to his former goalkeeper Chris Turner, extended his hand and congratulated him on a trophy-winning moment.

Wednesday's players, led by a tearful Pearson, filed up the 39 iconic Wembley steps and to the presentation area, each one of them grinning from ear to ear. In a bizarre quirk the trophy was handed over not by royalty or a high-ranking FA figure, but Tracey Bateman, the Rumbelows employee of the year. "It seemed forever before we went up the steps," Pearson remembered. "People say it wasn't as good to receive it from Tracey, but frankly I couldn't give a monkey's who gave it to me. It was such a great feeling to lift it.

"It was the realisation of a dream. Something you see other people do, but to do it yourself takes some believing. There was just a great roar. Everybody can see from the pictures how I was feeling. But you only become aware of the achievement once you return to the pitch. We were looking for friends and family in the crowd; the scenes were so emotional and you could see how much it meant to everyone. Winning meant a lot for the players' pride, but it was also very satisfying for the players to see the happiness we brought to the fans."

Unfortunately those watching on television back in Sheffield missed much of the post-match festivities when, to their untold horror, ITV controllers switched to a repeat showing of an episode of *War of the Monster Trucks*. Although it did provide Wednesday fans with the title of one of their most iconic fanzines, it was a bizarre call that rankles to this day and for many shows the most brazen example of a bias towards West Yorkshire, particularly Leeds, by the county's media.

After a slow and adoring lap of honour the players wandered back into the changing-room for beers, champagne and a fistful of the cake delivered on behalf of Phil King's parents hours earlier. Viv Anderson dragged a crate of lager through to United's dressing-room in an effort to console his former teammates.

Across the corridor Wednesday's stars were getting used to the presence of cameras by now and responded in kind, playing up and offering their thoughts and emotions. Among the pleasantries and clichés came this from Sheridan: "I knew all the true fans would get behind me. So that goal was for them. It's a nice feeling."

***

Ron Atkinson's plans for the Wembley weekend had gone far beyond the final whistle. Regardless of the result, he had arranged for the party of all parties back at the Royal Lancaster Hotel, where the players were back to spend the night drinking, singing and celebrating. Paul Carrack, a passionate Wednesdayite and musician with chart-topping band Mike and the Mechanics, was on hand to provide the tunes with his friend Glenn Tilbrook from Squeeze.

Among the tracks dropped – several times – was *It's a Praise for Sheffield Wednesday*, a title inspired by the BBC Radio Sheffield show *Praise or Grumble* that embraced the "Barmy Army" chant, mentioned every player by name and immortalised regular caller "Paul from Wisewood."

With the rest of the reserve-team players, wives, girlfriends and club employees in attendance, the squad walked into the venue's vast Westbourne Suite to incredible applause. These, remembered several players, are the private moments that stay with them. The squad gathered on tables and shared beers and laughed long into the evening, another of Ron's comic friends, Mick Miller, joining Boardman in holding court.

Before long, with the drink flowing, Phil King was encouraged to grab the microphone. Carrack was a friend of his and would from time to time hand over cassette tapes of unreleased music. The left-back was one of the first people in the world to hear *It's a Praise for Sheffield Wednesday* and played it on repeat in his car with his young daughter. Before long he knew every word and it became his party trick. What better party for it? With the entire squad standing behind him, some wearing sombreros, King beamed with delight as he delivered every line.

Ron made a passionate speech during which he commented that the only thing that he would change about the day would be to have had Palmer playing. There were other star turns, too. John Sheridan sang the Beatles classic *I Saw Her Standing There* to a great reception and 12 years before his appearance as Frank Sinatra on *Celebrity Stars in Their Eyes* Big Ron delivered his karaoke classic *New York, New York*. And then King sang again. And again. The mood was one of pure elation. For most.

With the stinging words of Atkinson that morning burnt into him, Kevin Pressman could not get into the spirit of celebration, try as he might. Having watched on at Wembley as Turner made that incredible save from McClair, having watched his teammates collect their medals, he remembered a feeling of melancholy. As the night wound down, an evening of pints consumed, the young 'keeper took himself off for a moment of private reflection that changed his life.

"We were celebrating, all our wives were there and it was great, but I couldn't get into it," he said. "It was really hard to see the players. You're part of it, but at the same time you're not part of it. I got myself a big carafe of lager and a glass and I walked across to Hyde Park and sat on a bench by myself, looking across the Serpentine. I was miserable. That was the moment it clicked.

"I had to change. Nobody else was going to do it. It was either I work hard and improve my attitude and have a career or I go to nothing. That 4am, sitting there on my own, changed my life. From there I knuckled down. And I owe that to Ron." Kevin Pressman's Owls career spanned 19 years and he became Sheffield Wednesday's fourth-highest appearance holder.

In the Westbourne Suite an exhausted David Hirst noticed that the mood had gone from one of elation to content. "We had the band on the stage, a few of the lads got up and it was great, but I just remember being shattered," he said. "It was the euphoria of the game, the result and what we'd achieved. I actually had a quiet night sitting at a table. I went up to the bar, got a crate of lager, sat at the table and drank that through the night. It went late, mind; at four or five o'clock in the morning I was still sat up with Big Ron, Mick Miller doing his routines, Stan Boardman telling gags. That was probably the most enjoyable part of the night, to be fair."

Phil King remembered getting to bed after the sun came up, Gordon Watson fell asleep in the hotel lobby and Nigel Pearson had just about enough time to take a nap and grab a shower before appearing on breakfast television early the next morning. All this with a vital league match against Leicester just three days away. Atkinson did not mind. In fact, he revelled in it.

"I was a great believer in a club getting a feel for Wembley," he said. "I was trying to build for the club to be used to going there. You never know where football is going to take you. It's no coincidence that Sheffield Wednesday went there two or three times soon afterwards; it whets your appetite. I wanted to make it as much of an event as we could.

"That final was a bizarre feeling, given everything. It was one of only two games I had in my career when I went in knowing for absolute certainty that my team was going to win the game. It's strange. A lot of times you go in thinking: 'I'm confident we'll win this,' but for that one I just absolutely knew it was going to go our way. I don't know why. Our performances in the cup had been terrific. We'd played ever so well at the Baseball Ground; the two semi-finals against Chelsea were as good as my sides had played. It was written."

Rising the next morning, those who could stomach it reported for breakfast and wandered over to Hyde Park, just as they had two days earlier. Roger Spry and Alan Smith led the players on a very light jog and Ron Atkinson, Richie Barker, Albert Phelan, Frank Barlow and Clive Baker wandered through the trees like a tracksuit-wearing Avengers. It was like the last morning of a close friend's wedding weekend; the happy headache-riddled calm before the return to work on Monday.

Saddled back on to the coach, players slept off the booze and posed for photographs with the morning papers. John Sheridan's eyes told their own story and Nigel Pearson, who had stolen a pair of Ron's trademark sunglasses, snoozed on the shoulder of Chris Turner. Up the M1 the Rumbelows Cup sat on full display in the front window of the bus.

Wednesday's arrival in Sheffield was the stuff of legend. Hundreds of supporters had gathered at Hillsborough to see the return of their cup-winning heroes and grab a sight of the trophy itself. Such an achievement could not be overstated. Although it was felt that their divisional status was false, they had become the first non-top-flight team to win the League Cup since Aston Villa in 1975. In the 30 years since no side from outside the top division has won any major trophy.

With the cup tucked under their arm, with their name up in lights, there were no more distractions for Wednesday's players, who had the tune of *It's a Praise for Sheffield Wednesday* stuck in their heads throughout the journey back to Sheffield after it had been played on repeat for much of the night before. Promotion, as it suggested in Carrack's song, was priority number one and it was time to get back to the day job.

"When things were feeling black," the lyrics said, "Big Ron told us we'd be back.

"Tell everybody that the heat is on, now we're going to Division One."

17

"WE'RE BACK"

If black bin-bags could have been handed out to the Sheffield
Wednesday players ahead of their home clash with Leicester City,
just three days after their Wembley heroics, you can guarantee
one or two would have taken them. Atkinson had shocked staff
by naming an unchanged side from the final, making it clear that there
was no time to waste when it came to refocusing their ultimate goal of
promotion to back to the First Division.

Several players, greeted by those excited crowds at Hillsborough on
the Monday, had found the lure of a hero's welcome too irresistible
and had continued the celebrations with a few pints, although in pubs
outside town where they thought they were less likely to be spotted. It
hardly worked. They were the talk of South Yorkshire, after all, and the
coaching staff knew full well that the drinking would continue.

All these years on Atkinson laughed at the suggestion that he was
unaware of his players continuing the celebrations. "It was great," he
said. "I always made a point of enjoying the big occasions and the boys
had done it right, let me tell you. But quickly things turned, in my mind
at least, to going back and getting the job done.

"I'd spoken to them on the bus on the way back from Wembley –
those of them who could keep their eyes open, that is – and told them
that it was important we didn't let anything unexpected happen in the
next six matches. It wasn't mathematically finished, the title, but in our
heart of hearts we knew Oldham and West Ham were bloody good
sides and it was going to take a lot for us to overtake them. But we had
to get the job done."

Arriving at the ground ahead of the Wednesday evening kick-off
against Leicester, it was clear several hours before kick-off that some-

thing special was occurring. Across the city Dave Bassett's Blades were well on their way to finishing a remarkable great escape from First Division relegation, having gone 16 matches without a win at the outset, and some supporters begrudgingly congratulated one another on a mutually memorable season.

With the Student Games on the horizon, Sheffield had a little sporting zeitgeist in its hands. More than 31,000 supporters on the blue side filed in to a sell-out Hillsborough to greet their Rumbelows Cup gladiators, those who had not been able to make the trip to the capital there on the promise not only of a handsome win over the relegation-threatened Foxes, but a first sight of the trophy itself. The three-handled cup was paraded around before the game – first by Lawrie Madden and Carlton Palmer to a full rendition of the Wednesday songbook and then by Nigel Pearson and the team on the night.

This time adrenaline could not carry Wednesday through. Leicester, who would eventually stave off relegation with a win over Oxford United on the last day of the season, kicked them around the pitch from the first whistle. The threat of the drop had led to future Owls boss David Pleat being sacked in January and under the whip-hand of their caretaker manager, disciplinarian former Newcastle and Everton boss Gordon Lee, the Foxes had decided their best route out of their predicament was pugilistic.

Paul Williams came under a series of strong challenges from Gary Mills, who had played England Schoolboys rugby and knew how to leave a bruise or two. John Sheridan was closed down at every opportunity and Hirst received a nasty gash on his left leg, but the talking-point of the disappointing 0-0 draw was a head injury to Nigel Pearson that would end a truly incredible season.

Phil King remembered a tired performance. "Three days after that cup final we just could not muster a gallop in the legs," he said. "It was like we had lead weights on. We were absolutely gone. You're so up, up and up and then your adrenaline drops so far down and you have to sort yourself out in three days. It's after the Lord Mayor's show stuff, isn't it? The other lot were fighting for their lives and we were just blowing."

"They were a bit of a comedown, the days after the final," said Hirst.

"You're up and flying, playing at Wembley, lifting the trophy, all those beers and celebrations and then you're playing at home against Leicester. You shouldn't say it, but it is a little bit difficult to go again in that situation."

A man-mountain of a player and an inspiring leader on and off the field, Pearson contributed one of the finest and most consistent seasons ever produced by a Sheffield Wednesday player. A rock at the back, he contributed six league goals and five in their Rumbelows Cup run to Wembley, claiming that man-of-the-match accolade at Wembley. He was quite possibly the least gifted technical footballer in the side, Atkinson remembered, but there was absolutely no doubt who deserved the player-of-the-season award, which was duly handed over at dinner at the end of the campaign to a standing ovation from his teammates.

When Atkinson briefly returned as Wednesday manager in 1997, he had planned to bring Pearson in as his assistant, grooming him for ascension to the top job. The move fell through in acrimonious circumstances – it is Atkinson's belief that the episode is a central reason for Pearson's modern-day reluctance to consider taking the Owls job on.

"Nigel Pearson was a great skipper and a great bloke, tough as old boots and he led by example every day in everything he did," Carlton Palmer said of his captain. "People talk about myself and Shez and Hirsty and people like that, but Nigel Pearson and Nigel Worthington...they're the backbone of your team. They're the ones with the really strong personalities, the mentality that is infectious and they get around people. If people aren't at it – and there were days that we weren't at it – they'd be straight at you."

The coiled fixture schedule refused to let up and just four days later a Pearson-less Wednesday were back at it, with the league table showing a clear picture of what was available to them. Occupying the third and final automatic spot in a rejigged promotion picture, the Owls went into their home clash with local rivals Barnsley four points clear of Notts County with a game in hand. They had one in hand over second-placed Oldham and promotion-assured leaders West Ham, too, seven and 10 points ahead respectively.

Ninth-placed Barnsley had been enjoying an encouraging season themselves although a run of one win in five and two consecutive defeats to Blackburn and Ipswich had damaged their play-off aspirations.

The Tykes fanbase have long felt a fierce rivalry with their perceived "big brother" neighbours and arrived in full voice, hoping to push County back into automatic contention while rescuing their own season. As if to enhance the derby atmosphere, a local soft toy company, Cuddles Galore, had provided hundreds of teddies for the home crowd to fling from terrace to terrace. The party atmosphere from six days earlier had remained.

Atkinson, perhaps mindful of the performance against Leicester, made a handful of changes, resting dependable duo Nilsson and Worthington just a few weeks on from their return from serious injury. With Pearson out, Viv Anderson deputised at centre-half with Harkes shuffled back in at right-back. Wilson pushed wide to facilitate Palmer's return to midfield and Trevor Francis stepped in on the left for Worthington. And in bright Sheffield sunshine, with fresher legs, Wednesday turned it on.

It had been largely unspoken that David Hirst had gone 11 matches without a goal, such was his telepathic ability to bring others around him into the game. And if it had been playing on his mind, you would never have known as he twisted and turned his way through the Barnsley defence to claim his 26th of the season. But Wednesday did not have it all their own way.

The home crowd were stunned when Mark Smith, he of 282 matches for the Owls in a previous life, headed home the free-kick of future Hillsborough coach Steve Agnew to make it 1-1. "For a moment I thought I was offside because it was so quiet," Smith later admitted. "But then I realised I wasn't playing for Wednesday anymore."

Any nervousness in the terraces did not translate on to the pitch as Wednesday continued in their search for a vital second into the second half. Barnsley goalkeeper Clive Baker was on his best form, saving twice from Williams and from Francis at close range, but the dam broke in spectacular fashion when Harkes hammered the ball into the top corner from 20 yards.

"My manager and coach had been screaming at me to stop cutting inside and using my left foot, but on this occasion I chose to ignore them," he grinned to reporters afterwards. His penchant for the spectacular had reportedly attracted interest from the scouts at Arsenal, who travelled to watch the final games of Wednesday's season.

The Owls remained in control and continued to force saves from Baker until late on when a classy ball from Hirst, somehow finding himself deep on the right-wing, reached Steve MacKenzie unmarked. MacKenzie, on for vice-captain Peter Shirtliff who had gone off with an injured back, finished confidently to unleash scenes of relieved jubilation in S6. "They sense the First Division is getting closer and closer," quipped John Helm on commentary. With Blackburn recording back-to-back wins over first Oldham in midweek and then West Ham that day, it might well be that something even grander was in the offing.

The issue was that Notts County were showing no signs of slipping whatsoever. By April 27 they had won four consecutive league matches – they would go on to extend that lead to seven – and were keeping Atkinson's Owls peering ever so tentatively over their shoulders. Heading into May, Wednesday were served up with a vital matchless midweek, their first since March, and used the time to regroup and recharge, with Alan Smith's physio room a busy place. Promotion was very much in their own hands.

Neither Pearson nor Shirtliff could return for another Hillsborough clash, this time with Millwall and the league's top marksman Teddy Sheringham, and the fear was that Wednesday may have to play out the remainder of their run-in without either of their bedrock central defenders. They need not have worried. With Anderson stepping in as captain, a confident performance at the back was capped by a Hirst special, two goals either side of the break.

Sheringham's 90th-minute effort arrived too late as any lingering Millwall hopes of automatic promotion at Wednesday's expense were dashed with a 2-1 win for the Owls. All of a sudden, having seen off two play-off contenders in a week, Sheffield Wednesday required one win to seal promotion.

"Wednesday are a delight," Millwall defender Mick McCarthy said after the game, reiterating a message delivered by opposition players and staff all season. "In Hirst they have one of the top strikers, not only in this division, but in the business altogether. I haven't come across a tougher opponent all season. I could happily watch them every week because Big Ron's approach is spot-on."

Three points from three games would seal the promotion which would cap off a truly remarkable season for Wednesday and, with the top four set to play each other on the final day, suddenly a late dart at the league title was still mathematically possible. Victories in their next two games, away at Port Vale and home to Bristol City, would mean that Wednesday travelled to red-hot Oldham for a one-off shoot-out if wobbling West Ham were to lose their final two matches. Having been on the outside of the conversation for the majority of the season, it would be quite Wednesday to steal in late on and add the league title to the League Cup nestled nicely in their trophy cabinet.

At his usual pre-match meeting before they made the trip to Port Vale, Atkinson addressed his players calmly with an ever-clear idea of exactly what he was going to say. "I think you'll draw lads," he dead-panned. Players looked at one another confused, waiting for a motivational twist in his delivery. It never arrived.

Nowadays Atkinson does not remember the confusing team talk, so whether he was attempting to calm expectations, suggesting promotion would be enough, or whether he was laying the gauntlet down to his players, is lost in the ether. He may or may not have been serious, but unfortunately he was right.

As was the case with Wembley, a Wednesday ticket for Port Vale had been the hottest in town; those fans scrambling for the few that had not been snapped up by season-ticket holders had queued through the night. Wednesday's players travelled in high spirits, playing cards on the coach and watching a VHS of their Wembley weekend highlights. This, it was felt, was the night when Atkinson's Barmy Army would return to the top tier. And for 11 minutes – 11 glorious minutes – that was exactly what a noisy rabble of 6,000 were seeing after Hirst again scored a superb goal, heading in Francis' classy cross just after half-time.

"We are going up," roused the travelling support with teddies again being flung from end to end of a packed away section. Wednesdayites had made up almost half the attendance and out-sang the Vale home fans throughout, even when Robbie Earle nodded home the equaliser on the hour after Chris Turner had made a hash of his punch. Although they tried and tried, a clearly tired Owls side failed to find another breakthrough, surviving a scare of their own when a Vale goal was disallowed in the dying moments.

Richie Barker, usually such a calm and collected figure on the touch-line, screamed an obscenity or two into the dulling Staffordshire sky as Wednesday failed to find a winner. The draw ended their lingering title hopes, but, thanks to a far superior goal difference than that of Notts County, did take them to within a point of a famous return to the big time with two matches remaining. With a daunting last-day trip to old foes Oldham looming large, there was a tingle of nervousness in the changing-room at the thought of a home clash with Bristol City just two days later.

But there was no such vision of shakiness from Atkinson. "I'm quite content with that," he said afterwards. "If you'd said at the start of the season that we'd need one point from our last two games to get back in the First Division I think we'd have been more than happy with that. We've still got it to do; we've crept another point closer. What we do know now is that we don't have to win either of our last games now, although we'll try to win them both. A point will be sufficient from our last two games."

"It was difficult not to have a feeling of disappointment," said Nigel Worthington, who sat out the Port Vale trip because of a flare-up of his ankle injury. "We were on the crest of a wave from Wembley and we felt we had been mounting a really good push at the end there. But looking back, it was always going to be a long shot. It was clear we were out on our legs, absolutely shot, and we'd picked up a few injuries which didn't help us. After Wembley we spoke about promotion being the ultimate and how important it was that we finished the job off. Really we'd left ourselves too much to do to win it."

With no time to train between matches, Wednesday faced newly-promoted Bristol City who, despite picking up only one win in their last four games, were fighting for a play-off place. With Pearson and Shirtliff still under the care of Smith, Lawrie Madden was drafted in alongside Viv Anderson to make up a 69-year-old pairing at centre-half and Francis provided even more experience in place of Williams. If much more fuel could be added to the fire of an expectant, 31,709-strong crowd, then a canister was thrown on when the iron-jawed Mark Aizlewood took out Francis in full flow early on to earn what must surely have nearly been a red card even then. During the course of the season the atmosphere was bettered only for Chelsea.

Fitting it was then, after Palmer had galloped forward in trademark fashion to start an incisive counter-attack, that Francis' jink and drop of the shoulder to beat Aizlewood found the instep of David Hirst's in-form left boot. A couple of weeks earlier he may not have attempted what followed, he said, but his confident, first-time finish left the former Sheffield United goalkeeper Andy Leaning arching his neck backwards to see it hit the back of the net. It was the striker's 30th goal of the season, it sent him to superstardom and it started a party in the stands that could have been heard from the city centre.

"That was us back at home off the back of a couple of results that weren't so good," Hirst said. "We felt we had a point to prove. We were in the mindset to do it with a bit of style, as Ron always said. And at the end of a long season the Bristol lads were coming off the back of that long trip. They caught us on a good day, to be fair. It was good fun, that one."

Facing wave after wave of Wednesday attacks, the Robins hardly had a kick as the Hillsborough crowd roared on every pass, tackle and shot with a tsunami of appreciation. In and out of half-time there was no sense of caution and the Owls romped on when Lawrie Madden, of all people, deflected one into the City net. But referee Paul Harrison, showing no sense of appreciation for the occasion, ruled it out for a foul in the build-up. Madden had not scored since 1986.

There was still no stopping Wednesday. A quick corner routine – Atkinson loved those – led to Wilson crossing to the head of Viv Anderson at the back post. It might well have been that his effort crossed Leaning's line, but Francis was there to head the return goalwards and celebrate in front of a manic Kop end. With a two-goal lead and only one point needed to secure a stepladder into the big time, the job was all but done. Wednesday had not conceded three at home all season – and not since a certain match against Nottingham Forest just a year earlier and three days earlier.

"Surely that'll be enough to take Sheffield Wednesday back into Division One," danced the words of John Helm on commentary as the cameras panned through rapturous South Stand celebrations. "They think so." When Hirst belted his second after an Aizlewood error at the back, the publicans of north Sheffield began rubbing their hands together and the crowd barely registered Wayne Allison's spectacular consolation goal a few minutes from time. After the whistle had been blown and after the crowd had rushed on to the pitch, Carlton Palmer strode down the tunnel with celebration in his eyes.

"Get in there," he shouted. "We're back!"

The night belonged to Sheffield Wednesday.

Cameras were granted access to the changing-room again and 37-year-old Francis – a European Cup winner – spoke of the season as a career highlight while sharing jokes with John Harkes, at 24 less than nine months into his career in the English leagues. David Hirst, fresh from the shower and sporting a Clark Kent-style curl on the brow, had scored two to take his run-in form to six in four.

The return to form of Wednesday's own Superman after 11 matches without a goal had inspired a comfortable last few matches that could have been anything but. "It feels brilliant, absolutely brilliant," he grinned into the camera with teammates singing Monty Python's *Always Look on the Bright Side of Life* in the background. "A lot better than last year, believe me."

Josephine's was again the venue of choice and, although the celebrations did not quite match the legend of the Chelsea second leg, the players drank long into the night. As was becoming something of a pleasant coincidence, it landed on the club's karaoke evening and the usual suspects sang their usual songs. It was again an evening shared with the community, both within and outside the club.

Those with wives, girlfriends and families called it a night about midnight; others continued until the early-summer sun rose through the city-centre buildings. As was the theme on nights of celebration, closing time did not apply to those players at Dave Allen's. And who could blame them?

"The fact we got promotion covered not winning the league," Hirst remembered all these years on. "We'd have loved to have won it obviously, but I think just getting promotion was the target in a season when we played an awful lot of games and worked really hard. We got what we deserved in winning the cup and getting promotion. That's anybody's priority, playing in the top flight. You look back now and the cup doesn't seem to be as important as it used to be, but it was certainly a big, big achievement. Promotion was the one thing that everybody wanted."

Palmer offered a similar sentiment. "The cup was one thing," he said. "But as professional football players promotion back into the First Division always had to be the main aim. That's where you want to play your football, you want that First Division status and to test yourselves against these top players, to go to Old Trafford and Anfield. We found it easy to switch back into league mode and you could see that from the results, I think. We had a good, strong group. We just all felt there was no point in us winning the cup and having all that fanfare if we didn't go back and get the job done at the end of it all. That's what you play all year for."

Wednesday still had one game to play in the Second Division, a trip to Oldham's plastic pitch on the day that the league's top four would all come together. Arriving with a goal difference level with their hosts, Atkinson's side could take the runners-up spot with a win regardless of what happened down at Upton Park in the match between leaders West Ham and Notts County. What followed was an afternoon of madness – although for once it fell not in favour of Wednesday's 1991 fairy-tale.

Billy Bonds' West Ham had the meanest defence in the division that year by some distance, conceding only 34 times in their 46 matches, and had only to better the Latics' score to lift a famous title. When news of a 2-0 Wednesday lead filtered down from Lancashire, it mattered little then that a Mark Draper double had put the Hammers up by the same scoreline within half-an-hour.

At Oldham, Atkinson's much-changed side included Jon Newsome being handed his first senior appearance of the season and Kevin Pressman back into the side to level up the appearance tally between the two stoppers, while Gordon Watson started upfront. The much-talked-about artificial pitch at Boundary Park, installed because of long-held drainage issues and so it could be hired out by clubs and schools during the week, was a major issue for visiting teams. Palmer remembers the ball bouncing "as high as a house" from clearances.

It caused logistical problems, too. Setting off for the game, a handful of players realised that they did not have adequate footwear for the conditions. Newsome, not long since an apprentice who knew every nook and cranny of Hillsborough, remembered that there was an old postman's sack kept in one of the storage rooms and returned with several pairs of moulded trainers that would be shared out ahead of Howard Wilkinson's more gruelling running sessions.

Incredibly, in a professional football match in which the hosts were competing for the Second Division title, Wednesday players wore cobwebbed footwear not touched in two years that might well have belonged to the long-departed Imre Varadi or Mel Sterland. The game has moved on.

Wednesday's two-goal lead had arrived via a David Hirst header, his 32nd and final in all competitions, and Danny Wilson, who continued his penchant for the aesthetic with a well-struck volley from the edge of the box. As it stood, a West Ham defeat was immaterial unless Oldham could score three goals. Wednesday, it was thought, could not possibly oblige. But with the minutes ticking down Roland Nilsson was dispossessed cheaply by a hungry Andy Barlow on the Owls' right and Ian Marshall poked it past Pressman at the second attempt.

John Sheridan, a future Oldham legend in his own right as a player and three-time manager, hit one wide; Hirst the same as Big Ron refused to spoil the spirit of the occasion by instructing his players to sit back and soak up the win. West Ham's goal down in London would be all she wrote at Upton Park as they lost 2-1, knowing that even the equaliser of 17-year-old Oldham midfielder Paul Barnard would not be enough for the Latics. And then, with every other game in the division completed after crowd trouble at Boundary Park had caused a slightly delayed kick-off, came the final twist of an incredible season.

Referee Vic Callow denied the Latics a penalty for what looked like a clear handball by Anderson and with protestations still ongoing, Sheridan brought down the onrushing Barlow in the box seconds later. Callow pointed to the spot and, with the very last kick of the entire season, Oldham midfielder Neil Redfearn, on as a sub, slotted home the penalty to hand his side a 3-2 win and a breathless league title. Wednesday watched on as Oldham lifted the silverware, a feeling of slight melancholy at what might have been.

West Ham's position as champions-elect was so certain just minutes before the trophy presentation that the Football League had dispatched it with the Hammers' name engraved on its side. They had been beaten

4-0 by Nottingham Forest in the semi-final of the FA Cup just three weeks before and it is still seen by some supporters as the ultimate slap in the face. Luckily, Oldham had an engraving business on-site and the error was changed in haste.

"We would've won the league that year had it not been for the cup and the number of games we had to play," remembered Atkinson, who hardly begrudged the great achievement of his mate Joe Royle in taking the unfashionable Lancashire side to the top tier for the first time in their history. "We would've been runners-up but for all that drama at the end there. We were the best team in the league that season and we played in a manner that people really liked. You could see that from conversations I was having with managers and coaches as the season went on. We were fantastic. It was an incredible season for us and such fun."

Although the season ended on an ever-so-slightly sour note for the Owls, Atkinson's sentiments echoed throughout the squad. And after all, for all the glory and all the achievement, they had played their part in a spectacular end to a spectacular season. In many ways it might have been seen as the Wednesday Way.

Looking back, Wednesday's 1990/91 season truly ended on May 8, three days before the madness on the plastic. From Aizlewood's vicious tackle on Francis to Hirst's classy opener; to the pure, unbridled emotional release of the pitch invasion. And it went back further, to a cold and uncertain midwinter, to vital wins, to Harkes' goal, to the sale of Dalian Atkinson and the signings of Wilson and Williams. It stretched back to Marbella and Acqui Terme and that desperate red-hot defeat to Forest. And to a dink, a trophy, a promotion and footballing immortality.

***

In the minutes after promotion was sealed that night against Bristol City, a television reporter accosted Atkinson in the mouth of the tunnel – in the exact spot he had been interviewed not long after that shock relegation a year earlier. "It was a nice game for us," he said, struggling to hear over the pandemonium, breathless and with a croaking voice. "We played very well and we may have won by several. It's a lovely way to come back and we've come back in style. This is the culmination of all season and working hard. Wembley was a one-off, but this is something we've worked for all season."

In May 1990 he answered alone in a stadium swirling with sadness, the lone shouts of two supporters breaking the long, emotional pauses in his answers. In May 1991 he was surrounded by nearly 35,000 disciples in a scene of joy that only football, only a football club such as Sheffield Wednesday, can deliver. Carlton was right. They were back.

18

REXIT

S heffield Wednesday chairman Dave Richards pulled open the curtains of his bedroom window on Thursday, May 30, believing the day ahead would be one to remember. Already a successful businessman and chairman of a football club that was awakening from a slumber and looked set to challenge towards the top of the First Division the following season, Richards was one of the local dignitaries invited to meet the Queen that afternoon.

It was Her Majesty's first visit to Sheffield in nearly five years and only her third in a quarter-of-a-century. The previous trip had been made to open Hillsborough's newly-roofed Spion Kop in December 1986 and she was back in the Steel City to open another sporting venue, the £35m Sheffield Arena, ahead of the World Student Games taking place later that summer. In its coverage of the royal visit, city newspaper *The Star* noted the Duke of Edinburgh's interest when told of Sheffield's want for a sporting legacy.

Alongside the cash plunged into facilities for the Games, Sheffield United had staged a remarkable rally to stay in the First Division and would be joined in 1991/92 by Wednesday, who had sealed promotion back to the big time less than three weeks earlier. The two clubs were scheduled to play the first top-flight Steel City derby since 1968.

Duties undertaken, photographs captured, memories made, Richards allowed his mind to drift to the next big event; one he in many ways expected to be more of a highlight than the first. The next day Wednesday were scheduled to embark on an open-top bus tour of the city in front of tens of thousands of adoring fans. It would be a 48-hour highlights package for anyone.

Life was good for Richards – at least until the tranquillity was shattered that afternoon, when he received a message from his secretary urging him to call Ron Atkinson. The messiah-like manager had led Wednesday's glorious 1990/91 season and brought them back into the big time, and Richards' secretary had received calls asking for comment about rumours that Atkinson was leaving for Aston Villa. The chairman's stomach dropped through the floor.

It was Villa's third attempt to bring Atkinson to the club he had a strong affinity for. A year earlier, when Wednesday had been relegated to the Second Division in those shock circumstances, he had been approached by Graham Taylor to take his place as he moved on to the England top job. He could not leave Hillsborough at that time; not those fans, not those colleagues. The club wasn't strong enough and without him could have easily fallen apart. He felt he had played his own role in their divisional demise and had already set about fixing it. "Thanks, Graham," he said, "but no thanks."

But 12 months later Wednesday were in a different place. Villa were, too. The season before Taylor's departure they had finished second in the league behind Liverpool, seven points ahead of Spurs in third. Under Dr Jozef Vengloš, the first manager born outside of Britain or Ireland to take charge of a First Division club, only the nature of the two-down relegation policy meant that they had not become too embroiled in a relegation dogfight, finishing fourth-bottom.

Unsurprisingly the Czechoslovakian was moved on at the end of the season. And as Villa's hierarchy gathered in the meeting rooms of Villa Park to discuss his replacement, there was only one candidate on their lips.

The call came from legendary Villa chairman Doug Ellis and, after a couple of days wrestling with the idea, this time Atkinson entertained it. Villa, after all, was his club. Making the two-hour drive to Sheffield on dark February mornings, he would pass signs for Aston Villa's Bodymoor Heath training ground, less than half-an-hour from his home. Once in Sheffield he would spend days, sometimes a whole week, in the Hallam Towers Hotel away from his beloved wife, Maggie. He loved Sheffield Wednesday dearly, but circumstances were not easy. Plus, he had reasoned, show any disdain this time and the Villa call may never come around again.

Unknown to Richards and the good folk of Sheffield Wednesday, their totemic manager was in talks to take charge of Aston Villa. Three decades on Atkinson describes the days that followed as "a right bloody mess."

He said: "I'd met the Villa people and it was agreed that nothing would be said until after the open-top bus and all that, so I could then go to see the club, speak to the chairman and explain my decision face-to-face. I stress that nothing was agreed with Villa, but I was more or less set on the move. They were in good shape and really, I needed to move back down. These things take a bit of toing and froing and it was all in the days before digital phones. My accountant was dealing with some inquiries with someone from Villa. Well, somebody picked up the phone and was listening in on the line. And they rang the bloody radio."

On a pleasant summer evening Atkinson was at his home in Barnt Green. He planned to make the trip to Sheffield the next morning in plenty of time for the parade and civic reception. He wanted to speak to Richards, with whom he had an excellent working relationship, and to the directors, particularly his great friend Cliff Woodward.

It would be a tough few days, but he wanted to do it right. They deserved that much. He recalled: "I was wandering down the road to grab some fish and chips for me and the wife and I got home to this phone call from Radio Two asking me to confirm that I was off to Villa. My heart just sank. I wouldn't confirm it, but I wouldn't deny it if it was true. I never lied to reporters."

Reporters rang Sheffield Wednesday in their attempt to get a definitive answer and were met with confusion. Under duress Aston Villa gave the story credence and it was broadcast on Central Television that evening. Richards, his regal day in the sunshine by now a distant memory, went about organising an emergency meeting with Wednesday's board that evening. It had been felt the club had not worked hard enough to persuade Howard Wilkinson to stay three years earlier and they would not be willing to make the same mistake again.

As if he needed clarity on the seriousness of the situation, Richards was aggressively verbally abused by a frustrated supporter on his way into the ground. Wednesday, it was decided, would pull out all the stops to keep their man.

Atkinson's white Mercedes arrived at the ground at nine o'clock the next morning ahead of a half past 10 media conference to be held in Wednesday's Press room. Scores of reporters, including those from the nationals, arrived during the morning, expecting to hear confirmation that Atkinson had left. It soon became clear that Villa were organising a Press conference themselves in the afternoon.

Fans could not believe what was happening and in the days before social media and 24-hour rolling news began to gather outside Hillsborough for any glimmer of information. Half 10 came and went. Atkinson and Richards were locked in conversation in the chairman's office.

After an hour Atkinson came out of the room and made his way down the corridor. Ever the showman, he smiled at the gathered reporters and asked: "What are you lot doing here?" before making his way to the little boy's room. After another hour Richards came out smiling, offering an indication that perhaps the situation was clear-cut and that Wednesday were winning the battle to keep Big Ron in their dugout. Soon afterwards Atkinson came out to ask staff members for bin liners, presumably to collect his things and leave.

By now scores of supporters were waiting outside the ground. Try as they might, reporters tried to speak to contacts for a whisper of what might be happening, but it was impossible; the story was developing behind the closed door in front of them. There were no winks, nudges or tip-offs to be had.

And then, movement. There would be a Press conference at one o'clock, the pack were told. Right on cue both Richards and Atkinson appeared with the chairman opening with the immortal line: "I am delighted to tell you that Ron Atkinson is staying." Supporters gathered outside listening to *BBC Radio Sheffield's* live coverage erupted in cheers, breaking out into a passionate chorus of "Atkinson's Barmy Army." "That reaction is typical of what this club is about," Atkinson said.

"The fans have been sensational and they have a passion for this club and for football. Really it was the feel of the place, the people around it and those fans out there that have been decisive." One supporter had shinned his way up a drainpipe and was listening to the proceedings from an open window. "Tha's done reyt, Ron," he strained, much to the amusement of everyone present.

"The last 24 hours have been devastating," said Richards, "but now I'd be happy for Ron to stay for life." The words were definite, if not the tone. Somehow, despite the pre-parade celebration taking place outside, something was not quite right in the feel of the room. The words were positive, but the demeanour was not one of a club that had sealed the manager's future. "You might not have heard the last of this one," it was quietly suggested to reporters at the back of the room.

The lunchtime news only heightened the sense of celebration at the parade. The event had been organised at relatively late notice, so winding through the Sheffield streets, several senior players were missing because of international call-ups and holidays. But it mattered little. Sheffield Wednesday had done something truly incredible that season and they intended to celebrate appropriately. A civic reception with the high-society types was held and thousands gathered at the foot of the town hall as players, directors and Atkinson himself paraded the trophy. "I must've been barmy to think of leaving," he told those gathered, saying he could never leave those fans. "I've got the best job in the world."

Little could get in the way of what was a huge celebration, but those who were there sensed something was amiss with Ron. So well-known as a personality larger than life, telling stories, sharing jokes, he was strangely subdued. "He wasn't himself," remembered Phil King, who later joined Atkinson at Villa Park. "I was next to him on the bus and I knew something wasn't right. We all knew the background of it, he'd speak about Villa from time to time and it was just so much closer to where he lived. He tried to put on a brave face, but the light wasn't behind the eyes."

Atkinson now remembers a feeling of caution despite the occasion and despite the adulation: "I'd had those conversations with Dave Richards, who quite frankly offered me a king's ransom. He offered to buy me a Bentley and all sorts. But it ended up with a very good offer to stay. They broke me. Aside from the money, the thing that really did it was something that Cliff Woodward said to me. With Martin Edwards, he was my favourite director I ever worked with. He was so funny, the only director I wanted on the team bus because it was like having your own permanent Stan Boardman.

"He said: 'If you don't stay, I'll pack up.' In hindsight I was a little bit browbeaten and in the end I said I'd stay. But when I had time to think, I thought: 'If I don't go now, it might be an opportunity that never comes around.' It was one of those things. You know, if I could have moved Sheffield 80 miles south, I might still be there now. I felt I was leaving them in good shape and I still feel that, if I hadn't taken that job, then I would never have managed Villa."

It was reported that the offer Wednesday tabled would have made Atkinson the best-paid manager in the history of British football. But the contract was never signed. A Press release that was circulated on June 6, less than a week on from his expression that any decision to leave his Hillsborough post would be "barmy," confirmed that Atkinson had left Wednesday. "The board of Sheffield Wednesday FC announce that late on Wednesday evening, 5th June, 1991, Mr Ron Atkinson presented his resignation to the chairman, Mr David Richards, with immediate effect," the statement read. "The club is now taking legal advice."

John Harkes, by now back in the US, found out by a call to his cell phone by his agent, Ian St John Jr. The pair had a great relationship and remain good friends. "I remember getting back and going down to the Jersey Shore," he said. "It was my first break from constant football; I'd played all the way through from Albany and into the World Cup and then into Wednesday. That whole season was a lot of football for me; it was absolutely incredible. I remember sitting there on a beach in New Jersey reflecting on what had happened to me in my life. It was like a film. It just all hit me at once. And then the phone call came from my agent to say that Ron Atkinson was leaving. And I was devastated.

"The way in which the code would come across from a UK number, it just had a lot of zeros. So I nearly didn't answer it. But I did and Ian told me Ron was going to Villa. I just said: 'No, come on, we just started!' I'd only worked from him in that one year and I felt I had so much more to learn from him and felt that the club would've been so much better with him. But in time you understand his reasons."

David Hirst – who said he still gets regular phone calls from Atkinson "when he's bored on the motorway" – was also abroad. His performances with Wednesday had earned him his first full England call-up on a glamorous tour of Australasia, where he made two of three international appearances and scored against what he always describes as "the footballing powerhouse that is New Zealand."

"I was in the lift going down for breakfast in Australia," he remembered. "Fred Street, who was the physio at the time, said Ron was going. I told him it was nonsense, newspaper talk. But during the trip it became clear he was going and eventually I got the call to say he'd gone to Villa. I was gutted. Ron had his reasons and I respected that, but we'd got a good team together and he could have taken us further. I was disheartened by it, I've got to say."

Carlton Palmer said that from the parade onwards he knew Atkinson would go. "I was really close to Ron," he said. "It was a difficult one for him. He was travelling from the Midlands, his missus didn't want to move and then he got a call from the club he always wanted to manage, right on his doorstep. Everyone said it was about the money, but the fact is he could've earned a fortune at Wednesday. Would we have gone on to achieve more? We'd have won the First Division, I'm sure of it."

Outside the relative understanding of a disappointed changing-room, there was a vitriolic reaction to Ron's departure. Supporters hung the words "Judas Atkinson" above the players' entrance at the ground and coverage in *The Star* reflected the feelings of their readers, pushing the theme of good riddance and greed. "It was bad enough that he should be contemplating leaving Hillsborough on the day they were to celebrate the season's triumphs," read an opinion piece, "but then he said what a great club Wednesday was, how he must be barmy to think of leaving, that he was staying loyal and all kinds of phrases that now stick in the throat. Now comes the ultimate in mercenary insults as, just a few days later, Atkinson confirms what many believe – he's chasing the money and has no loyalty."

It was a line of reportage that stoked the fire and the reaction cut deep into a man who deeply loved the football club and its people. "I made a mistake last week," Atkinson said. "I drove up to Sheffield on a highly-emotive day and did a U-turn when I should have pressed ahead with negotiations for my release. I will hold my hands up and admit that I let a lot of Wednesday supporters down. But a week can be like a million years in football and, when the dust has settled, I hope they can look back on some memorable days at Hillsborough. We won the League Cup and promotion in the same season and I would like to think that they will remember me for that."

It is now fair to say that they do. In no small part due to Atkinson's recommendation, Trevor Francis was named as his replacement and enjoyed two seasons of incredible First Division success, finishing third in his first campaign, qualifying for Europe and reaching two domestic cup finals in 1993.

Atkinson returned to Hillsborough on his first matchday with his new club on the first day of the 1991/92 season and received an acidic reception from the Wednesday faithful, who sang: "Judas, what's the score?" much in the same tone as the West Brom fans had done all those months earlier. And as Wednesday had done at West Brom, Aston Villa came back from behind to win. Finishing seventh in Ron's first season, Villa were runners-up to Manchester United in 1992/93 and won the League Cup a year later.

Time proved to be a great healer and Atkinson returned to manage Wednesday in November 1997, staving off the threat of relegation and guiding them to a 16th-place finish. Despite his desire to stay a Dave Richards-led board shocked everyone to appoint Danny Wilson instead. One for another book perhaps.

But on departure in June 1991 Ron's legacy was unquestionable. Only three players – Chris Turner, Nigel Pearson and David Hirst – had survived from the team he inherited on his arrival in February 1989 and his efforts in the transfer market laid the foundations of the success that was yet to befall them. He had successfully moved the club on from the Wilkinson years and, in returning them to the First Division at the first attempt, allowed for an eight-year stint in the money-spinning Premier League after its evolution in the summer of 1992.

There remains a sense of: "What if...?" among Owls fans. There perhaps always will be. From Acqui Terme to Ipswich, from that Hull hammering at Hillsborough to famous wins up and down that Second Division, there was a sense of something special happening at Wednesday. There were Harkes' goal at Derby, the Chelsea semi-finals, Hirst's awakening as one of the country's finest goalscorers and Sheridan's redemption. There was the moment when Nigel Pearson lifted the Rumbelows Cup and the evening when promotion was sealed against Bristol City. There was Josephine's, laughs and glory. There was a barmy army. Despite all the success that followed in two years of Francis, the manner of the 1990/91 season will always leave fans wondering what might have been if Ron's sliding door had been pushed in the other direction.

Two years later, at the end of the 1992/93 season, Francis' Wednesday squad headed out on a post-season trip to Marbella, where they were celebrating the oh-so-nearly of having played and lost in the two domestic cup finals. Wandering the Puerto Banus strip for what Carlton Palmer would describe as a "starter bar," they noticed another set of footballers enjoying one another's company and drinking in the hot Spanish sun. The group of footballers were from Aston Villa.

The players shook hands, shared a drink and a laugh. Ron Atkinson was at the centre of it, embracing his old friends; Carlton, Hirsty, Shez. When Wednesday finished their drinks and moved on, Atkinson nudged Paul McGrath and leant in. "Look at that lot," he said, watching them walk away in fits of laughter. "They stick together all the while."

Atkinson had joined Sheffield Wednesday almost accidentally. But boy, is he glad he did.

ACKNOWLEDGEMENTS

E xcuse the Oscar-style ramble, but it has been a long-held ambition of mine to write a book, I'm not shy of a bit of melodrama and there are plenty of people I need to thank.

I suppose the only place to start is with family and friends for their love and support not only during the process of writing, but in all the years leading up to it, particularly the rough times; my loving parents Stewart and Debbie, Phil, Viv, my brother and best pal Robbie, his wife Georgina as well as my beautiful Nana Joy and the daft old bugger this book is dedicated to on another page. The rest of the Miller-Bryett clan, the lads and the rest of you, you know who you are. Thank you.

To any and all of the 62 people I interviewed across the world from my kitchen during the Covid-19 lockdown, from players to staff to fans and opposition figures, thank you for your time, memories and patience; especially when the Zoom meetings cut out. Particular gratitude must go to Ron Atkinson, who has been hugely generous with his time and has shared incredible stories and spoken about things he may not have felt particularly comfortable talking about. For all that, as well as the foreword, thank you.

Thanks to my colleagues at *The Star* who have given me the opportunity to fulfil a dream in becoming a sports writer and fall in love with a mad wee football club in South Yorkshire; in particular Liam Hoden for the phone call I thought would never come, Joe Crann for covering me every time I was elsewhere and the gaffer Chris Holt for his constant support. Thanks also to Dom Howson for his guidance in showing me the ropes, although he still owes me several coffees.

Untold thanks must go to my publisher Danny Hall at *Vertical Editions* – also a fine and respected colleague at *The Star*, albeit on the dark side – for putting up with me throughout the process. Despite every deadline missed – which was all of them – every 3am email and every dodgy line of punctuation, you were a legend throughout and deserve a sainthood for your patience. I must extend my appreciation to Dave

Bond for his help, Albert Pearson for his support with some of the research and Nancy Fielder, Richard Markham and Steve Ellis for allowing us to use their photographs in the book.

I can't thank the godfather of Sheffield football journalism, Alan Biggs, enough for his guidance and support throughout this project and beyond. Asked to provide a few words at short notice, nothing was too much trouble – as is typical of the man.

Finally, and most importantly, to my beautiful soon-to-be wife Naomi, who has put up with countless tantrums, late nights and who, as I write this, has yet to see our new dining table for programmes, newspapers, books and scraps of paper. I'm not sure where I'd be without you.

WAWAW?

Alex Miller, 2021

ABOUT THE AUTHOR

lex Miller is a Sheffield Wednesday writer for the *Sheffield Star* newspaper. Covering the Owls home and away, he has slowly but surely fallen in love with the club and '91 is his first book.

After realising at a young age he was going to fall a very, very long way short of a career in professional football, he set about getting as close to the action as he possibly could; which meant gaining lawful access to the Press box. A graduate of Leeds Trinity University, where he completed an undergraduate and master's degree in journalism, Alex wrote for newspapers including *the Yorkshire Post* and *Halifax Courier* before he was seconded to *The Star* in 2019.

After two months his posting was made permanent and after quickly realising the role covering Sheffield Wednesday was somewhere close to a dream job, he's been humming along to *Hi-Ho Silver Lining* ever since.

In his downtime Alex can be found scrolling Twitter, listening to dodgy indie music and averaging low scores at his beloved Ben Rhydding cricket club. He lives in West Yorkshire with his fiancée Naomi and has ambitions to write more books in the future.

FINAL 1990/91 DIVISION TWO TABLE

		P	W	D	L	GF	GA	Pts
1	Oldham Athletic	46	25	13	8	83	53	88
2	West Ham	46	24	15	7	60	34	87
3	**Sheffield Wednesday**	46	22	16	8	80	51	82
4	Notts County	46	23	11	12	76	55	80
5	Millwall	46	20	13	13	70	51	73
6	Brighton and Hove Albion	46	21	7	18	63	69	70
7	Middlesbrough	46	20	9	17	66	47	69
8	Barnsley	46	19	12	15	63	48	69
9	Bristol City	46	20	7	19	68	71	67
10	Oxford United	46	14	19	13	69	66	61
11	Newcastle United	46	14	17	15	49	56	59
12	Wolverhampton Wanderers	46	13	19	14	63	63	58
13	Bristol Rovers	46	15	13	18	56	59	58
14	Ipswich Town	46	13	18	15	60	68	57
15	Port Vale	46	15	12	19	56	64	57
16	Charlton Athletic	46	13	17	16	57	61	56
17	Portsmouth	46	14	11	21	58	70	53
18	Plymouth Argyle	46	12	17	17	54	68	53
19	Blackburn Rovers	46	14	10	22	51	66	52
20	Watford	46	12	15	19	45	59	51
21	Swindon Town	46	12	14	20	65	73	50
22	Leicester City	46	14	8	24	60	83	50
23	West Bromwich Albion	46	10	18	18	52	61	48
24	Hull City	46	10	15	21	57	85	45

*Notts County promoted after beating Brighton in play-off final

ROLL OF HONOUR

S
even Sheffield Wednesday players made more than 50 appearances for the Owls in their historic 1990/91 season, with John
Sheridan featuring in all 46 league games and 59 in all and
Carlton Palmer playing 58 times across the season. David Hirst
scored 29 goals in league, FA Cup and League Cup, supported by Paul
Williams' 17 and a dozen each from Sheridan and centre-half and skipper Nigel Pearson.

Kevin Pressman and Chris Turner, both boyhood Wednesdayites
who battled all season for the club's No.1 shirt, both finished it having
played 23 league games apiece, while Roland Nilsson's stellar campaign
on the right of defence was hampered by injury. Veteran Trevor Francis, a football legend in the twilight of his career, made countless contributions to the season, many from the bench.

Viv Anderson arrived in January to add experience to their promotion push and there were important, understated efforts from players
such as Steve MacKenzie and Steve McCall, both of whom scored vital
goals. The efforts of the Owls' reserve side, which won the Pontins
League that year, were important in always keeping the first team on
its toes.

*Excludes Zenith Data Systems Cup	League		FA Cup		League Cup		Total	
	Games	Goals	Games	Goals	Games	Goals	Games	Goals
Carlton Palmer	45	2	4	1	9	0	58	3
John Sheridan	45+1	10	4	1	9	1	58+1	12
Phil King	43	0	4	0	9	0	56	0
Peter Shirtliff	39	2	4	1	10	1	53	4

David Hirst	39+2	24	4	2	9	3	52+2	29
Nigel Pearson	39	6	4	1	9	5	52	12
Paul Williams	40+6	15	2+2	0	7+3	2	49+11	17
Danny Wilson	35+1	6	2	0	10	1	47+1	7
Nigel Worthington	31+2	1	3	0	10	0	44+2	1
John Harkes	22+1	2	3+1	0	7	1	32+2	3
Chris Turner	23	0	4	0	4	0	31	0
Kevin Pressman	23	0	0	0	6	0	29	0
Trevor Francis	18+20	4	2+1	1	5+1	1	25+22	6
Viv Anderson	21+1	2	3	1	0	0	24+1	3
Roland Nilsson	22	0	0	0	2	0	24	0
Steve McCall	13+6	2	1	0	2+3	0	16+9	2
Steve MacKenzie	5+7	2	0	0	0	0	5+7	2
Lawrie Madden	1+4	0	0	0	2+2	0	3+6	0
Jon Newsome	1	0	0	0	0	0	1	0
Gordon Watson	1+4	0	0	0	0	0	1+4	0
Steve Whitton	0+1	0	0	0	0	0	0+1	0

STATS AND SCORERS

Date	Opponent	Score	Position	Crowd
Sat 25 Aug	Ipswich Town	2-0	4	17,284
	Peter Shirtliff, Paul Williams			
Sat 1 Sept	Hull City	5-1	2	23,000
	David Hirst 4, Paul Williams			
Sat 8 Sept	Charlton Athletic	1-0	2	7,407
	John Sheridan			
Sat 15 Sept	Watford	2-0	2	22,061
	Nigel Pearson, Nigel Worthington			
Wed 19 Sept	Newcastle United	2-2	2	30,628
	David Hirst, Steve McCall			
Sat 22 Sept	Leicester City	4-2	2	16,156
	David Hirst 2, Paul Williams, Danny Wilson			
Wed 26 Sept	Brentford	2-1	LC2	11,207
	David Hirst, Nigel Pearson			
Sat 29 Sept	West Ham United	1-1	2	28,786
	David Hirst			
Wed 3 Oct	Brighton & H. Albion	4-0	2	10,379
	Nigel Pearson, John Sheridan, Paul Williams, Danny Wilson			
Sat 6 Oct	Bristol Rovers	1-0	2	6,413
	Trevor Francis			
Tue 9 Oct	Brentford	2-1	LC2	8,227
	Trevor Francis, Nigel Pearson			
Sat 13 Oct	Plymouth Argyle	3-0	1	23,489
	John Sheridan 2, Danny Wilson			
Sat 20 Oct	Port Vale	1-1	2	24,527
	Paul Williams			

Tue 23 Oct	Barnsley	1-1	2	23,079	
				Carlton Palmer	
Sat 27 Oct	Millwall	2-4	3	12,835	
				David Hirst 2	
Wed 31 Oct	Swindon Town	0-0	LC3	13,900	
Sat 3 Nov	Oldham Athletic	2-2	3	34,845	
				John Sheridan 2	
Tue 6 Nov	Swindon Town	1-0	LC3 R	9,043	
				Nigel Pearson	
Sat 10 Nov	Blackburn Rovers	0-1	3	13,437	
Sat 17 Nov	Swindon Town	2-1	3	22,715	
				Nigel Pearson, Paul Williams	
Sat 24 Nov	West Brom	2-1	3	16,546	
				Trevor Francis, Peter Shirtliff	
Wed 28 Nov	Derby County	1-1	LC4	25,649	
				David Hirst	
Sat 1 Dec	Notts County	2-2	4	23,474	
				David Hirst, John Sheridan	
Sat 8 Dec	Bristol City	1-1	3	11,254	
				Danny Wilson	
Wed 12 Dec	Derby County	2-1	LC4 R	17,050	
				John Harkes, Paul Williams	
Sat 15 Dec	Ipswich Town	2-2	3	20,431	
				Trevor Francis, Nigel Pearson	
Sat 22 Dec	Oxford United	2-2	3	6,061	
				David Hirst, Danny Wilson	
Wed 26 Dec	Wolves	2-2	4	29,686	
				Steve McCall, Carlton Palmer	
Sat 29 Dec	Portsmouth	2-1	3	22,885	
				David Hirst 2	

Tue 1 Jan	Middlesbrough	2-0	3	22,869

David Hirst, Paul Williams

Sat 5 Jan	Mansfield Town	2-0	FA3	9.076

John Sheridan, Peter Shirtliff

Sat 12 Jan	Hull City	1-0	3	10,907

Paul Williams

Sat 19 Jan	Charlton Athletic	0-0	3	22,318
Wed 23 Jan	Coventry City	1-0	LC5	20,712

Nigel Pearson

Sat 26 Jan	Millwall	4-4	FA4	13,663

Trevor Francis, David Hirst

Wed 30 Jan	Millwall	2-0	FA4 R	25,140

Viv Anderson, David Hirst

Sat 2 Feb	Watford	2-2	3	10,338

John Harkes, Paul Williams

Sun 10 Feb	Chelsea	2-0	LC SF	34,074

David Hirst, Peter Shirtliff

Sat 16 Feb	Cambridge United	0-4	FA5	9,624
Tue 19 Feb	Swindon Town	1-2	3	8,274

David Hirst

Wed 27 Feb	Chelsea	3-1	LC SF	34,669

Nigel Pearson, Paul Williams, Danny Wilson

Sat 2 Mar	Notts County	2-0	3	15,546

Paul Williams, OG

Sat 9 Mar	West Brom	1-0	3	26,934

John Sheridan

Wed 13 Mar	Brighton & H. Albion	1-1	3	23,969

Viv Anderson

Sat 16 Mar	West Ham United	3-1	3	26,182

Paul Williams 2, David Hirst

Tue 19 Mar	Plymouth Argyle	1-1	3	7,806
	Steve MacKenzie			
Sat 23 Mar	Bristol Rovers	2-1	3	25,074
	Paul Williams, OG			
Sat 30 Mar	Wolves	2-3	3	18,011
	Nigel Pearson 2			
Mon 1 Apr	Oxford United	0-2	3	28,682
Sat 6 Apr	Portsmouth	0-2	3	10,390
Wed 10 Apr	Blackburn Rovers	3-1	3	23,193
	John Sheridan 2, Viv Anderson			
Sat 13 Apr	Middlesbrough	2-0	3	30,598
	Paul Williams 2			
Wed 17 Apr	Newcastle United	0-1	3	18,330
Sun 21 Apr	Manchester United	1-0	LC F	80,000
	John Sheridan			
Wed 24 Apr	Leicester City	0-0	3	31,308
Sat 27 Apr	Barnsley	3-1	3	30,693
	John Harkes, David Hirst, Steve MacKenzie			
Sat 4 May	Millwall	2-1	3	30,278
	David Hirst 2			
Mon 6 May	Port Vale	1-1	3	13,317
	David Hirst			
Wed 8 May	Bristol City	3-1	3	31,706
	David Hirst 2, Trevor Francis			
Sat 11 May	Oldham Athletic	2-3	3	18,809
	David Hirst, Danny Wilson			

FA: FA Cup
LC: League Cup
R: Replay

POSTSCRIPT

by Alan Biggs

The sun is shining on a glorious spring day. Sheffield Wednesday's opposition is in red. The result is a shock. It's an abiding image of those triumphant times of three decades ago – but maybe not the one you're thinking about. This technicolour flashback features a yellow shirt as bright as the weather. It is worn by the manager of the Owls on an afternoon of cheerful, "it won't happen to us" optimism.

In my mind's eye this striking image of Ron Atkinson on what turned out to be one of Wednesday's darkest days is as indelible as his besuited sombrero-wearing celebration at Wembley 11 months later. In the first he is a rare picture of misery; in the second a more familiar depiction of swaggering joy.

These utterly contrasting spectacles bookended the League Cup and promotion-winning exploits of season 1990-91. The significance is that you couldn't have had one without the other. Not the beating of Manchester United without the losing to Nottingham Forest. This was a graphic illustration of football's ups and downs, neatly packaged in one remarkable calendar year.

Neither the Owls' relegation from the top flight nor their lifting of a major trophy were remotely expected. And yet the two events were tightly bound together. That's how I recall those times, having been privileged to be at both games, and many in between, as a member of the club's media corps. And it remains the only piece of major silverware I've seen lifted at either side of Sheffield across 45 years on the Steel City beat. The memory is even more special in that context and all the sweeter for the supporters who remember it because of all the suffering on either side.

You can't truly appreciate the highs without enduring the lows; none more sickening than Wednesday's relegation on May 5th, 1990. This was the formative moment of everything that followed.

It was then that Ron Atkinson showed his special quality as manager. In truth, he was thunderstruck. Relegation was unthinkable and he was probably as much, if not more, responsible for it than his players. This really was the team that was too good to go down. I know they say that's an impossibility and that the table never lies. I swear that on this occasion it did.

Wednesday relegated themselves. With a few games to go they looked more than safe. Unfortunately they believed it and mentally headed for the beach, winning only one of the last seven games and losing five. Cue Hillsborough, the seaside weather of early May and a shirt-sleeved crowd of 29,763. Wednesday had contrived to put themselves in a position of still needing effectively just a point against Brian Clough's Nottingham Forest. Even then, the combination of results required to relegate them looked remote.

But Forest's stroll to an embarrassingly comfortable 3-0 win and Luton's 3-2 victory at Derby left the stadium in stunned disbelief. The abiding memory for this reporter, working for the BBC's *Sport on Two* (later *5 Live*) that day, was of being part of the last day drama.

Back then, fans kept in touch with other games via transistor radios glued to ears. Every time I reported a Forest goal I was told of loud cheers from Luton followers at the Baseball Ground. Equally, news of Luton goals from there left the Hillsborough faithful quaking. You were actually cued each time to relay the reaction of the crowd. It seesawed back and forth. From being 2-0 up, Luton were pegged back to 2-2 and a relieved Hillsborough erupted.

The fateful moment came 15 minutes from the end of both games when Kingsley Black's second goal for Luton edged the Hatters to three points and safety. Wednesday were down – on goal difference.

Filtering through also was news of a brilliant promotion parade for Sheffield United who stormed to a 5-2 win at Leicester to take Wednesday's place in the First Division. Never have the Blades inflicted a more ruthless twisting of the knife. Atkinson, who had been hired to head off relegation the previous season before strengthening the side quite substantially, struck a forlorn and penitent figure in that incongruous gleaming daffodil shirt. As well he might perhaps.

That team, with an addition or two, was good enough to have been top half in the top flight the following season – and events subsequently bore that out. But first, Big Ron faced his quit or stay moment. Sacking was never on the agenda. Not only was he staying to make amends but so were his equally chastened players. All of them. That was his dress-ing room decree, met without a murmur of dissent. Imagine a manager being able to force through such an edict today! It couldn't happen and was unusual even then but that was the power of Atkinson's personali-ty. Maybe, too, it was a measure of the characters in that dressing room.

Wembley and a return to the top league 12 months later can be traced right back to that bright and frightful afternoon. Redemption was needed and the fans were owed it; so were the players who had sold themselves short. What followed exceeded that demand as a tal-ented team applied itself to what at the time was a real culture shock. Wednesday had spent the previous six seasons in the First Division, more than once competing at the top end.

Yet there was a belief in both the manager and the team. The mood was far removed from the social media meltdowns of today. The for-mer West Brom and Manchester United boss fronting the club boasted both the career and charisma to convince supporters that a team which should never have been relegated would surely right the wrong.

Winning the first four games – including a 5-1 romp over Hull in which David Hirst hit four – made that conviction unshakeable. There were testing spells, of course; five without a win in the autumn, five successive draws in December and three straight defeats as March turned to April. But I remember a team without an obvious weak link whose only occasional vulnerability was borne of a desire to play purist passing football at all times.

Everything was in the context of retribution. In early March I met Atkinson in his office for a series of articles called "The Making of Big Ron" for the *Daily Express*, with whom I had a freelance contract at the time. "Nobody was more disappointed than me," he recalled of relega-tion. "It was such a shock to everyone and a lot of people outside the club couldn't believe it. All we've done is start to put the record straight for the supporters who've stuck with us."

There were private moments at that meeting that demonstrated his aura of command. He'd just had one of several clashes with "that scal-lywag" John Sheridan but conspiratorially suggested: "I don't mind that – I like a bit of mischief around the place."

Then the internal phone at his elbow rang and a relaxed and beaming Ron was informed that the *Express* photographer assigned to take an office picture for our series was waiting to come in. As the guy entered, Atkinson's persona changed in an instant. Standing up and clapping his hands, he barked: "No trick shots, no snapshots, let's get on with it."

Suspicious of snappers or not, or at least ones he didn't know, you'd see Big Ron's ability to change the mood on a whim throughout that season. It was a deliberate trick. Concerned by those aforementioned three successive defeats in the run up to the Rumbelows Cup final, he fed me a line that he was threatening to cancel a familiarising trip to Wembley, otherwise known as a jolly. Then, after his team responded with a couple of wins, they flopped at Newcastle four days before the final. Atkinson was fuming afterwards and said so, underlining that promotion was the main priority.

Within hours of returning from that late night trip to Tyneside, the whole squad was on duty at Hillsborough the following day for a pre-Wembley media session. Big Ron behaved as if the previous night had never happened, quipping, laughing and repeating the "lovely jubbly" line from *Only Fools and Horses.* How he behaved, and why he did it, made an impression on everyone; not least, you suspect, his previously chastened players. The idea that they could go on and beat Alex Ferguson's Manchester United the following Sunday was not so incredible.

I think everyone in and around the club was psyched into believing it was more than possible. On the day itself Wednesday parked panache for pragmatism. Sheridan cracked the only goal and Fergie's flair players were cramped for time and space. Watching from the Press box, it's strange that I don't recall much anxiety, only a sense of destiny.

There were two of us on the *Express* team assigned to write up the quotes story and North-West staff man John Bean would lead it if, as most anticipated, Manchester United won. Ever the gentleman, "Beano" turned to me at the final whistle, held out his hand and, with a magnanimous smile, said: "It's your story, matey."

Some story it turned out to be as Atkinson regaled us with how he had drafted in comedian pal Stan Boardman to relax the team with a wisecracking routine on the journey to the stadium. The rest blurred into an alcohol-induced blackout after seeing Big Ron take the mic at the official reception at the Royal Lancaster Hotel to belt out *New York, New York,* sometime early Monday morning.

But, for me and many others, there were many untold twists to this tale and much credit to Alex Miller for unearthing them. When I read this book I will see stories us lot missed and think: "Why didn't I know that?"

I'd also like to thank Alex for honouring me with the pleasure and privilege of reciting my own memories. Journalists don't get to see everything but back then you were much closer up than now. You'd arrive at the ground to see Ron but first catch players in the dressing room corridor after training; relationships were formed that were natural and chatty.

You could put your finger on the pulse. It was a happy place where people enjoyed coming to work. There were smiles around every corner, an atmosphere generated by the manager's fun-loving but competitive personality. The past tells us that success comes in cycles and that something of the like will be repeated again in the future. But the rarity of it, certainly in the experience of Wednesday fans and my own, tells us one thing.

Never take it for granted and enjoy it to the full. And in the case of 1991, may it last forever.